SLEEPING WITH THE ANCESTORS

SLEEPING WITH THE ANCESTORS

HOW I FOLLOWED THE FOOTPRINTS OF SLAVERY

JOSEPH MCGILL JR.
AND HERB FRAZIER

BOOKS

NEW YORK

Hachette Books
Hachette Book Group
1290 Avenue of the Americas
New York, NY 10104
HachetteBooks.com
Twitter.com/HachetteBooks
Instagram.com/HachetteBooks

First Edition: June 2023

Published by Hachette Books, an imprint of Perseus Books, LLC, a subsidiary of
Hachette Book Group, Inc. The Hachette Books name and logo is a trademark of the
Hachette Book Group.

The Hachette Speakers Bureau provides a wide range of authors for speaking events.
To find out more, go to hachettespeakersbureau.com or email HachetteSpeakers@
hbgusa.com.

Books by Hachette Books may be purchased in bulk for business, educational, or
promotional use. For information, please contact your local bookseller or Hachette
Book Group Special Markets Department at special.markets@hbgusa.com.

The publisher is not responsible for websites (or their content) that are not owned by
the publisher.

Library of Congress Control Number: 2023934251

ISBNs: 9780306829666 (hardcover), 9780306829680 (ebook)

Printed in the United States of America

LSC-C

Printing 1, 2023

Griot: a member of a class of traveling poets, musicians, and storytellers who maintain a tradition of oral history in parts of West Africa.

Joseph McGill Jr. dedicates this book to the enslaved ancestors whose voices were muted when they were on this earth. Slave dwellings can be preserved, but as already proven, they can be lost. It is the responsibility of archaeologists, archivists, genealogists, scholars, and griots to resurrect the voices of the ancestors and give them the respect they rightly deserve.

To my mom and dad, the late Susie Mae McGill and Joseph McGill Sr., I honor your memory. To my daughter, Jocelyn, a recent graduate of the Tuskegee University College of Veterinary Medicine, you reached your quota of sleeping in "one" slave dwelling with me. To my lovely wife, Vilarin McGill, thank you for allowing me the time to sleep with the ancestors and follow the footprints of slavery.

When I was in the military, I visited in 1984 the living space where Anne Frank hid from the Nazis. Seeing that cramped space taught me the importance of historic places. It planted a seed that would grow three decades later into the Slave Dwelling Project.

Herb Frazier dedicates this book to Jim Campbell, Jack McCray, L. R. Byrd, and Horace Mungin, dear friends who have joined the ancestors, and to the next generation—grandchildren Lauryn, Nicholas, Kinsley, and Connor Thomas; Nathaniel Perry Hamilton; Roman Lee Frazier; and Roman Averion White.

Contents

Contents

FOREWORD BY HERB FRAZIER

AS A BOY I UNKNOWINGLY SPOKE THE NAMES OF WHITE MEN WHO enslaved Black people. Streets named for slave trader Henry Laurens, slave-owning US president George Washington, and Vice President John C. Calhoun, a staunch defender of chattel slavery, bordered my tiny neighborhood on the east side of Charleston, South Carolina. My home was a public housing project built in the 1940s as a slum-clearing effort. Within it I lived mostly unaware of the racially segregated city and dangerous Jim Crow South.

I also didn't know that riverside land just beyond a rusty chain-link fence that bordered my neighborhood, Ansonborough Homes, had been the site of Gadsden's Wharf, where captured Africans had arrived three centuries before. Up to 40 percent of the Africans brought to North America came through Charleston, and one of those entry points was across the street from where I grew up! The International African American Museum plans to open on June 27, 2023, on the site of Gadsden's Wharf, with an opening ceremony on June 24. Its mission is to instill empathy and understanding of the African American experience. After two decades of planning, the museum's construction began just before the fall of the nearby towering Calhoun monument.

As a boy in the cradle of slavery, the echoes of Africa surrounded me, but I was too young to know it. My father and grandmother were either too ashamed of that history or didn't know it well enough themselves to share it with me. Africa was evident in the African-style rice dishes we ate, the African words we spoke, like *tote*, *okra*, *cooter*, and *biddy*, the syncopated hand claps in church, and the West African–inspired coiled sweetgrass baskets Black women sold to tourists. The face of Africa morphed into the faces of Black women who strolled gracefully along city streets with heavy loads balanced with dignity on their heads.

Decades later as a daily newspaper reporter, I walked where captured Africans were held before they were shipped to Charleston and other American seaports. Then I connected my childhood memories with an African source and the ancestors who brought their customs to America, giving rise to Gullah Geechee people along coastal South and North Carolina, Georgia, and parts of northern Florida.

In the crumbling ruins of Bunce Island near Freetown, Sierra Leone, I heard how Africans were branded like cattle to help buyers on the other side of the ocean identify their origin. In the Gambia on Kunta Kinteh Island in the shade of towering baobab trees, Africans were graded like animals. Those considered the best were loaded on ships while others were tossed in the River Gambia to die. At Elmina Castle on Ghana's coast, a room marked with a skull and crossbones held those who resisted. Locked in without food or water, they perished. A guide called them the "freedom fighters."

When I left daily journalism, I became the unlikely freelance marketing consultant and later full-time marketing director for Magnolia Plantation and Gardens, a Southern plantation where Africans were sold to white enslavers like those whose names are on the streets of my old neighborhood. This led to a reunion with Joseph McGill. Joe said he wanted to spend a night in one of Magnolia's slave cabins.

As a recovering newspaper reporter, I knew immediately that if he did that simple act of sleeping in a slave cabin, journalists would flock to his story. Doing so also would lead to a much wider discussion on chattel slavery and this country's fraught and prolonged relationship with it. I helped him spread the word. After a few months of sending press releases to the local media, announcing the growing number of cabins where he planned to sleep, he no longer needed my help.

After a decade of braving the elements, adjusting to hard wooden floors, cajoling property owners, and assuaging critics, Joe has become well-known nationally for his crusading effort to draw attention to the preservation of former slave cabins and other structures where enslaved people lived and raised their families. He's the first and only person in the United States who has routinely slept in extant slave dwellings to carry out a sustained campaign to save these structures. He preaches that these places, and the stories of enslaved people who lived in them, are important to telling a complete narrative of one of America's original sins—slavery.

Since launching the Slave Dwelling Project, Joe has slept in more than two hundred cabins and larger structures in twenty-five states and the District of Columbia to change the American narrative one slave dwelling at a time. He's bedded down in likely and unlikely places where slavery existed across a third of the United States, stretching from the deep South to the Western and New England states and the upper Midwest. He's traveled to rural and suburban landscapes, college campuses, private homes, the homes of US presidents, national and state parks, barns, churches, and the modest residences of Northern merchants. There's no place in this country that has not been touched by slavery, just as the entire country has been shaped by the ingenuity and tenacity of enslaved people who were once counted as three-fifths of a person as a result of a compromise with Southern colonies that led to the ratification of the US Constitution.

Joe has worn many hats. He's followed the paths of a historic preservationist with the National Trust for Historic Preservation, a Civil War reenactor, a museum director, and a tour guide. When I first met him, he was dressed in the heavy blue woolen uniform of a Black Union soldier. It was an unusually cold April night in 1992 when a tour boat pushed through light swells in Charleston Harbor toward Fort Sumter. On board were dozens of African American journalists from southern news outlets attending a regional conference of the National Association of Black Journalists. I and other conference organizers wanted to show our visiting colleagues important Black history sites in Charleston and the African influences of Gullah Geechee culture. The tour boat churned through the darkness toward the federal fort that in April 1861 received the first shots of the American Civil War.

Joe waited for us at a small campfire that did little to ease the finger-numbing cold. The fire's dim light revealed him standing erect against a black background as he personified a soldier who joined to fight with the Fifty-Fourth Regiment of the Massachusetts Volunteer Infantry. Those Black Union soldiers may have been enslaved or free men before they came south to ultimately face Confederate troops in an epic battle on Morris Island within view of Fort Sumter, itself on a wedge of land at the entrance to Charleston's harbor. Joe spoke of the Black soldiers who knew if they were captured, Confederates would sell them into slavery or execute them instead of abiding by military custom to hold them as war prisoners.

The next time I encountered Joe, he was a historic preservationist with the National Trust for Historic Preservation. He was one of several advisors guiding Magnolia through the renovation of four nineteenth-century slave cabins at the former rice plantation on the Ashley River upstream from Charleston. In the eyes of many Black Americans, Magnolia and other former plantation sites are places to avoid because of their troubled histories. As African American men with a passion for history, however, Joe and I were eager to use our unexpected ties with Magnolia to tell the stories of our ancestors and honor the enslaved people whose sacrifices built this nation.

Joe launched his Slave Cabin Project at Magnolia. As the project grew, he was usually alone. But others eventually joined him, young and old, Black and white. Some gathered around campfires to talk about the lingering effects of slavery in America before finding a place in the cabins to sleep. When Joe embarked on this journey, he did not know what he would find beyond the fleeting experience of laying his head in a slave cabin on a southern landscape or in a building in an urban northern city. He wanted to shine a light on the places where our enslaved ancestors lived, which today are often hiding in plain sight.

Joe's followers include readers of his social media posts and blogs and viewers of his Facebook live feeds, made even more necessary in 2020 by the spread of the coronavirus that shut down in-person gatherings. Before the pandemic, advisors to his nonprofit Slave Dwelling Project helped him organize academic conferences. He's given keynote talks nationally on what he does and why he does it.

Just as in the beginning, Joseph McGill has a story to tell. Unlike the beginning, it is now a much larger story. I've rejoined him to help him tell it on the pages that follow.

INTRODUCTION

THE OLD WOMAN MAINTAINED HER USUALLY JOLLY DEMEANOR AS she lovingly performed her daily task at a slave cabin she called the "chillun's house." Too stooped to toil in the field, the granny watched the plantation's children who were too young to do field work alongside their able-bodied parents. On this day the gray-haired caregiver told the children how she, as a girl, was enticed to a ship bound for America.

Pale-faced strangers laid pieces of red cloth on the ground. She and others in her community grabbed them. Then larger pieces were placed farther on until they crossed a river. On the other side, everyone rushed toward bits of red cloth until finally the trail of fabric stopped on a big ship. When the gate was chained shut, she and the other Africans couldn't flee. The ship's crew had herded the unsuspecting captives to a large iron cage in the belly of the boat. "Five or six hundred all together down under the first deck where we was locked in," the granny told the children. They were caged with other Africans who spoke unfamiliar languages. "So we signed with our hands."

Days later she saw the glorious blue sky again along with horrifying sights of people jumping in the water in futile attempts to swim home. "Lots of them still lost down there in the sea." On the ship she and the others were given enough red flannel to wrap around themselves, the granny remembered. When the big boat reached America, they stepped up on the auction block they called the "banjo table" to be sold to the highest bidder like land, cattle, or mules. "The white man took you to your new home in America," she told the young ones. "That's how I come to be on this here plantation."

The old woman removed ash bread baking in the fireplace. She served it to the children with cups of sassafras tea. Wiping sweat from her brow with a red cloth tied around her head, she announced it was time to bundle the infants. At one o'clock every workday, she and the older children took the infants to the field, where their mothers breastfed them. When the mothers finished their work, they fetched their babies from the "chilluns' house," a slave cabin that served as the plantation's center of young life.

This account as a singular event did not occur. Instead, it is a compilation of recollections of formerly enslaved people on plantations in South Carolina who, after decades of freedom, talked about their enslavement with writers from the Works Progress Administration (WPA) Federal Writers' Project. In the 1930s, the writers collected more than twenty-three hundred firsthand accounts of slavery in seventeen states, mostly in the southern states. Several people shared the "red cloth" story with the WPA writers. These accounts provide a window into the past to possibly understand what our ancestors felt and endured.

The "red cloth" tale is an example of how our African ancestors used the oral tradition to pass on their experiences in slavery to the next generation. They also describe a horrific Middle Passage across the Atlantic Ocean, the largest forced migration in human history, that transferred millions of captured West Africans to the Western hemisphere. That event ushered in chattel slavery in the United States. Historian Michael A. Gomez argues the seducing or tricking of Africans was the "most important aspect of the [slave] trade to understand and the most consequential lesson to learn about dealing with white folk." The use of "red cloth" is also part of a pattern of deception that continued after the Emancipation Proclamation freed enslaved people in the slaveholding states.

In 2017, Ohio State University undergraduate Carley Reinhard became fascinated by a red cloth narrative. Her curiosity led to research grants that allowed her to delve into the various ways slave traders tricked Africans into captivity. "As slavery expanded throughout the United States and the fear of kidnapping rose, the stories of being seduced by red trinkets were modified to warn children of the dangers of kidnapping within America," she said. "Even after slavery ended, the stories were kept alive in new ways, and the red cloth became a tool for empowerment and protection. Different contexts changed the specifics and generalities of the myth, but West African folk culture survived across time, oceans, and continents."

For six years, I was a program officer for the National Trust for Historic Preservation. For seven decades the Trust has led the movement to save America's historic places. A privately funded nonprofit organization, the Trust has worked to protect America's historic sites, tell the full American story, build stronger communities, and invest in preservation efforts. Those places that received the Trust's attention were grand buildings such as enslavers' antebellum homes. If the dwellings in which the enslaved lived and worked were mentioned at all, they were often labeled as outbuildings or dependencies, polite euphemisms that masked their true purpose.

People of African descent—considered legal property—were bought, sold, and owned until the day they died. It is my desire to give humanity to these enslaved people as I present the places where they lived. In these places they experienced the full range of human emotion while they adapted to slavery and their forced estrangement from Africa. These structures are some of the most visible artifacts of slavery and, as such, should be viewed as sacred spaces, a concept that might not be embraced universally.

While slave cabins for African Americans may be painful symbols of exploitation, they can also engender pride that our ancestors survived slavery. George Washington University historian James Oliver Horton observed that for white Americans slave cabins "should produce sobering shame, but for some they summon the nostalgia for the myth of the Old South." Preserved slave dwellings also serve as important evidence of what Maya Angelou calls "the huts of history's shame," he added. "Confronting or avoiding the shame of history's huts constitutes the central preservation issue that must be addressed at public exhibits of slave habitation."

Slave cabins were more than a place to live. They were a gathering place to hear the latest news, as in the case of two formerly enslaved men, Sam Mitchell and Alfred Sligh. At the Woodlawn

Plantation on Ladys Island in Beaufort County, South Carolina, eighty-seven-year-old Sam Mitchell described the cabin he lived in and its decrepit condition. "De slave lib on de Street, each cabin had two room. De Master don't gib you nutting for yo' house—you hab to git dat de best way you can. In our house was bed, table and bench to sit on. My father mek dem. My mother had fourteen chillen—us sleep on floor." Alfred Sligh, enslaved in Newberry County in central South Carolina, was a centenarian when he recalled the day in 1863 that he heard of the Emancipation Proclamation. "We gang up at his grandmother's cabin and she tell us it . . . We look scared, lak mules in de midst of a hornet nest, as we stood dere" not knowing what to do next until the wife of the plantation owner confirmed that freedom had come. Barbara Burlison Mooney, an associate professor at the School of Art and Art History at the University of Iowa, notes that "some cynics may scoff and condemn this idea as naïve or romantic, yet places where slaves slept and were beaten, raped, exploited, and yet survived must be marked as extraordinary memorials, not as adjuncts to white gentility."

Architectural historians have found it difficult to detail the types of structures used to house enslaved people during the colonial era because so few of those poorly constructed dwellings—built for Black slaves and white indentured servants—survived beyond the early nineteenth century. Other more well-constructed buildings are still standing. In some instances the enslaved were quartered in the homes of the enslaver, and as such, those habitats are available for study. My travels have taken me to some of these locations, which to the surprise and dismay of some people exist in states outside the South.

Initially, I called my work the Slave Cabin Project. But early on I realized that places where enslaved people lived were not limited to cabins on rural Southern landscapes. I eventually changed the name of my work to the Slave Dwelling Project, which is not about reparations or hunting for ghosts and artifacts. Instead, I want to tell the stories of the people who lived in these structures. If I had not changed the name and scope of my work, I would have restricted what I've accomplished in the decade since launching the project in May 2010. I've encountered dwellings in urban centers—small towns and big cities—in the South and in major cities across the country. Enslaved people lived in houses of worship, campuses of higher education, and plantations owned by former US presidents. Twelve of the first eighteen presidents owned slaves at some point during their lives.

My use of the word "slave" in the title of my work is admittedly startling for some people. I am intentional in my desire to be as frank as possible and not sugarcoat American history and its system of chattel slavery, an inhuman institution supported during the sixteenth through nineteenth centuries by this country and European powers.

This history of slavery and knowledge of the types of spaces where enslaved people lived was not part of my education when I was growing up in rural South Carolina. My full understanding of slavery didn't begin until my professional life as a historic preservationist and my weekend hobby as a Civil War reenactor. More than two hundred thousand Black men joined the US Army and Navy to end slavery. Southern states formed the Confederate States of America to maintain slavery, the backbone of the Southern economy.

Civil War historian Gordon Rhea, who lives in Mount Pleasant, South Carolina, near Charleston, is the descendent of a Confederate soldier. Rhea's great-grandfather Captain James David Rhea commanded a company in the Confederate Third Tennessee regiment and survived a series of unfathomable hardships during the war. Although Rhea admires his grandfather's bravery and fortitude, he is not proud of the cause his grandfather's nation represented, preserving human slavery and fostering that institution's propagation into new territories. Rhea points to several examples in which the Confederate founders clearly stated their motives. Among them is South Carolina's expressed concern that "the non-slaveholding states have assumed the right of deciding on the propriety of our domestic institutions . . . [and] have denounced as sinful the institution of slavery."

My simple act of sleeping where enslaved people slept has broadened my awareness of their history, but it cannot replicate the pain and suffering they endured. I hope that my travels have brought attention to the need for a deeper study and understanding of this history. It is rare for African Americans to own former plantation sites where slave cabins still stand.* Therefore, we must find ways to gain access to these historic places through sleepovers, special tours, interviews, and research. Only then can we truly tell the complete story of America.

---

* Keith Waring, an African American member of the Charleston City Council, is part owner of a former plantation site on Slann Island, south of Charleston. A slave cabin that once stood there was demolished before he and his partners acquired the property. Its foundation is still visible.

Slavery in the New World was unlike any other form of human bondage that had existed in the world before it, even slavery in Europe. The arbitrary classification of race determined who was enslaved. The root of the word "slave" is found in Europe. In the premodern era, Slavic people were enslaved by other Europeans. But when Europeans began the New World conquest, none of the people enslaved in the Western Hemisphere were other Europeans. The enslaved were people of color and predominantly Africans.

Most Black people in modern-day America are familiar with the "one drop rule." One drop of Black blood classifies a person as Black. That arbitrary idea dates back to slavery, when the slightest hint of African ancestry classified a person as Black. Even the word "black" has importance in demeaning a person of African descent, particularly for the English, whose location in the North Atlantic placed them more distant from people of color than other Europeans. The dark complexion of Africans was called "black," a term meaning dirty and foul, as opposed to "white," suggesting pure and wholesome. In broad terms, the Europeans also didn't give credence to anything Africans had accomplished prior to their capture and forced exodus to the New World. The American brand of slavery ensured the offspring of enslaved people were also held in bondage, a practice that undermined the financial and social foundation of succeeding generations and established a perpetual transfer of wealth for slave-owning white families. These fundamental patterns existed across the country in spite of slavery's regional variations. People held in bondage lacked individual freedoms and generally had no recourse in the courts.

Native Americans were enslaved, too. But their labor was not the backbone of New World plantation slavery. Indian slavery early on was illegal, but nonetheless it persisted. Over time, white America developed subversive means to benefit from the coerced labor of Native Americans through displacement, indebtedness, and violence or the threat of it.

Indentured European workers made up part of America's colonial workforce, but indentured servitude ultimately was not the most profitable option for the enslaver. During my encounters with people who mention this, I stress the difference in indentured servitude and chattel slavery. Indentured workers indentured themselves. Their servitude had a beginning and an end. Enslavement for Africans, however, had no end, and their offspring would provide free labor for generations. Enslaving Africans was legal for centuries and sanctioned worldwide by states and empires before the practice became prevalent in the New World. Because of the fear of uprisings, American colonial laws later laid the foundation for the control of people of African descent. It was a lesson I encountered at Bacon's Castle in Surry County, Virginia.

My search for slave dwellings satisfied a childhood lust for travel beyond my hometown of Kingstree, South Carolina, that I didn't consciously realize I had. This retrospective on my decade of sleeping in slave dwellings, however, is more than a travel memoir of historic locations. It is a look back on my frank campfire conversations on race and my unexpected role as counselor and sometimes referee when the topic of racism caused emotions to run hot. Join the conversation as I visit dwelling places that housed our enslaved ancestors to explore how slavery has stained America.

ONE

DUSTING OFF AN OLD IDEA

I WAS AMONG HUNDREDS OF UNIFORMED MEN—SOME DRESSED IN gray, others in blue—who charged across a grassy field with scattered palmettos and oaks. Like life-sized pieces on a giant game board, we moved on command. "Second line forward! Ready, aim, fire!" Saber-wielding horseback riders galloped among us. Booming cannons and crackling rifles wafted smoke into the wind. Faux blood stained those who fell in dramatic displays of injury and death.

We were Civil War reenactors before cheering spectators accustomed to blue Union and gray Confederate units staging battles. Few, however, had seen my unit of "colored troops," the Fifty-Fourth Massachusetts Volunteer Regiment, Company I. We honored the memory of the Black Union soldiers who gave their lives at the epic 1863 Second Battle of Battery Wagner on Morris Island, South Carolina. The other side had no Black reenactors. They waved the Confederate banner while wishing the real war had had a different outcome. The mostly white audiences treated us with respect, asking if we'd pose for pictures. We represented a history they weren't accustomed to seeing.

As a reenactor, I had developed an appreciation for historic places and had become comfortable sleeping outdoors, sitting around campfires, and listening to stories, music, and lies told by macho men. Before a reenactment we camped on historic grounds like Olustee Battlefield Historic State Park near Jacksonville, Florida, the site of the state's largest Civil War battle in 1864 that involved the Fifty-Fourth Massachusetts. But then I realized at an annual regional reenactment at Boone Hall Plantation near Charleston, South Carolina, that we were ignoring a history on the other side of the big house.

Founded in 1681 by Major John Boone, an Englishman, the site is a former brick factory and pecan farm that enslaved thousands of people of African descent. Today it is a major tourist attraction, suggesting something concrete to visitors curious about the meaning of the loaded terms "plantation" and "slavery." By 1817, Henry and John Horlbeck had acquired the 1,450-acre property. During the Horlbeck years, the Boone Hall brickyard produced four million bricks annually with the free labor from fifty men and thirty-five women, said Mount Pleasant historian Suzannah Smith Miles. The cabins were made of those rejected bricks not sold to the federal government to build Fort Sumter or the stately Charleston mansions of plantation owners. When I slept in a tent the night before reenactments at Boone Hall, I'd wonder about the people who lived in those cabins beyond the big house. Those cabins stand as silent reminders of what caused the Civil War, yet they and the enslaved were ignored.

My thoughts of those cabins returned years later and prompted a bigger idea, an opportunity for me to sleep in one of them on a still night in May 1999. I tapped into my desire for exploration to gird myself for a night alone in a slave cabin at Boone Hall. I replaced any fear of the unknown with thoughts of the enslaved ancestors. I had just arrived in Charleston on an early morning flight from Cedar Rapids, Iowa, feeling good that the History Channel didn't reject my night-in-a-slave-cabin idea.

I first recognized the power of historic sites when I was a military policeman in the US Air Force, guarding nuclear arsenals on air bases in England, Washington state, and Germany. While stationed in Germany, I joined a sightseeing tour of Amsterdam with a group of my air force buddies. During that tour we visited a place that reminded me of a tenth-grade world history class in Kingstree, South Carolina. The teacher showed us a film strip about Anne Frank, a Jewish girl who hid in an attic during World War II with her family before they were discovered and killed by the Nazis. Now I was in the place where Anne Frank lived. I would not have gone there had I been alone. Seeing that space made the Anne Frank story real for me. Being there connected that space to her and her diaries that told of her life in hiding and a futile fight to live. That tour taught me the importance of preserving historic places.

After six years in the military, I returned to South Carolina to enroll at South Carolina State College, now South Carolina State University, a predominantly Black campus in Orangeburg, an hour-and-a-half drive from Kingstree. I followed my older sister and my mother's sisters to SC State. Like them, I majored in English. I wrote for the campus newspaper and joined the yearbook staff. I flirted with the idea of a journalism career, but fate had another career choice waiting for me. There was another flirtation, too. During my junior year, two female colleagues on the newspaper staff introduced me to Vilarin Mozee, a psychology major from Newberry, South Carolina. I proposed to her in 1990. The following year, we were married.

One of the paper's perennial stories was about the Orangeburg Massacre, an event on the campus I had not heard about before arriving there. On the evening of February 8, 1968, SC State students Samuel Hammond Jr., Delano Middleton, and Henry Smith were shot to death on campus by South Carolina Highway Patrol officers during a protest of a segregated bowling alley. Twenty-seven others were injured. Their deaths have become known as the Orangeburg Massacre. It occurred three months before student protesters were killed by law enforcement officers at Jackson State University, a Black campus in Jackson, Mississippi. These fatal shootings at Black campuses are lesser-known events than the deaths of white students at Kent State University, shot dead on May 4, 1970, by the National Guard while they protested the Vietnam War. I was shocked to learn about the Orangeburg Massacre, seventeen years after it happened. I was also disappointed that I was not taught about it in school. So close, yet so far away.

After graduating from South Carolina State University in 1989, I joined the National Park Service (NPS). I was recruited by an old friend and distant cousin, Michael Allen, who I had known when we were boys in Kingstree. We had worked side by side in the tobacco fields, picking the broad green leaves and then hanging them in barns to dry. Michael had graduated from Kingstree Senior

High the year before me, then matriculated at SC State. Following high school, he became an NPS ranger at the Fort Sumter National Monument at Charleston, South Carolina. For two summers before I graduated, I received park ranger training at the fort. After I earned my degree, Fort Sumter's superintendent Brian Varnado offered me a full-time job. Excitedly, I accepted, knowing I would work at the place where the Civil War began. I enjoyed standing in front of audiences, telling people about history. However, trepidation stirred within me. I'd be the point person who told visitors about the fort's war history.

While the Park Service provided a general script, I did additional research to ensure I would give an inclusive and accurate story beyond just military tactics. An African American park ranger before mostly white audiences also would assuredly spark criticism and correction if I misspoke. Therefore, it was important to me, Michael, and the other Black ranger to be armed with all the facts.

Within minutes of visitors disembarking from the tour boat, I could spot the ones who might have a problem being led around by an African American park ranger. Their eyes and body language were immediate clues. The most common question I received was "How does it feel as a Black man giving this history?" The white rangers didn't get a comparable question.

At the entrance to Charleston's harbor, Fort Sumter is flanked by two sites important to the city's history before the American Revolution and during the Civil War: Fort Moultrie, another former federal fort and NPS site on Sullivan's Island, and Fort Johnson on James Island, owned by South Carolina and used as a marine resource center. Some days I led tours at Fort Moultrie on

Sullivan's Island. While there, I heard a story crucial to understanding the Black experience in America, but one not taught to me in high school or college.

Today, Sullivan's Island is an affluent ocean-side community, once the site of pest houses, or quarantine stations where Blacks and whites suspected of having contagious diseases were held before they were allowed into Charleston. This colonial-era practice ended in the late 1790s after the Revolution. This delay was mandated to ensure that domestic and international travelers and enslaved Africans were free of infectious diseases such as smallpox, yellow fever, and measles. Only those travelers and Africans who showed signs of being ill were held in quarantine. This Sullivan's Island history is the product of Elaine Nichols's research for her master's degree in public service archaeology at the University of South Carolina.

Nichols discovered that a number of different pest houses were located on the island at various locations. Travelers were held an average of ten days before they were released. Sometimes people were quarantined on small boats and ships. The tiny pest houses have long since vanished from the island's landscape, but Nichols's research opened a window to the role the island played in Charleston's early medical history. Because Africans were brought through Sullivan's Island, the site is often called the Ellis Island for African Americans. It is a crude comparison. Africans came by force, not by choice.

After I led a tour at Sumter, a guest approached me. Tony Horwitz, a *Wall Street Journal* journalist, asked to interview me for a book he was writing.* I stood out to him because he was not

---

* Tony Horwitz died May 27, 2019, in Washington, DC.

expecting to see a Black man leading a tour at Fort Sumter. Horwitz was curious if I felt awkward taking tourists through Sumter, a shrine to the slaveholding Confederacy. I told him I would feel awkward if that was the only story I told. But I explained that whenever I had the opportunity, I pointed south to Morris Island to direct visitors to the nearby island where Black Union soldiers in the Fifty-Fourth Massachusetts Infantry Regiment followed orders to engage the Confederates in a doomed assault on Battery Wagner. The movie *Glory* told that story, and its portrayal of that attack changed the attitudes of whites on both sides of the conflict about the Black soldiers' battle readiness. In 1998, Horwitz's book *Confederates in the Attic: Dispatches from the Unfinished Civil War* was released. The book became a bestseller and caught the eye of readers nationwide. It also led to my night at Boone Hall.

I enjoyed my work at the Park Service, but after six years an online job posting grabbed my attention. One of South Carolina's most historic African American institutions, the Penn Center on St. Helena Island, had created a new position. I was hired as Penn's director of history and culture. The Penn Center grew from the former Penn School, which opened in 1862 as one of the country's first schools for formerly enslaved people freed before the end of the Civil War. In the 1960s, the Penn Center was a safe haven for the Reverend Martin Luther King Jr.'s civil rights planning sessions. Today, it supports education, community development, and social justice programs in the Gullah Geechee community. My duties included creating a museum named for York W. Bailey, a Penn graduate and St. Helena Island physician. At Fort Sumter I told a specific story; Penn presented an opportunity to tell a broader story of African American struggles and achievement. Three employees and about two dozen volunteers helped me tell those stories.

Three years later, I was lured away to the next challenge when I saw an online job posting for the executive director of the African American Historical Museum and Cultural Center in Cedar Rapids, Iowa, a new facility that opened in 2003. I supervised the fundraising, collection of artifacts, and construction of a new museum. While I was there, the History Channel called me.

The producers of the national television network had read Tony Horwitz's book with its references to me. They had conceived a television documentary, *The Unfinished Civil War*, and wanted to contrast two reenactors, one white, honoring the Confederacy, and one Black, representing the Union. They selected me and John Krausse, a white Confederate reenactor from Hagerstown, Maryland. They said that sometime during the filming I would meet Krausse.

The documentary producers wanted to know if I would talk about the war from the perspective of a Black reenactor. I agreed to be interviewed because I saw it as an excellent opportunity to tell the story of Black Union soldiers who fought and died on Morris Island. Further, they wondered if I would participate in one of the protest marches in South Carolina against the Confederate flag, the battle flag of the Confederate army, which flew above the South Carolina State House. The flag had been the focus of the National Association for the Advancement of Colored People (NAACP) and others who consider it a symbol of hate. I said I'd do that, too.

The producers needed something else to expand the story, but they weren't sure what it should be. Without much forethought I suggested sleeping in a slave cabin. They quickly embraced the creative genius of my unique and simple idea. They made the arrangements for me to spend a night at Boone Hall. Not everyone has the privilege to sleep at a historic site. From my reenacting experiences, I had become comfortable sleeping outdoors at historic places. Those outdoor places, however, are not the same as historic indoor spaces, like the cramped quarters Anne Frank shared before the Nazis found her. When the producers said they wanted something more, the idea of spending a night in a slave cabin came spontaneously. It was the first time I had expressed it openly since I wondered about the silent cabins standing beyond the big house at Boone Hall when I was a Civil War reenactor there. In 1999 the cabins were being renovated. The wooden floors had been ripped up to expose the earth. I randomly chose a cabin, which, like the others, had a brick platform that formed the base of the chimney. It was large enough for my sleeping bag.

I had never before camped alone in a building, certainly not one like Boone's brick slave cabin. No doubt those bricks were made by Black hands, so by staying in that cabin I honored the enslaved workers who built it. The producers asked me repeatedly whether I was afraid and wanted to back out. Each time I replied I was going through with it. Backing out was not an option. The producers purchased my flight ticket to Charleston. I did not want to appear in the documentary as chickening out of this opportunity and challenge. I lit two candles so I could see to write in my diary. I closed the wooden door and left open two shutters to increase the air flow, much as Abbey, an enslaved woman at Boone Hall, might have done in one of the cabins before she ran away in 1783 with her six-year-old daughter, Bright, and her three-year-old son.

Being there alone with my thoughts, I began to understand how enslaved families felt when they were forced to live in these cabins. The structures were substantial, but the brick floor was uncomfortable. It's unlikely the enslaver provided furnishings or a bed. It is likely, however, the enslaved residents fashioned beds called "pallets" out of straw, hay, or moss stuffed inside fabric. I thought about the forgotten workers who built the cabins or those who lived there enduring the heartache of children or a spouse being sold and shipped away. But in a strange twist of caring, Boone stipulated in his will that his estate "be kept together," which Smith Miles interprets as meaning an enslaved family should be kept intact.

I was concerned that I wouldn't be able to sleep, but I quickly drifted off. When the sun rose to burn away a misty morning, it also relieved me of a desire to again sleep alone in a slave cabin. I left that experience with the satisfaction that I stood up to the challenge and braved the unknown as my tribute to the ancestors.

That night in Boone Hall's slave cabin was the first of three trips back to South Carolina for the documentary. On the next two trips, I was not alone. I marched with hundreds of people calling for the South Carolina legislature to lower the Confederate flag from atop the state capitol building in Columbia. The flag had sparked a long debate in South Carolina over whether it is a symbol of hate or of heritage. In the late 1930s, more than half a century after the end of the war, the state's legislature first raised the flag in the house chamber. Two decades later, the senate followed suit. The 1960s civil rights era heated passions further when the flag was hoisted over the State House on April 11, 1961, during the Civil War's centennial and four months before I was born. Raising the flag was considered a clear action against desegregation and the civil rights movement. No date was specified when it would come down, so it just stayed there, decade after decade. The flag continued to flap in the wind in spite of a lawsuit and a threatened NAACP boycott. In the mid-1990s lawmakers passed a law giving the legislature complete authority over the flag. In 1996 the Republican governor David Beasley likely lost a reelection bid due to his suggestion to remove the flag.

On January 1, 2000, the NAACP imposed a boycott of South Carolina. Sixteen days later, on the anniversary of Martin Luther King Jr.'s birthday, nearly fifty thousand demonstrators marched in protest against the flag. That event dwarfed a subsequent pro-flag rally of six thousand. Then in April 2000, Charleston mayor Joseph P. Riley Jr. led a five-day, 110-mile march from the port city to Columbia to demand the flag's removal. The marchers were within three miles of the State House when I joined them with the film crew in tow and a wireless microphone hidden under my T-shirt. Some people in the procession asked why the camera crew was following me. I turned the question back to them and asked when they had joined the march.

Those protest efforts had an effect. That spring the state senate and the house voted to lower the flag in a compromise arrangement signed into law by Democratic governor Jim Hodges. But they didn't get rid of the flag—they just moved it from the State House dome to a ground-level flagpole in front of the capitol. In many ways it would be more visually prominent than ever. The film crew was with me when I returned to Columbia for the transfer ceremony.

At noon on July 1, 2000, I squinted to focus my gaze on the flag, silhouetted against a bright sky, to watch it slowly disappear from view. Pro-flag supporters chanted, "Return our flag! Return our flag!" The chant turned to cheers when a smaller version of the flag was hoisted up a thirty-foot pole at the monument to the state's Confederate dead in front of the State House along a busy downtown street.* Tension in the crowd heightened as people on both sides of the flag debate yelled at one another. At that moment, I was afraid violence would erupt.

Then John Krausse, the Confederate reenactor from Maryland, approached me wearing a gray Confederate uniform and fake blood smeared on his face. Over the previous two years, the film crew had separately interviewed Krausse and me. We had never met. When we embraced, he apologized if the faux blood stained my white T-shirt. "The blood is symbolic for all the blood that was spilled from 1861 to 1865," he explained. As he spoke, his hands tightly gripped a pole attached to a Confederate flag. I revealed that I appreciated that the flag had been taken down and placed on the monument. Lowering it, however, brought it closer to eye level, a

---

* The compromise didn't quell the flag debate. A poem penned by the state's poet laureate Marjory Wentworth was banned from the January 2015 inauguration of Republican governor Nikki Haley because it mentioned the flag and the civil rights issues it represents. The flag was finally removed from the State House grounds and placed in the state's museum after a young white supremacist in June 2015 murdered nine members of the Emanuel AME Church in Charleston.

move that I thought was insufficient. I'd prefer that it be placed in a museum. If it were sent to a museum, I would honor it there, I told him. Krausse always thought the flag should stay atop the State House. Those who were pro-flag had won the day because it remained on the grounds in a location giving it greater visibility. Krausse said the flag was being removed from cemeteries in Maryland. He feared the flag backlash would go beyond just removing it from buildings. What would be next? Removing Confederate monuments? Renaming streets? I countered that I was opposed to any effort to eradicate the flag. I honor soldiers. They fought and died for a reason they believed in. Each side is in their separate corners, and we need to come together to have a dialogue, I said. "That is what happened here," Krausse said. "The dialogue became lost." Then he stepped back to say, "God bless you, Joe!" He saluted. I returned the salute. Then we shook hands.

When the show finally aired on the History Channel, I was shocked. Confederate reenactors voiced a reverence for the Southern white soldiers with strong sentiment that the war was not fought to preserve slavery. That was counter to all of the research I had done, back when I worked at Fort Sumter, studying the official documents of that time. Maintaining the institution of slavery was at varying degrees a consistent theme with Southern states' decision to secede from the United States to form the Confederate States of America. Primary sources show that each Confederate state issued an "Article of Secession," explaining its break from the Union. Texas, Mississippi, Georgia, and South Carolina issued additional documents, often called "Declarations of Causes." These documents laid out their reasons. Slavery is mentioned in all of them.

After working at the museum in Cedar Rapids for several years, I saw an online job posting that presented my next challenge. The National Trust for Historic Preservation, based in Washington, DC, was seeking a program officer to advocate for the protection of historic sites in Alabama and Louisiana. The work required travel from the Trust's office in Charleston. I joined the Trust in February 2003. Ironically, I had started my journey with a desire to leave South Carolina, and now I was returning to my home state with a need to increase my income to support my wife, Vilarin, and our daughter, Jocelyn.

The Trust grounded me in the important work of finding money to save historic buildings, such as the General Joe Wheeler House in Hillsboro, Alabama. Wheeler was one of only two Confederate officers promoted to the rank of general in the US Army after the Civil War. But soon I realized a shortcoming of my duties with the Trust. Time and money were being spent to protect iconic Southern homes, wealthy white Southern homes, but few property owners acknowledged the economic system—slavery—that made some of these structures possible. Preserving historic Southern homes was popular. The slave dwellings standing nearby received little or no attention. I decided that the Trust was not putting enough emphasis on those structures that housed the people whose stolen labor supported the Southern economy that built those grand homes. I wanted to do something that would bring attention to those people, the work they did, the lives they lived, where they lived, and the agency they possessed in spite of a system attempting to rob them of their soul, will, and existence. My DNA compelled me to interpret the lives of enslaved people who once inhabited historic sites.

In 2007 Charleston's Magnolia Plantation and Gardens, America's oldest garden, received a $100,000 grant from the Annenberg Foundation to restore four slave cabins that had been lived in before Emancipation and into the twentieth century. During that span of time, the workers—enslaved and free—lived in four 1850s cabins. With the money, Magnolia hired archaeologists to survey the area around the dwellings. While other historic sites have restored similar slave cabins and houses for interpretation, no site had ever rehabilitated a series of structures that convey African American history from slavery to freedom and beyond. As part of that effort, Magnolia assembled a team of advisors in 2008 to oversee the restoration work. I was one of them.

A few years before, I had seen Magnolia's dilapidated cabins when I participated in a march with Revolutionary War and Civil War reenactors. We arrived at Magnolia from the neighboring Drayton Hall plantation, which has a family connection with Magnolia. As we emerged from the woods, the cabins came into view. I had no prior knowledge of them, but somehow they appealed to the historic preservationist within me. When I saw the four white clapboard dwellings again, I knew they would be central to a story that needed to be told.

My night in the brick cabin at Boone Hall came rushing back to me, as did my visit to Anne Frank's house in Amsterdam many years before. For much of the previous decade, I had been away from the South and removed from opportunities like the one I now had at Magnolia. I knew there were other structures like the Magnolia cabins across the South that also needed just as much attention.

Then I seized on the opportunity to dust off my original idea. I asked Craig Hadley, who supervised the cabin restoration for Magnolia, if I could sleep in one of the cabins. He passed me on to Tom Johnson, Magnolia's garden director, who had the final approval. Without hesitation, Tom said yes. I was on my way to making the idea of sleeping in slave cabins my own and not part of a producer's video project.

TWO

Embarking on a Yearlong Project

Magnolia

On February 28, 2009, I was one of the lucky invitees to a private riverside ceremony to honor the African ancestors, but the closer I got the more I wondered if this was the right place. A turn just off a main highway west of Charleston led to a 1960s subdivision of modest ranch-style homes. The simple decor of porches and yard items screamed *white neighborhood*, where residents would more likely opt for reruns of *Ozzie and Harriet* than episodes of *Roots*. Why is an African ancestors' worship being held here, of all places?

At the river a group of Black people mingled in a crowd near a boat ramp. I recognized a number of local academics and history buffs, who waited as the swift current rushed inland from the distant sea. I knew then that I was not lost. Another familiar face stood out too, but one I had only seen on television—actor Isaiah

Washington. As I gathered with the others, I decided that I was in good company after all.

Centuries ago this place was Ashley Ferry Town, a colonial-era community located at a narrow point in the Ashley River, where a flat-bottom boat tethered to a rope pulled tight across the river shuttled people, livestock, and crops from one bank to the other. Other larger boats docked here too, with human cargo captured from West Africa. Bypassing a 1760s smallpox epidemic in Charleston, slave ships sailed up this river to auction the Africans to nearby plantations. This was probably the first place where those Africans stepped on American soil after their harrowing Middle Passage journey— hallowed ground. The surrounding acreage today is stamped with the names of those plantation-owning families, such as Drayton, Middleton, and Bee. Schools and subdivisions like this one— Drayton on the Ashley—carry those colonial identities. However, there is no visible recognition of the Africans who landed here.

The sky grew dark. I feared rain would spoil this prelude to a larger public ceremony planned upriver at Magnolia Plantation and Gardens to dedicate four restored slave cabins there. At the river, the social chatter gave way to Amadu Massally, a Dallas resident, who came to mourn the ancestors' arrival here. As a community activist, Massally connects African Americans with his homeland, the country of Sierra Leone on Africa's west coast. At least three slave ships arrived at Ashley Ferry Town from Sierra Leone. Massally's lineage is Mende, Sierra Leone's largest ethnic group. At the shoreline, he gazed across the waterway to call on "the common ancestors to acknowledge our presence here today, as descendants of Sierra Leone from Africa and America, to honor you and others who left our country unwillingly to set this country on the trajectory it still enjoys today!" Because of the ancestors' inability to return home he offered them a *sara*, a token of comfort. It came in the form of sand and pebbles from the British slave-trading post at Bunce Island on the Sierra Leone River. He gripped a fistful of sediment from the African river and sprinkled it in the American river. At Bunce Island the ancestors likely took their last steps on African soil before the voyage to Ashley Ferry Town.

During Massally's tribute, Isaiah Washington stood by, impressively dressed in a loose-fitting, green-highlighted robe that fluttered in the brisk wind. A genetic test had shown that Washington descended from the Mende. Since then, the actor known for his role on *Grey's Anatomy* had used his celebrity to inform and inspire people about the ancestors and millions of Americans with genetic links to Africa. He contributed to the building of a school in Sierra Leone and efforts to preserve the crumbling Bunce Island ruins where historians say history sleeps. In return, the Sierra Leone government granted him citizenship based on the DNA results and his philanthropy.

The audience of some thirty people formed a two-line human chain along an L-shaped pier over the river. A white wreath moved along slowly until it reached Thomalind Martin Polite, a local teacher. Martin Polite's seventh-generation grandmother was captured in 1756 in Sierra Leone and sold to a South Carolina rice planter, who named the ten-year-old Priscilla. Martin Polite extended the wreath to Washington, who hurled it into the Ashley River. As if it had been planned, the incoming tide pushed the floral ring upriver toward Magnolia. The attendees returned to their cars for a short drive to the plantation along the oak-lined scenic highway called Ashley River Road, past an elementary school and a plantation named Drayton Hall. The ground along the highway and the entrance into Magnolia bear witness to the Southern economy before and after slavery. Trenches and mounds of soil along the tree-lined road are remnants of phosphate mining after the war, which saved some property owners from financial ruin. Along Magnolia's entrance road, ditches coated with green duckweed once carried fresh water to nearby rice fields where African hands tilled the soil.

Not far from an overgrown rice field, a giant open-sided white tent was set up near the slave cabins at Magnolia in anticipation of rain. The crowd from the riverside ceremony joined a much larger gathering under the shelter. They mingled as VIP guests arrived, among them Charleston's mayor Joseph P. Riley Jr., who had marched a decade earlier against the Confederate flag atop the South Carolina state capitol. With the four renovated cabins as a backdrop, Washington told the audience, "Yes, DNA has memory," but the stories of those "powerful souls" who lived in the cabins must be remembered. Magnolia has been Drayton family property since 1679. The dedication ended with four voices of the Bennett Singers' spirited gospel rendition of "I Done Done What You Told Me to Do." The Bennett Singers are descendants of Adam Bennett, an enslaved gardener at Magnolia.

After Emancipation, Magnolia's garden staff and their families, including Adam Bennett, continued to live in the cabins through the twelve-year period called Reconstruction after the Civil War and beyond. During that time, many Black Americans, some of them once enslaved, held positions in the US Congress, state legis-latures, city councils, and police forces. And Magnolia opened its gardens to the public in the 1870s as Charleston's first tourist attrac-tion, employing formerly enslaved gardeners. Built in the 1850s, the cabins remained in use until the early 1990s. Each of the restored cabins tells a different story. Following the dedication, the audience toured each of them. Standing in the cabins, I wondered about all the people—the families—who had lived in these spaces, where they slept at night, woke up in the morning, loved, argued, wept; those intimate human moments. Too many distractions around me, however, disrupted my ability to contemplate those fleeting thoughts.

At the ceremony the excitement of sleeping in one of these cab-ins grew within me. Few others knew what I was planning. More planning was necessary to make my crazy idea real, if it was even possible. Working with the National Trust, I had interacted with state preservation offices in Alabama and Louisiana, part of a national network of federal and state agencies with the mission to preserve America's historic buildings and sites. The Trust's attention—and that of the preservation offices—went to the archi-tecturally significant buildings, such as the antebellum mansions of the enslavers. But my interest was the overlooked slave cabins and their survival.

The state preservation office in Columbia was the logical first step to secure a list of extant slave cabins. I received early support from Elizabeth Johnson, deputy state historic preservation officer at the South Carolina Department of Archives and History. I was assured that she and her staff would help because we were kindred spirits. About a week after my initial contact, I received a list of twenty-one plantation sites on the National Register of Historic Places.

Most of the professionals who preserve historic structures embraced my idea. Others, however, saw some risk. That pushback even came from my own relatives, who were concerned that people would want to harm me. One of my aunts asked, "Isn't there another way to commemorate our ancestors? Why do you have to go to that extreme?"

As I prepared the list of properties where I wanted to stay, I called my friend Herb Frazier, a former newspaper reporter, to help me connect with the media. Herb was a freelance writer and public relations consultant who helped Magnolia with the February 2009 cabin dedication. When Herb sent out that initial press release in the spring of 2010, announcing the first five cabin stays, I saw my idea maturing beyond that one night in a slave cabin at Boone Hall in 1999. The Slave Cabin Project was taking shape. My goal was to sleep for as many nights as possible in one year—2010—in buildings constructed by enslaved people in South Carolina.

My first three overnight stays were scheduled for Magnolia Plantation and Gardens, the Heyward House in Bluffton, and McLeod Plantation on James Island near Charleston. All lie within a culturally important geographic region for Gullah Geechee people, the descendants of enslaved West Africans. In 2006 Congress passed an act that created the Gullah Geechee Cultural Heritage Corridor along the coastal lowlands from Wilmington, North Carolina, through South Carolina and Georgia to St. Augustine, Florida. In Georgia and Florida, people of African descent prefer the term Geechee to describe themselves and their culture.

I set Saturday, May 8, 2010, as the night I'd sleep at Magnolia. Being on the team that evaluated Magnolia's renovated cabins gave me a preview of Magnolia's history. As the time approached to sleep there, I also pondered slavery's lingering implications and contradictions in Charleston, marketed to tourists as the Holy City, an ironic moniker for this cradle of human bondage.

Charleston's unique Gullah history reflects the influences of our African ancestors through food, religious worship, language, and craft, especially the coiled sweetgrass baskets that have become a Lowcountry icon. However, that link to our bloodline hasn't erased the corrosive interaction between the slave owners and the enslaved. Free Blacks, the offspring of the slave owners, even themselves enslaved people of African descent. Mistrust divided the dark-skinned and fair-skinned Black offspring of the enslavers, who sometimes extended to their mixed-race children privileges denied to the darker-skinned slave-cabin dwellers. The skin-color divide within the nonwhite community was most evident through the Brown Fellowship Society. The society provided social aid and a place to bury the dead but only to mulattos. Even into the middle of the twentieth century, skin color in the city's Black community was a pernicious social threshold to the right club, church, or school. Today, thousands of African Americans carry surnames of slave-owning families— Middleton, Drayton, Pinckney, and Huger among them. Some celebrate these connections, while others may not be aware of the history of those names. Newcomers and tourists to Charleston can't fathom these contradictions or slavery's lingering generational trauma of rape, racism, and disenfranchisement. For visitors it's all blurred by the architectural charm of a city built with Black hands.

These ironies are lost, too, on the uninitiated traveler drawn to the historic gardens and the plantation past at Magnolia.

According to family history, Thomas Drayton Jr. and his wife, Ann Fox, established Magnolia in 1679. He and other subsequent owners did not, of course, wield a hammer or saw. He and other relatives owned scores of enslaved Africans, who provided most of the labor to clear the land and build the house. Some spent their entire lives there. Some fled. In 1816, Myrah, enslaved at Magnolia, emancipated herself, albeit briefly. She was eventually caught miles away in Colleton. That same year, Thomas Drayton Jr.'s fourth-generation grandson, John Grimké Drayton, was born. At a young age, he inherited Magnolia following his older brother's death from an accidental gunshot wound. John Grimké Drayton became an Episcopal minister, presiding for four decades before and after the Civil War over the nearby St. Andrew's Episcopal Church. In the 1850s through the 1860s, he enslaved at least forty-five people, who lived in eleven wooden cabins. Each building held two families in a room on either side of a brick chimney. By the 1840s, Drayton enlarged Magnolia's gardens. He is credited with establishing Magnolia's romantic-style gardens, where there is minimal human interference and nature rules. As with the house, it's unlikely he did much of the work, instead directing enslaved gardeners in the tasks of turning a raw landscape into an internationally celebrated collection of azaleas and camellias.

At Magnolia Chapel, reserved for Black worshipers, he ministered to the enslaved, calling them his "black Roses." His ministry was thought to represent yet another contradiction of slavery.

Reverend Drayton conducted marriage ceremonies between enslaved men and women, including an April 8, 1855, service at his home where Gabriel and Ruthy, owned by a neighbor, exchanged vows. Despite the presence of an Episcopal minister, the marriages weren't recognized by the law. As a man of his time, it is likely that Drayton struggled with the dual realities of slavery and his religious beliefs. Were his actions a subtle defiance of society's norms? Was he seeking atonement for enslaving people? Reverend Drayton's aunts Sarah and Angelina Grimké were leading abolitionists whose activism placed them at odds with whites in South Carolina and in other Southern states and even some Northerners who felt the sisters should avoid speaking about something as controversial as slavery. They eventually settled in Boston. It's possible their antislavery crusades influenced their young nephew, although as an adult he didn't emancipate his "black Roses." John Drayton Hastie Jr., one of seven members of Magnolia's board of directors and a tenth-generation Drayton, said that Reverend Drayton's racism was the unfortunate "norm." He was a conservative man not ready to confront intransigent social issues in Southern society. "His aunts were banished," Hastie said. "He did not want exile for himself or his family. He took comfort in 'paternalism.'"

The four renovated Magnolia cabins are all that remain of the eleven slave dwellings that once stood in a line some distance from Magnolia's main house, at the end of a long oak-lined entrance. One dwelling reflects the 1850s and slavery. It has whitewashed wooden walls and a pitched ceiling and loft, stained black from fireplace smoke. A wooden mortar and pestle, essential rice-cleaning tools, lean against the hearth. Another cabin reflects the 1870s, the Reconstruction era; it is brighter, with white walls and a pitched ceiling. A heavy, unvarnished wooden table with two matching benches and two cabinets take up much of the space in an adjoining room. The Jim Crow–era cabin depicts segregation in the 1930s, a decade when at least eight African Americans were lynched in South Carolina. Originally, the walls were covered with newspaper to seal cracks; during the restoration, the wallpaper became newspaper facsimiles. A black potbelly stove's flue joins the brick chimney. The other side of the cabin opens to a sleeping space with a crude bed formed by interlacing rope to support a mattress. The fourth cabin, tied to an electrical line, celebrates the civil rights era's local protest movement in Charleston. For nearly four decades, until 1969, the cabin, expanded to four rooms, with wallpaper and linoleum flooring, was the Leach family home. Johnnie Leach was Magnolia's senior gardener until his death in 2016 at age ninety-three.[*]

Taylor Drayton Nelson, Magnolia's chief executive officer and an eleventh-generation Drayton, told a local newspaper reporter the three-year cabin restoration provides "a tangible link with the intangible past." Those ties might have been lost had it not been for Nelson's chance encounter with a senior executive of the Annenberg Foundation, who took a liking to the tall, youthful Nelson, who sports a ponytail and plays rock guitar. That friendship led to

---

[*] A photo of him, his grandson, a son, and their cousin, all Magnolia employees, currently hangs on a wall above a white wreath.

Magnolia receiving an unprecedented $100,000 grant to restore the cabins and survey the area around them.

I didn't choose the Reconstruction-era cabin for the launch of the Slave Cabin Project. A Magnolia staff member made the selection for me. He had lit a fire in the hearth on a mild night when heat was not really necessary. Nevertheless, it added to the ambience. My inaugural cabin stay received local print and broadcast media coverage. As the sun was setting, a reporter with the local NBC affiliate arrived and gave me reason to be afraid. He told me about his experience of sleeping in a tent in South Africa when a large spider dropped onto his chest. Then Magnolia's nature center director Chris Smith warned me of the alligators lurking in the nearby swamp. I would think of both admonitions often through the night.

As a program officer with the National Trust, I was accustomed to media interviews, but this was different. This was my first on-camera questioning about why I wanted to travel South Carolina to sleep in slave cabins. If a television station sent a reporter to interview me, then I knew my plan had value. It wasn't crazy after all. When the reporter left, I was alone. Some had suggested that my experience would be like staying in a haunted house, but it wasn't unpleasant at all. Hearing my own breath, I could imagine the men, women, and children who had lived in the cabin during the decades of Jim Crow, when the opportunities of Reconstruction were pulled away from Black people. The evening was enhanced by the sounds of music and nature. A wedding had been booked on the property. The band's music mixed with nature's reverberations—crickets, frogs, birds. When the musicians stopped around midnight, the piercing screams of patrolling peacocks filled the air. I couldn't sleep. Admittedly, it was a little spooky being alone in a former slave cabin and uncomfortable physically and psychologically. That night I pondered what drove me to do such an odd thing. The ancestors! Several times I ventured into the darkness, hearing a sound on the wooden shingled roof, but it was a tree branch swaying in the wind, not the restless spirits some people had warned me to watch out for. Putting a fresh log on the fire, I finally drifted off to sleep, snug in my sleeping bag on a hard wooden floor that reminded me the ancestors had found a better way to sleep in their cabin than on the hard floor. Older folks laid on rope beds made of tightly drawn ropes. Children sometimes curled their little bodies on a pallet, huge pillow-like bags stuffed with fluffy material such as straw, hay, or moss. Most enslaved people slept on pallets.

The morning call of shrieking peacocks signaled I had made it through the first night of my one-year plan. A blue sky with warm breezes provided the perfect weather to get off the cabin's hard wooden floor and stroll through Magnolia, before almost all of the employees arrived for work. Unlike all the years when scores of enslaved people lived and worked here, I had the place almost to myself. I followed an asphalt drive to discover a burial ground on the edge of the nearby swamp that's home to alligators and snakes— the kind that might have discouraged enslaved people from attempting a nighttime escape. The site is near water, a sign that it's the resting place for Black people. According to custom, people of African descent buried their dead near water, believing the water would return the deceased's soul to Africa. The dates on the headstones showed that some of these people were born into slavery but died free. What a transformation in one lifetime. Although given the opportunity through freedom, did these people ever leave Magnolia? Could it be that they left only to have their bodies returned to the place of their birth and enslavement? I found depressions in the soil and wondered if they could be the unmarked graves of the enslaved. Were the ancestors my guide to their final resting place? I felt connected to them, as if they approved that I would tell their stories.

Large gray headstones for Adam Bennett and his wife, Hannah, are prominent features at the site's entrance, befitting the Bennetts' importance to the Drayton family. Bennett was the revered garden superintendent before and after the Civil War. According to the Bennett and Drayton family lore, he traveled more than two hundred miles on foot and other means to Flat Rock, North Carolina, where the Reverend John Grimké Drayton had fled before Union soldiers marched into the area. He told Drayton the main house had been burned, but the gardens were untouched. And then the two men, once owner and enslaved, now both free, returned to Magnolia, where they would live for the rest of their lives, though in very different circumstances.

Heyward House

Before noon on a clear day in November 1861, a massive armada of eighty-four Union navy ships carrying twenty thousand army troops steamed into Port Royal Sound on the South Carolina coast below Charleston to launch a sea invasion seven months after Confederates took Fort Sumter. Brigadier General Thomas Drayton, commanding the four thousand Confederates at Port Royal, fought against his brother Captain Percival Drayton at the helm of the Union gunboat *Pocahontas*. Both men are related to the Drayton family at Magnolia Plantation in Charleston, where I launched the Slave Cabin Project.

During a fourteen-mile journey inland to capture the nearly defenseless Beaufort, the Union's big shipboard guns sent percussive waves of booming sound rippling across the flat marshy lowlands. Whites in Beaufort, who depended on enslaved people to maintain their genteel lifestyles, quickly fled the state's second-oldest city after Charleston.

Their swift exit was the second-greatest skedaddle behind the Union's defeat earlier that summer at the First Battle of Bull Run, a clash that drew curious spectators to the rolling Virginia countryside. When whites fled Beaufort, they left behind eight thousand to ten thousand enslaved people stunned by the Union's swift invasion and perplexed about their future. Black people long remembered that noisy day as "the big gun shoot." When the smoke cleared, the US government, with the aid of Northern abolitionists, tested whether Black people could function on their own, free of the burdens of slavery. The formerly enslaved people farmed confiscated lands and opened schools during this prelude to Reconstruction called the Port Royal Experiment. The Penn School on St. Helena Island was one of the early centers of learning. Today the Penn Center is a community center and museum on the rural St. Helena Island. Beginning in the mid-1990s, I was the center's director of history and culture. I was able to join my passion for history with my hobby as a Civil War reenactor. I staged a mock battle between Confederate and Union reenactors. I brought a demonstration to Penn that had never been seen before to illustrate that during the war, Black people—those who had been recently freed and others who were born free—were proactive in the liberation of enslaved people.

With my sleeping bag stowed away on May 25, 2010, I headed south along US 17 toward Bluffton, South Carolina, on a route I had traveled often when I was on the Penn Center staff. The highway slices through a dense forest before crossing open wetlands with signs naming the people here before the Europeans and Africans. The roadway skirts Yemassee, a small railroad junction named for a Native people who warred against the English settlers. The river names echo the Indigenous inhabitants: Ashepoo, Combahee, and Edisto. These rivers form the ACE Basin estuary, the largest incubator of aquatic life on the Atlantic coast. At points along the highway the estuary's carpet of golden grasses extends to a blue-sky horizon. Then the view returns to dense woodlands at the Combahee, where a bridge named for abolitionist Harriet Tubman spans the waterway. The Underground Railroad and Civil War hero was with a US Navy gunboat during a raid along the Combahee that freed about 750 enslaved people. Closer to Bluffton, a Civil War symbol reminded me of the haunting warnings from friends and family who cautioned me to be wary of people who might do me harm. I saw Confederate flags on vehicles that seemed to stand out more than ever during the ninety-mile drive that gave me time to decide whether spending a night alone in a slave cabin was something I really wanted to do.

Those concerns vanished at Bluffton, a quaint community on a bluff along the May River that once served as an inland river port near today's popular Hilton Head Island. Bluffton's peaceful surroundings exude the feeling of a safe, walkable tourist town, with sidewalks and slow speed limits. At the Heyward House, the staff also helped to settle me as they showed me the tiny cabin, about the size of a one-car garage. They said they accepted my idea to sleep there because they wanted to bring more attention to the house and cabin, and they believed my presence would help. It had a bed, replicas of the tools used to build the Heyward House, and minimal space.

At the Heyward House, the wooden slave cabin is thought to have existed before the white family's main house. The cabin, with white weatherboard siding, on a brick foundation, was built around 1840, a year before enslaved craftsmen completed the main house. The small lot with the cabin and house in a compact urban setting contrasts dramatically with Magnolia's cabins, surrounded by five hundred acres of gardens, woodlands, and a waterfowl haven. It is believed that an all-male crew of enslaved carpenters lived in the cabin while constructing the house for John James Cole, a Beaufort County rice planter. He and his family used it during the hot summer months of the rice-growing season as a retreat from their plantation, near mosquito-infested marshes, breeding grounds for yellow fever and malaria. Enslaved female domestic workers lived in the cabin until the end of the Civil War. Nearly two decades later, the descendants of Thomas Heyward Jr., one of four South Carolina signers of the Declaration of Independence, acquired the house. The Historic Bluffton Foundation purchased the property in 2000 and converted it to the community museum and visitor's center.

Shortly after the Union navy's initial assault, General Drayton retreated with his men to a new headquarters at Bluffton, thirty miles south of Beaufort. Eventually, Union gunboats bombarded Bluffton in June 1863. Much of the town was destroyed, but the Heyward House and the slave cabin were among the twenty-one structures that survived. Incorporated in 1825, Bluffton was formed with five hundred people in a heavily wooded one-square-mile area. Life in Bluffton was timed by the May River tides that gifted a bountiful harvest of shrimp, fish, and oysters for the local shelling factory. Crushed oyster shells bleached by the sun turned the main streets into gleaming white thoroughfares. Today, a population of nearly twenty-five thousand resides within a meandering town boundary that resembles an oddly gerrymandered US House district. Surprisingly, in spite of its legacy of slavery, people in the town have lived somewhat peacefully.

The Heyward House staff invited some locals to meet me. Following my brief talk about the Slave Cabin Project, most of them left, except for Jacob "Jake" Martin, who engaged me for about an hour about my work and his childhood in Bluffton. I told him I didn't plan to sleep in cabins into the following year. Martin had returned to Bluffton after he retired from the Detroit police force. When he was a child, Black children like him and white children did everything together except attend the same schools and churches. Whites, however, had a habit of visiting Black congregations unannounced. Martin had known the family that lived in the Heyward House, where he now volunteered as a docent.

Martin represents the closeness between Blacks and whites in a southern town that once had a thriving Black business district with a movie theater, icehouse, and general store, supported by the entire community. In the aftermath of slavery, Black families weren't regarded as ex-slaves, but were judged on their own personal strengths and fortitude. It was never perfect, but Bluffton was never just a little white town.

After Martin left, I retreated to the cabin. I placed my sleeping bag near the door, but wondered how many enslaved workers had been crowded into this space while they worked on the Heyward House. For one person—me—it was comfortable, but how cramped might it have been for four or six, along with whatever minimal personal possessions they were allowed? I kept the door open to let in some cool air. With a club by my side, in case of a wandering raccoon or two-legged intruder, a hooting owl serenaded me to sleep. The next morning the door was open just as I had left it, but the hooting owl was gone, replaced with sounds of commuter traffic and joggers passing by. Small crawling worms had invaded my space.

Before I returned home, the staff arranged for me to meet a small group of elementary school children. I shared with them a brief talk about slavery that I purposely limited because I knew from experience as a National Park Service ranger at Fort Sumter that young children have very short attention spans. When the students left, I drove away, still heeding warnings to be on high alert for people who waved Confederate flags. I also departed with a sense of accomplishment. I had completed my first cabin stay away from Charleston, a major step that convinced me I could do this alone in an unfamiliar place. I was far less stressed and better able to think clearly about the next adventure to carry my message of slave cabin preservation across the harbor from Charleston.

THREE

Honoring the Ancestors

McLeod

Singing sustained Pompey Dawson as he and other enslaved people at McLeod Plantation picked Sea Island cotton under a blistering hot sun amid heavy humidity that drenched them in sweat. Bent over to pull fluffy cotton balls from short prickly bushes, Dawson belted out the old Negro song "Motherless Chillins See a Hard-time." It soothed him and the others, who, because of the lyrics, tagged Dawson with the basket name "Hardtime." In Gullah communities on the Sea Islands of coastal South Carolina, it was common for people to have a basket name or nickname like "Dimmy," "Apple," or "Man," used exclusively within close-knit Gullah enclaves.

Born in 1821, Dawson and his wife, Judy, and their children, William, Titus, and Mima, also were born enslaved at McLeod, one of more than two dozen plantations on James Island across the harbor from Charleston. By 1860, McLeod's Black population of seventy-four people lived in twenty-three cabins. Many of them were part of the agricultural workforce that grew peanuts, watermelons, and potatoes. In the 1860 census, McLeod was the island's fifth-largest plantation but first in the production of Sea Island cotton, popular for its extra-long fibers that made it a lucrative European export.

After the Civil War, Dawson briefly became a leading cultivator of Sea Island cotton on James Island. Through the Freedmen's Bureau, he and forty-three other formerly enslaved people received up to forty acres at McLeod and other plantations. But later the law was rescinded, crashing the independent Black farmers' hopes. The federal government returned the property to the original owner. Some Black people, descendants of people at McLeod, remained there to work the fields and live in five cabins that survived into the twentieth century. A squat brick cistern between a line of cabins and oaks is a reminder of the water source that once served the enslaved community. Behind the cabins a leaning outhouse struggles to defy gravity. Robersina Gathers lived in one of the cabins. When Gathers became old enough, she helped the elders harvest beans, tomatoes, peas, collard greens, and other produce. When Gathers was eight years old, her mother gave birth, likely in their cabin, to a baby girl. One year later, the baby died. "Her name was Julia," Gathers remembered. "My father built a coffin made of board and buried her in the woods behind our cabin."

McLeod, one of the plantations on the list I received from the state preservation office in Columbia, sits at a high embankment near Wappoo Creek, named for one of the Native American tribes on the island as far back as 600 BC. McLeod's history dates back to 1741, when Samuel Peronneau Sr. farmed and raised livestock there. By 1851, William W. McLeod purchased nearly seventeen hundred acres. McLeod preferred to call his property Inverness, possibly a reference to a city in the Scottish Highlands. During its heyday it was simply called McLeod's.

Made of clapboard siding and topped with tin, the cabins parallel an adjacent oak allée that provides a stunning tree-lined view of McLeod's main house from Folly Road, the island's main highway that ends at the Atlantic Ocean. A much larger sixth cabin closest to the road was constructed after the Civil War. Surrounded by wide tidal marshes and crooked creeks and rivers, James Island is typical of the sea islands that hug South Carolina's Atlantic coast, isolated until bridges joined them with the mainland following World War II. That isolation allowed people of African descent—Gullah Geechee people—to retain more of their African ways, especially their Gullah language, than Black residents on the mainland.

Confederate troops at Fort Johnson on the opposite side of the island fired on Fort Sumter, beginning the Civil War at 4:30 a.m. on April 12, 1861. Soon the cannon volley was heard in my hometown of Kingstree, seventy-five miles away. In Kingstree, the barrage "could be distinctly heard, which for a time everybody took to be thunder."

On July 16, 1863, the Massachusetts Fifty-Fourth, a volunteer regiment of free Black men, camped on the island at the Sol Legare community, where they engaged the Confederates in a skirmish. The Massachusetts Fifty-Fourth later battled the Confederates on nearby Morris Island. Restaurateur and Civil War relic hunter

Robert Bohrn made a startling find in 1987 on the sandy shores of Folly Beach, a popular oceanfront tourist destination near Charleston that was once off-limits to Black beachgoers. While scanning the ground with a metal detector, he stumbled on the graves of nineteen Black Union soldiers killed during the war. They were members of the Fifty-Fifth Massachusetts Infantry Regiment.*

Two years after the remains were found, Hollywood released the movie *Glory*, which depicts the Civil War's first all-Black volunteer fighting force. The assault on Battery Wagner was the film's climactic scene. The story of that battle sent me on another deep dive in the history books to uncover those Black warriors who had a say in the war's outcome.

As a park ranger, I was accustomed to fielding questions. But one query knocked me back. At Fort Moultrie, Confederate reenactors camped and presented living-history demonstrations. Some wore gray Confederate uniforms. Others wore Union blue. I was invited to join them. Knowing the real Confederate forces waged war to keep people who looked like me enslaved, I declined. I also suspected that the reenactors felt they needed my Black face to validate their actions. I resented what they were doing. However, they were honoring their ancestors and heritage. I could respect that. Then I saw their sincerity. They were honoring soldiers.

Declining their offer got me thinking about forming a group of Black Civil War reenactors. I spoke to Bohrn about the movie *Glory* and the absence of Black groups locally. Atlanta, Boston, and

---

* Those remains have since been reinterred at the National Cemetery in Beaufort, South Carolina.

Washington, DC, had Black reenactors; why not Charleston, where the war started? His encouragement to organize a group heightened my desire to do so. About a year after the movie was released, I joined several others in starting the Fifty-Fourth Massachusetts Volunteer Infantry, Company I. The idea took hold immediately, attracting prominent members of the Black community, including the city's first Black police chief, a funeral home director, the owner of a Gullah art gallery, and the director of the African American research center at the College of Charleston.

We didn't play war games when we donned blue woolen uniforms and slung reproduction-model rifles over our shoulders. We were living historians portraying brave Black Union troops who fought to end slavery. I sought to present an accurate history, to wear the uniform properly, and to well represent the two hundred thousand Black volunteer soldiers and the women who aided them. Ironically, the Confederate reenactors needed Black reenactors as much as we needed them. They trained us on military tactics and weapons safety, enabling us to gain our certifications as reenactors. We could have traveled to Atlanta to train with Black reenactors, but the time and distance would have delayed our plans. The local Confederate reenactors benefited from having us around for reenactments because then they'd have an enemy to shoot at. Later on, we mingled with the Confederate reenactors to understand what motivated them. Some said they wished the real Confederates had won the war.

During the Civil War, when the Southern army ordered the evacuation of James Island, plantation owners were allowed to select one male and one female enslaved person to remain behind to watch over their property during the war. At McLeod, Stephen and Harriet Forest were tasked to stay behind as the McLeod family fled to Greenwood, South Carolina, located two hundred miles inland from Charleston. During the war, McLeod's was a Confederate field commissary, headquarters, and hospital.

After the war, another volunteer Black Union unit, the Fifty-Fifth Massachusetts, was possibly among a larger contingent of Union forces camped at McLeod. The site was used for three years as local headquarters for the Freedmen's Bureau, a federal government agency that assisted newly freed people.

McLeod and James Island are important to Black Civil War reenactors like me. I participated in two mock battles at McLeod long before I began the Slave Cabin Project. I asked my fellow reenactors if any of them would join me to sleep in a cabin at McLeod. James Brown and Ernest Parks raised their hand. Parks was quick to accept my invitation. He was reared in the Sol Legare community, a fiercely independent Black community named for a former slave-holding farmer who sold house plots on a narrow strip of high ground to newly freed people. The offer to sleep in a McLeod cabin meshed with his yearning to feel the ancestors' spirit. It was his African-centered upbringing at Sol Legare that prepared him when he and others left the community to integrate a white high school.

Parks was a scrappy ninth grader when he left his nurturing Black world at Sol Legare in the late 1960s for bare-knuckle encounters at a white school grappling with an end to race-based segregation. Like the school, Folly Beach, the island's main attraction with a boardwalk and amusement center, would eventually admit beachgoers with black skin. Parks and his neighbors, however, had for generations had their own entertainment and more in the Sol Legare community. A century after Emancipation, Sol Legare had a community school, hotel, restaurants, nightclubs, and a gathering place with a riverside boardwalk. A farmers' cooperative, the Seashore Farmers Lodge, provided cultural activities, religious services, meeting space, and a fundraising organization. Back then, elders taught farming and fishing, necessary skills to sustain businesses.

Parks and other Black students with strong identities left this safe haven in 1968 to integrate James Island High School. During the following two years, frequent clashes between students of both races disrupted campus life. Parks remembered:

The white boys had never really experienced blackness to the depth to which we gave it. So they started hurling racial epithets at us, particularly toward our women, and we weren't having it. The next thing we faced off and rocks started flying and then we got into actual fisticuffs. The cops came. Some students, black and white, were arrested but later released. The next year the white boys were prepared; they brought the [Ku Klux Klan]. The police came again and intervened and stopped them. We were staunch in the Civil Rights Movement that was very active in Charleston at that time. So it was all built up to the point that you had to explode.

I set June 19, 2010, as the date for the cabin stay at McLeod. I chose that date for a reason. June 19, now called Juneteenth, is an annual observance across the nation to commemorate the date when news of the Emancipation Proclamation reached enslaved people in Texas, the most remote of the slaveholding states. Although the Emancipation Proclamation took effect on January 1, 1863, President Abraham Lincoln's executive order only freed enslaved people in the Confederate states. Two and a half years later, in Galveston, Texas, on June 19, 1865, two months after the war ended, enslaved people learned of their freedom. Later that year the Thirteenth Amendment to the US Constitution abolished slavery.

As I had done with the two previous cabin stays, I met with staff of the property owners, the Historic Charleston Foundation, to discuss the dos and don'ts of my visit.* The property had no physical boundaries, and the staff told me to be aware of people who might come on the property late at night in search of Civil War artifacts. Then they showed me the cabin closest to the main house. The night of our cabin stay, Ernest, James, and I sat outside under long oak boughs wrapped in moss and topped with welted resurrection ferns that spring to life after rain. We talked about our ancestors' struggles, how far we've come as a people, and our role to portray freedom-fighting Black soldiers. Although Ernest's ancestors had been enslaved on the island's Dill Plantation, not far from McLeod, some of them may also have worked at McLeod, which had a bartering relationship with Dill. Being familiar with McLeod and having Ernest and James with me raised my confidence beyond the levels reached following the two previous stays at Magnolia and the Heyward House in Bluffton.

---

* McLeod is currently owned by the Charleston Parks and Recreation Department.

McLeod is a blend of Magnolia and the Heyward House. While it is nestled among a grove of oaks like Magnolia, McLeod is also alongside a busy road, similar to the Heyward House. Later in the night, the traffic noise subsided. The following morning Ernest woke before me. The crickets' clicking echoed across the field. Hovering mist created a soft white blanket just above the ground. He imagined how our ancestors had been greeted with similar sights and sounds as they rose to plow the soil.

The roar of morning traffic soon returned along with a surprise: breakfast delivered by my National Trust coworker and our mutual friend. Both are white women. Their affirming gesture convinced me that what I was doing had an appeal to the wider community.

Several days after our stay at McLeod, Ernest met with James Island historian Eugene Frazier, who told him, "I know your people!" Frazier said that Harrison Wilder is Parks's paternal great-great-grandfather. He was enslaved in Sumter, South Carolina, where he escaped and joined the 104th Regiment of the United States Colored Infantry.

When Parks became a Civil War reenactor, he took on the persona of an unnamed foot soldier. "I love being able to tell the story from the perspective of the foot soldier, who went from being a slave to being a soldier fighting for America. But now my name is Harrison Wilder," he said. "I tell the story of how I escaped from McLeod Plantation [and] traveled down to Beaufort where I met Robert Smalls, who commandeered the Confederate boat the *Planter* and turned it over to the Union Navy. Smalls took me to Boston where I joined the Massachusetts Fifty-Fourth and then I ended up back on James Island to fight on Morris Island where a lot of my comrades died. In my story, however, I don't die on Morris Island."

Goodwill

I never would have imagined a scrap of circus history at Goodwill Plantation if property owner Larry Faulkenberry had not pointed it out to me. He stepped across a shallow ditch along the main road into Goodwill to pinch shards of silver wire embedded in a tree, a reminder of a flamboyant showman who coined "the greatest show on earth." P. T. Barnum quartered camels, zebras, and horses on two hundred acres enclosed within wire fencing at this sprawling property east of Columbia in central South Carolina. Barnum purchased Goodwill in 1888 as a wedding gift for his granddaughter Julia H. Clark.* Animals accustomed to prancing before cheering crowds roamed the forest for several years near Goodwill's main gate. I enjoyed Faulkenberry's tales of Barnum's connection with Goodwill, but these were not the stories that drew me to this thirty-three-hundred-acre plantation site, established before the American Revolution. The main event for me stood in a grassy meadow beyond the trees. Nearly three decades before Barnum purchased Goodwill, it had been the temporary home for nearly two thousand enslaved people displaced by the Civil War when the Union navy took control of Port Royal Sound. In the areas beyond federal control, slavery continued under the Confederate government.

---

* Julia Clark died in the main house at Goodwill Plantation from childbirth complications on February 10, 1894.

In response to Beaufort's capture, the Confederacy ordered rice planters within twenty-five miles of Beaufort to move their enslaved workforce to the state's interior to continue the production of food for civilians and soldiers. The winding Combahee River, flowing into Port Royal Sound, divides Beaufort and Colleton Counties, where rice plantations lined the tidal waterway used to irrigate rice fields at high tide then drain them on the outgoing current. Later in the war, Harriett Tubman participated with the Union navy on a raid that ushered in a new kind of scorched-earth warfare that left plantations in ruin but liberated hundreds of enslaved people.

A decade before the Union's invasion, South Carolina rice planter Nathaniel Heyward, likely the largest slaveholder in the South, died at age eighty-five and was buried at his Bluff Plantation in Beaufort County. Heyward had expanded a modest inheritance of property to some twenty plantations covering thirty-five thousand acres, mostly along the Combahee in Beaufort and Colleton Counties and Charleston County, where more than twenty-five hundred enslaved people had the capacity in 1849 to produce 16.7 million pounds of unmilled rice. By comparison, the much smaller Magnolia Plantation in 1850 produced 40,000 pounds of rice. Of course, Heyward's success came with the exploitation of enslaved West Africans whose Black hands were skilled at growing the white grain. They understood how to harness the tides to irrigate rice, a method that replaced the channeling of water from inland swamps that had been used widely in South Carolina prior to the Revolutionary War.

Responding to the wartime evacuation order, Charles Heyward—Nathaniel Heyward's son—rounded up enslaved people from four of his rice plantations on the Colleton side of the

Combahee. Among them was Betsy Anderson, a twenty-four-year-old field hand from the Myrtle Grove Plantation. Anderson and the others boarded the Charleston and Savannah Railroad that traveled on a rickety narrow-gauge rail line and trestles spanning marshes and rivers with Indian names: Ashepoo, Combahee, and Edisto. Today that massive estuary is known as the ACE Basin. At Charleston another rail line took them to Kingville train station near Gadsden, eleven miles west of Goodwill. Those who could walked to Goodwill. Those who couldn't boarded wagons for the last leg of the journey to Goodwill on the Wateree River's west bank.

The river is named for the Wateree tribe, whose presence was first recorded by Spanish explorers in the 1500s. Eventually, white settlers pushed Indigenous people out to claim the land. Daniel Huger, a wealthy rice planter and member of the Continental Congress, established Goodwill in 1785. Following his death fourteen years later, Goodwill's ownership was transferred to the Heyward family. The crops grown and lumber and bricks produced enabled Goodwill to prosper, and its location on the river gave it water access to the port at Charleston. The most notable achievement, however, was its success as the only large-scale rice producer in the state's interior more than one hundred miles from the rice-growing lowlands. Goodwill was so large that at one point, its seven thousand acres crossed into neighboring Sumter County and came close to the plantation of William Ellison, whose success came not from producing rice but from making and repairing cotton gins and growing the fluffy white fibers. At the start of the Civil War in 1861, Ellison's workforce of seventy enslaved people cultivated one hundred bales of cotton. Although Ellison, who died the year the war began, was a slave-owning planter like the Heywards, he came to the slave trade on a different path. Ellison, who was Black, was born into slavery in Fairfield County. He gained his freedom after apprenticing with a white artisan who taught him how to build and repair cotton gins. After Ellison's death his sons carried on the cotton gin shop and plantation to suffer the same economic doom as other white plantation owners. After the war the Ellison Plantation only produced five bales of cotton in 1869.

When the first shot of the Civil War was fired, Charles Heyward's son, Edward Barnwell Heyward, owned Goodwill. In 1858, the younger Heyward had bought Goodwill and its enslaved workforce of eighty-two people, who produced cotton and corn and a small parcel of rice irrigated by the Wateree River. The enslaved people from the Combahee knew very little about growing cotton and corn, but they were expert rice growers. Rice production at Goodwill came with a slight twist. Instead of irrigating the fields using the tidal flow method, the fields at Goodwill were nourished with water that flowed from a pond to the fields and then to the river. Nevertheless, the enslaved rice growers adapted to increase Goodwill's production in the sand hills of the state's interior, a vastly different landscape from the flat, wet coastal lowlands.

When the Combahee exodus stopped, Goodwill's enslaved population swelled from 280 people to some 2,000 people. Four years into the war, it began to close in on central South Carolina. In February 1865, the Union army, led by Major General William Tecumseh Sherman, invaded the state, arriving to face a mostly overwhelmed and decimated Confederate army. Entering from Georgia, Union forces cut a path of ruin as they advanced toward the capital city. When troops approached, old white men waved white flags of surrender as thousands of horse-mounted soldiers moved along briskly. The old men announced the rebels had left Columbia, adding that the "blue-clad army" would be welcomed as long as they weren't unkind to old folks, women, and children. The ground shook from the concussion of "big guns" that rained hot shells on Columbia. The next morning, few houses remained in a smoldering city. After laying waste to Columbia, federal troops proceeded toward North Carolina. Passing through Fairfield County, just north of Columbia, troops gleefully burned more homes. Enslaved people watched the destruction with teary eyes. Sixteen-year-old Ami Lumpkin joined the chorus of voices who pleaded with the soldiers "not to burn our white folks houses, and they didn't."

Days after the South surrendered on April 9, 1865, Edward Barnwell Heyward took a buggy ride to Columbia. He returned with a federal agent who had good news for the enslaved community. Standing high in the buggy, the agent told them they were free to come and go as they pleased. They didn't rejoice at the news that a Union victory had freed them. "Why, suh, dem 'ent done nutt'n!" said Betsy Anderson, who witnessed that announcement. "They didn't holler and shout and have a big time," she recalled. As one of the enslaved people brought to Goodwill from the Combahee, Anderson likely spoke in rich Gullah tones.

For much of that day, Goodwill's Black residents quietly lounged around without celebration and talked among themselves. They returned to work the next day on the promise the Heywards would specify how they'd be paid for future work. Eventually, the newly formed Freedmen's Bureau in Columbia helped Goodwill's

Black families negotiate a work contract with the Heywards. On June 5, 1865, the Heywards proposed varying shares of the crop sales based on the workers' classification. Freedmen would be clothed, housed, and fed, with the young, elderly, and infirm cared for. Heyward's proposal also included the right to punish workers for laziness, misconduct, desertion, and insubordination. The freedmen agreed to those terms until January 1, 1866. On that date, with the crops harvested and sold, they were no longer under the contract. Heyward arranged for them to return to the Lowcountry and somehow had them carried back up the Combahee River on the Union gunboat *John Adams*. It is the same vessel that accompanied Harriet Tubman on raids along the Combahee to free enslaved people. Those who returned to the Lowcountry from Goodwill discovered that enslaved people who had remained there had been free with the Emancipation Proclamation for more than two years before the war ended, while others were freed as early as 1861 when the Union navy seized Beaufort.

Not all of them, however, left Goodwill. Betsy Anderson was among those who stayed, refusing to return to the Myrtle Grover Plantation on the Combahee. She had married Henry Anderson, who was at Goodwill when she arrived with the other people from the Combahee. When asked in the mid-1930s why she didn't go back to the Combahee, she said her husband belonged at Goodwill, and she could not leave him. "Me marry Henry Anderson. Him belongs here, en me couldn't lef' um." In 1935, Betsy Anderson died at age ninety-one.

I didn't call property owner Larry Faulkenberry to ask for permission to sleep in one of the 1858 slave cabins there. Tom

Milligan, a Columbia real estate agent who handled Faulkenberry's purchase of Goodwill in 1994, contacted me to ask if I'd accept Faulkenberry's invitation to visit Goodwill. The invitation came after Milligan saw a story about the Slave Cabin Project in the Charleston newspaper. Goodwill is near the predominately African American town of Eastover, founded in 1880.

I arrived at Goodwill on Saturday, June 26, 2010, upbeat knowing my previous cabin stays were the result of my own efforts. But this time the publicity my work had received opened the door for Faulkenberry's invitation. His offer spoke clearly of his intentions to do the right thing to preserve Goodwill and tell the stories of the people who were enslaved there. When I met him and heard his passion for Goodwill, I could feel his sincerity.

Goodwill's main gate fronts the four-lane Garners Ferry Highway that connects Columbia with Sumter, South Carolina, on the other side of the Wateree River. The unpaved road beyond the gate stops at a remote-controlled iron gate supported by two massive brick columns. Beyond it the graveled road runs straight toward the old 1850s overseer's cottage, strategically positioned so watchful eyes could survey the comings and goings.

After I arrived at Goodwill, Faulkenberry took me on an informative tour of several nineteenth-century buildings that included a blacksmith shop, the main house built in 1858, and a replica of a water-powered millhouse with some of the machinery from the original 1700s millhouse built by Daniel Huger. The force of water from a nearby pond turns a large cast-iron waterwheel that engages the mill's machinery. Like a kid in a candy store, Faulkenberry gleefully explained the millhouse machinery had been removed from the original structure destroyed in 1989 by the massive Hurricane Hugo. Inside, waterpower turns massive wheels to bale cotton, grind corn, and cut cedar into shingles and pine into lumber. All of it debunks the myth, Faulkenberry insisted, that Black people couldn't cipher to track the transformation of raw material to finished product while operating equipment unsupervised.

The same applies to tending Goodwill's rice field, established by Huger but expanded with the free labor of skilled Combahee River rice growers. "The enslaved people have known how to grow rice and control water all their lives," said Faulkenberry, whose southern drawl rises in pitch when he emphasizes a point. "They weren't waiting around for somebody to tell them what to do. There were six white people here and two thousand slaves, and they knew what to do, and they did it."

Goodwill's ownership had changed hands several times before Faulkenberry purchased the 3,280-acre property for $3.5 million. The Goodwill restoration was not Faulkenberry's original idea. He had planned to harvest the pine and hardwoods, and to replant young trees to rehabilitate the scarred landscape before selling some of it. In 2005, Faulkenbery marketed a portion of Goodwill as a high-end development of thirty homes on million-dollar lots with connecting equestrian trails. The core of the property was subdivided, but only one six-acre lot was sold.

Born in Winnsboro in Fairfield County, South Carolina, Faulkenberry was raised by his grandparents in the adjacent Kershaw County town of Kershaw. His family has been in the land and timber business for generations. During the five decades he has acquired and sold large tracts of property, he has abided by a simple rule: don't fall in love with the land. He was aware that if he did, it would be difficult to sell. After searching local archives to reveal Goodwill's history and that of the people enslaved there, Faulkenberry violated that rule. He fell in love with Goodwill and its history. Now he's the devoted custodian of its land and structures and the memory of Goodwill's enslaved community. He obtained an eight-by-ten, black-and-white photo of Betsy Anderson. For Faulkenberry, Goodwill's history came alive with a photo of someone who survived slavery. Her framed picture is one of his most prized possessions.

When he decided not to sell the property, Faulkenberry realized it was more land than what he and his family needed. He joined with adjacent landowners and sold 2,500 acres of Goodwill to South Carolina to establish the Wateree River Heritage Preserve and Wildlife Management Area. On the 750 acres he retained, he built a modest-sized home for himself and his wife, Jerry Faulkenberry, which was completed a few months before my visit. He opens Goodwill for private tours that include rides on a mule-drawn wagon and, of course, a waterwheel demonstration.

Faulkenberry's enthusiasm, however, to tell the story of Goodwill's enslaved workforce was dampened when two Black women questioned his authority to convey that history because he's white. That reaction was disappointing. Any source of information about the enslaved that I can find is important. I must give these people the voice they didn't have in slavery. If it comes from Faulkenberry or someone else of his race, that's okay as long as it's accurate, documented, and offered with respect.

Much of what Faulkenberry has learned comes from Goodwill's historian and caretaker Grover Rye. When he was a boy, Rye listened intently to the memories of Lee "T." McLemore, born at Goodwill in 1870. Rye's father had been Goodwill's caretaker, and T. McLemore worked for him. McLemore showed Rye many of Goodwill's secrets, like the site of a forgotten cemetery where it is believed about fifty enslaved people are buried. The young Rye saw the pastor of Goodwill Baptist Church perform baptisms in a pond near the original millhouse on the road that leads to the caretaker's house where he lived with his family. Grover Rye played with the Black children at Goodwill. His pronunciation of a word spoken by Betsy Anderson is a haunting reminder of her and other enslaved people from Beaufort County. For instance, he pronounced Combahee as "Combee," just as Anderson pronounced it during a 1930s interview with former South Carolina governor Duncan Clinch Heyward, the son of Edward Barnwell Heyward, who owned Goodwill during the Civil War.

When the Combahee's enslaved workforce arrived at Goodwill in 1861, two dozen slave quarters, built a decade before the Civil War, were scattered throughout the property. Four of the original cabins that stood in a row survived to the twentieth century, but a 1947 fire destroyed the two middle cabins. In September 1989, the massive Hurricane Hugo heavily damaged the two remaining cabins, but Faulkenberry restored them.

During the tour Faulkenberry apologized for the rustic conditions of the tin-roofed slave cabins with unpainted and weatherworn wooden siding. I was thrilled, however, with what I saw. I was eager to lay my head on that floor. The square-shaped cabins, on brick pillars a foot above ground, appeared large enough for five to eight people. Both were structurally sound but bare inside. Although a crude wall divides the space into three rooms, the placement of the chimney on an exterior wall indicates the cabins were originally built for one family. If they had been designed for two families, like Magnolia's cabins, the chimneys would have been placed in the center of the dwellings to heat two separate living spaces. A well in front of the cabin I chose to sleep in suggested whoever lived there only had to walk a few paces for a cool drink. The thirty-foot well is enclosed in a concrete-like shaft that extends three feet above ground. It is covered with a cedar-shingled roof with a hand crank to lower a wooden bucket inside to scoop the water out. Faulkenberry covered the cedar roof with tin to protect the shingles, possibly milled on the property. It is also likely that wells were dug at the other cabin sites.

After the tour, Tom Milligan prepared a hearty steak dinner on the grill, and we dined on the patio of Faulkenberry's home and engaged for two hours in stimulating conversation about his reasons to preserve Goodwill and share it with others. I was surprised he invested the time, money, and thought into researching the enslaved and bringing the property back to life. Hearing Faulkenberry's sincerity to protect Goodwill and tell the stories of the enslaved endeared me to him beyond his invitation to sleep in one of the cabins.

After the meal, I drove to the cabins located about a quarter of a mile from Faulkenberry's house. I entered with my sleeping mat and club. As with the previous cabin stays, I brought a club to ward off four-legged intruders. My air force buddy in England, Philadelphia native Victor Bethea, gifted the club to me before I was transferred to Germany. Victor picked up the decorative souvenir, adorned with the words "regalo de boadas," in Spain. I am still wondering why he gave me a club with the phrase "wedding gift."

When I walked in the cabin, I heard a fluttering in the tall brick chimney, broad at the base that becomes narrow as it ascends through the roof. I was too afraid to poke my head inside to investigate. As much as I was unsure of that chimney, I chose to sleep near it, the most prominent feature in that space. When I stretched out on the floor, I soon realized I was not alone. With my flashlight, I saw a roach crawling on my arm. I squashed it. Then a spider dropped in. I squashed it too. I placed both of them next to me. In the morning, they were gone. Maybe they became a meal for whatever fluttered in the chimney.

At daybreak I had spent the night in a place formerly occupied by people who may have been the victims of two forced migrations, first the Middle Passage from West Africa and then the exodus from the Combahee River to a place called Goodwill, an unusual name for a plantation. But its twenty-first-century owner, Larry Faulkenberry, is someone who embodies goodwill. I didn't call him. He invited me to Goodwill. Faulkenberry's invitation inspired me to not give up.

I didn't know it at the time, but the cabin I slept in had been at different times the home of Henry and Betsy Anderson before Emancipation and after freedom came. T. McLemore lived there, too. As in life, they may be sharing the same resting place in death. Betsy Anderson died in the 1930s at the age of ninety-one. Local people tell me Betsy Anderson and possibly her husband, along with McLemore, are buried in the graveyard at the old Shiloh AME Church near Eastover, South Carolina. On the chilly morning of

November 6, 2021, Herb and I looked for them in the old graveyard at the original site of Shiloh Church, established in 1873, three miles north of Goodwill. We didn't find them, but that does not mean they aren't there. Depressions in the soil are signs of unmarked graves. They could be there, but we'll never know for sure.

*   *   *

So far, I've slept in four former slave cabins at plantation sites in South Carolina. Except for one night at McLeod Plantation, I have been alone. Except for that night at Magnolia Plantation and Gardens when I ventured into the darkness to investigate a strange sound, I've otherwise remained safely in the cabins until sunrise, bundled in a sleeping bag and always with my trusty club nearby. Warnings that restless spirits lurk in slave cabins haven't shaken my resolve to continue the Slave Cabin Project. But I am about to face my greatest challenge yet at Hobcaw Barony just north of Georgetown, South Carolina. For the first time a journalist will join me, seeking to experience what it's like to sleep in a slave cabin. The curious reporter and I are about to be tested in unexpected ways. We'll lean on one another during a night to remember.

FOUR

A Homecoming

Hobcaw Barony

As I neared Hobcaw Barony, a sprawling collection of a dozen former plantation sites just north of Georgetown, South Carolina, I saw familiar sights from my childhood. In the distant mist loomed the paper plant with its noxious fumes I could smell forty-five miles away in Kingstree. Then the highway seemingly came within arm's length of a steel mill, a sparking, clanking behemoth with its own metallic odor. I marveled at that tall, arching bridge over the broad Waccamaw River, named for the Native people who lost their land to European colonizers. Those eye-popping sites dazzled me when I traveled with my sisters, neighborhood friends, and Catholic nun Florence Kaster. She drove a van loaded with kids for our annual summertime outing to an Atlantic Ocean beach that welcomed Black people.

Kaster introduced us to Huntington Island Beach. Along with the nearby Brookgreen Gardens—a former rice plantation—it was among the few oceanside places where Black people could go.* The annual excursions were part of Kaster's year-round ministry at a predominantly Black Catholic church near Kingstree's Black community. She also gave impoverished families clothing and food. The aid came, however, only after we sat through Friday evening Bible study. Miss Florence didn't wear a habit as she mingled with her young parishioners, who, in many cases, were taller than her. Nevertheless, we looked up to her for support. I didn't know it then, but the church's aid helped my family through difficult times.

My parents, Joseph McGill Sr. and Susie Mae McGill, had six children, three boys and three girls. We shared one bedroom; a bed for the boys, another for the girls. I was the oldest boy. Our mother, a housewife, also cooked and cleaned at her parents' home. My father and grandfather worked together laying bricks, and at times, I'd help them. Although my father lived with us, I didn't have much of a relationship with him. He lived in the bottle until it took his life.

Beach trips with Kaster gave me and my sisters, Shirley, Lula, and Barbara, a brief escape from tiny Kingstree, about one-fourth the size of Georgetown, which had twelve thousand residents. Kingstree, Williamsburg County's seat of government, was settled by white pioneers who did the hard labor to tame the wilderness until Roger Gordon, in 1736, purchased an African named Dick. Soon

---

* Archer and Anna Hyatt Huntington, philanthropist and sculptor, respectively, left the park and adjacent Brookgreen Gardens as their legacy.

the settlers' attitude toward work changed. During the American Revolution, Williamsburg had more enslaved Black people than white people tasked with herding cattle and cultivating crops. No one white man enslaved a vast number of people, but each enslaved a few.

According to local lore, Dick, a fiddle player, was bequeathed to Gordon's daughter when she married Hugh McGill, an original settler. Whether I am related to him I don't know, but I know that at least one of my ancestors was enslaved. Dick was such an accomplished fiddler that he was called the best around or the "fiddler facile princeps." It is unknown how well the McGills danced before Dick came into their circle. But as the legend goes, after Dick began to fiddle for Hugh McGill, no McGill has ever been able to keep time with the fiddle.

That bit of local lore, whether true or not, is not a story I would have heard as a high school student. Much of the history taught in my school was a distorted version of reality, especially when it came to slavery. Teachers repeatedly fed students a "happy slave" narrative from textbooks written by writers like Mary Simms Oliphant, author of an elementary school history of South Carolina. She and others of her ilk sympathized with the defeated South, blaming the Civil War on the North while casting the "lost cause" as just and noble.

As a historic preservationist, Civil War reenactor, and slave cabin investigator, I was absorbing the history of slavery in new ways. My next lesson awaited at Hobcaw Barony on July 24, 2010, the fifth plantation visit of the Slave Cabin Project, still in its infancy but gaining increasing interest among my coworkers in the Washington, DC, office of the National Trust for Historic Preservation. They mused that the Trust should adopt my work. More media outlets had also begun to take notice. *Charlotte Observer* reporter Eric Frazier called to ask if he could join me at Hobcaw. Saying yes to Eric was easy, considering he's an African American journalist with Lowcountry South Carolina roots. If he were a white reporter, I would have been reluctant. My strong feeling at the time was that sleeping in a former slave cabin is an experience that should be reserved for Black people who want to connect with Black history and the ancestors. Having Eric along also presented an opportunity for someone else not only to experience a night in a slave cabin but also to write about it. My colleagues at the Trust had encouraged me to write a blog after each cabin stay. My blogs were shared on Lowcountry Africana, a website curated by genealogist Toni Carrier.

Hobcaw's entrance, just beyond the Waccamaw River bridge, fronts the four-lane US Highway 17 North. Beyond it lies a strand of beaches, including Myrtle Beach, a popular tourist destination closed in the 1960s to Black beachgoers. When I arrived at Hobcaw, executive director George Chastain greeted me. It was easy convincing the historic preservationist Chastain to understand my interest in Hobcaw. Then Chastain introduced me to Lee Brockington, Hobcaw's director of interpretation, who ushered me to a room in the visitor center where nearly two dozen local residents had been waiting to hear me tell them about my slave cabin experiences. Chastain and Brockington were eager to host the Slave Cabin Project at Hobcaw. They had hoped my visit would encourage scholars to research Hobcaw's enslaved community.

I soon fell under Brockington's spell. She snared me into her engaging and detailed yet speedy recitation of Hobcaw's colonial-era history, which she had done countless times before for visitors to the sixteen-thousand-acre research reserve. Hobcaw had been a coastal rice empire that became the winter retreat for Wall Street financier Bernard M. Baruch in the early twentieth century. Then the time came for me to see the slave cabins. I followed Brockington in my car along a two-mile sandy road to the dwellings I was eager to see. The more we drove deeper into a dense forest, however, the more the reality of what I was about to do began to weigh on me. Because of Hobcaw's isolation, I wondered if I could sleep in a remote cabin I had not yet seen surrounded by a dense forest.

Seven white buildings stand along "the street" in a wide clearing that had been the home to some two hundred enslaved people in Friendfield Village. The cabin reserved for me stood at the far end of the street. It is one of three surviving 1840 slave cabins that once numbered a dozen in the Friendfield Village at Hobcaw. All that remain now are three postbellum cabins, a doctor's office, and a church that existed nearby before 1865. In a 1905 photograph of the village, the church appears in its present location, Brockington told me.

Before 1865, people were encouraged to attend church services led by Episcopal minister Alexander Glennie, an itinerant pastor from the nearby All Saints Episcopal Church. He ministered to the enslaved communities on the Waccamaw Neck, a peninsula bordered by the Waccamaw River on the west and the Atlantic Ocean to the east. Friendfield, like some of the other plantations, is laid out as a narrow half-mile strip of land. On a map of the broad peninsula, Friendfield resembles a belt strapped across the wide Waccamaw Neck. On this land, plantation owners encouraged enslaved people to attend Glennie's services by offering a day off or additional rations. Glennie even performed marriages of enslaved couples, which, of course, South Carolina did not recognize. These fake weddings were likely performed to bond enslaved couples together to discourage escapes. If Waccamaw Neck plantation owners were true Christians, they would not have purchased and sold people.

The cabin was likely the most authentic structure I've seen, with the most original materials, including the nails that bound milled wood showing saw marks with some decay. Like the cabin in Bluffton, this cabin was about the size of a one-car garage. None of the other structures where I'd slept so far were as isolated as Hobcaw's. Magnolia's cabin experience was near a wedding reception that kept my mind occupied so I wouldn't dwell on the adjacent alligator-infested swamp. The busy street noise at the cabins in Bluffton and McLeod, where I was not alone, offered some comfort that people were nearby. The Goodwill cabin, although isolated, was within a short drive of the home of property owner Larry Faulkenberry, who had invited me to the site. But Hobcaw's vastness presented a different challenge in my now hypervigilant state of fretting that a wild animal might attack me and Eric. Hours could pass before help arrived. My unspoken tension, however, was abated knowing Eric would arrive soon.

My nervousness was also eased slightly when Brockington told the story of Laura Carr. I would spend the night in the cabin where she lived after Emancipation. Laura Carr was born in 1857, and her parents had been enslaved at Friendfield, where she became a mid-wife and childcare worker. She gathered Friendfield's children in the cabin as their parents worked in the surrounding forest and rice fields. I took delight in the story because of Carr's aiding the success-ful births of Black children, ensuring African genes would produce the next generation in America. I wondered if Laura Carr called her cabin the "chillun's house." I admired Hobcaw's preservation of the cabin, which never had running water and electricity even when Carr lived in it, into the 1930s. Laura Carr died on October 12, 1937, at age eighty. She is buried in one of two large known African American cemeteries at Hobcaw that hold more than fifty graves.

Eric arrived to hear some of Brockington's history presentation before she left us alone on "the street" in Friendfield to ponder what we were about to do. Before Eric joined the *Observer* in 1998 for a second time, he had been a religion reporter at the *Post and Courier* in Charleston. He was among the Black reporters at the 1992 regional Black journalists' conference in Charleston whom I met at Fort Sumter. When Eric learned about the cabin project, he imme-diately latched on to the idea of meeting me again to understand what motivates me. He thought I must be incredibly brave to sleep alone in a slave cabin given the emotional weight and history of oppression, pain, and misery the cabins represent.

Eric grew up in the Green Pond community in Colleton County, just south of Charleston. He knew one of his relatives, Paul Drayton, had been enslaved on Nathaniel Heyward's Pynes Planta-tion on the upper end of the Combahee River, where Betsy Ander-son had been enslaved on Heyward's Myrtle Grove Plantation before she and others were moved inland to Goodwill Plantation during the Civil War. Decades ago Pynes was bulldozed to build the rail line that links New York with Miami. Growing up in a Lowcountry home, Eric heard legions of haunted-spirits stories about the living being tormented by the spirits of those unjustly treated in life. His rational brain tried to convince him ghosts don't exist. But if they do, he thought, slave cabins are fitting receptacles for restless souls.

When Eric arrived, I asked, "Are you ready for this?"

He answered, "I think so."

Neither of us revealed any growing nervousness. I was bothered, however, by Hobcaw's isolation, although I found comfort having Eric with me. Otherwise, I would have been tempted to sleep in my car or just drive away. I later learned that Eric considered the whole affair a spooky scene in a spirit-filled Toni Morrison novel. He certainly wouldn't have been there alone. Eric left briefly to ensure his daughter and his fiancée, who had checked into a Georgetown hotel, had dinner. As he drove away, I wondered whether he would return. As a reporter who had promised a unique story that piqued the newsroom's interest, he had every reason to return. When Eric returned to Friendfield, darkness fell like a heavy blanket. With the darkness the forest came alive with menacing mosquitoes and clicking cicada sounds echoing through the trees. I told Eric, "I couldn't do this if I believed in ghosts." Eric still had not shared his unease, which grew even more intense as we took our places on the cabin floor.

I placed my sleeping bag near the fireplace at one end of the cabin in the room with an exterior door. Eric was on the other side of a wall that divided the dwelling. We could see one another through an opening. Eric shined his flashlight on the old bare wood in the tight cabin. He felt the draft through cracks in the floor. His thoughts made it difficult to focus on the story. He wondered about the people who had lived in that space. What were their stories? What happened to them? Did they know joy in their lives, or was it all just misery? As he grappled with those thoughts, he felt the people could still be there. He thought, "I honor you and hope you are in a better place." Fear began to creep in as the overwhelming experience became even more unsettling.

Shortly after my first cabin stay at Magnolia, producers with ghost-hunting television shows called me. I quickly rejected invitations to appear on their shows. I was more concerned about snakes, feral hogs, and other wildlife, not spirits. I was dispassionate about sleeping in the cabins. I feared that emotional burnout might make it too difficult to continue with my one-year plan to sleep in South Carolina's slave cabins. I focused instead on what I could control, like finding places to sleep and laying my head down where the ancestors had slept. Anyone who listened closely heard my repeated mantra that I slept in slave cabins to honor the ancestors. That message prompted one anonymous comment on a newspaper's website: "If you want to get in touch with your ancestors, go visit the ape section at the zoo."

After Eric ate a snack bar, he forced his mind to focus long enough to do a basic interview. The question-and-answer session was familiar ground that distracted his attention from being in a slave cabin. We also talked about our families before I announced, "I think I am going to sleep." That abrupt news startled Eric. He had planned to stay awake for as long as possible, but around 2:00 a.m., his body too said it was shutting down. He drifted off. Then he bolted up in his sleeping bag. He told me later that he heard what he thought was the mournful sound of a lone jazz trumpeter winding out of the dark woods. His skin crawled. He wondered whether he was really hearing a trumpet—or was he going crazy? Eric looked through the open door into the darkness. Was the spirit of a tortured slave in the woods playing a horn? He looked at me. I was snoring. Eric didn't want to wake me for fear I would think he was a wimp. Shortly before dawn, Eric finally fell asleep. The rising sun meant he could finally relax.

A month after the Hobcaw Barony cabin stay, I received another media call, likely in response to Eric's story. National Public Radio interviewed me for a program that aired in August 2010. At that point I was realizing my crazy idea might not be so crazy after all. Maybe I should continue beyond the first year and stop stereotyping slave cabins as being just on rural plantations. The Heyward House visit showed me that structures where enslaved people lived exist in small towns like Bluffton, and they aren't exclusive to isolated rural spaces like Hobcaw Barony.

Morris Street

On a summer day in 1937, Thomas Jefferson bent low to do unusual work for a man of his age. At 102, Jefferson was picking cotton, seven decades after the Civil War freed him from slavery. Jefferson, his mother, and his four siblings were wedding gifts to Mary Amanda Pauline Hammond when she married Elias John Earle, son of Samuel Girard Earle, one of the early settlers of Anderson County, two hundred miles inland from Charleston and along the Georgia

border. Jefferson had been enslaved on Earle's Evergreen Plantation. Decades later a writer with the Federal Writers' Project asked
Jefferson why he was picking cotton. "Just to take a little exercise,"
he answered.

Enslaved workers at Goodwill Plantation were ordered to grow
rice to help the Confederate war effort. As the miller of Earle's corn
and flour mill, Jefferson's free labor was used to feed the rebel army.
"We worked all night Saturday night, all day Sunday and Sunday
night, and Monday morning [we] had ten barrels of flour to send
the Confederate army," Jefferson said.

On Morris Street in the town of Anderson, Elizabeth H. Earle
owned three houses on long, narrow lots used to quarter enslaved
workers. The buildings were slated for demolition when Michael
Bedenbaugh, executive director of the Palmetto Trust for Historic
Preservation, purchased them to make them available for an inves-
tor to rehabilitate them under strict guidelines.* Land records
showed Elizabeth H. Earle owned the land in 1855. She was the
sister-in-law to Elias John Earle, who enslaved Thomas Jefferson at
Evergreen Plantation. Elizabeth Earle, who lived near the houses,
is believed to have hired the enslaved residents out for local jobs.
The house I was scheduled to sleep in was one of four structures
she owned. The fourth dwelling was likely built after 1865, said
Bedenbaugh, whose preservation group is headquartered in Pros-
perity, South Carolina, just northwest of Columbia. While the
demand for enslaved workers was high, Bedenbaugh said in rural
Anderson County the enslaved population also may have increased

---

* The organization is now called Preservation South Carolina.

in the town during a building boom that followed the 1850s completion of a railroad line.

Bedenbaugh invited me to sleep in the house nearest to the sidewalk along Morris Street. I would not be alone. On August 21, 2010, Terry James of Florence, South Carolina, met me at the tiny house. Terry also wears the blue woolen uniform of a Civil War reenactor. Like me, the movie *Glory* lured him into becoming a devotee of the Massachusetts Fifty-Fourth. He was aware of my early cabin stay invitation to my fellow reenactors. Terry remained hesitant, however, because he thought I was crazy. I must be crazy, Terry thought, to not take seriously threats I might face from mean-spirited people who don't appreciate messages that counter their belief that enslaved people were happy and well cared for. After fellow reenactors Ernest Parks and James Brown joined me at McLeod Plantation, Terry warmed up to the idea of sleeping in a slave cabin.

As my sixth cabin stay, in Anderson, approached, Terry realized that his great-great-great-grandparents Ervin and Nora James had gone through more than just one night in a cabin, so why should he be afraid. They were among a dozen enslaved people on the James Plantation between Marion and Darlington in South Carolina. In his 1830 will, plantation owner George James valued Norma James at $535.

Terry and I arrived about the same time at the house on Morris Street, where a dozen people surprised me with a red-carpet-like welcome. Bedenbaugh had recruited members of the local historical society to clean the three houses. The only Black man in the racially mixed group gave me a battery-powered lantern. I was beginning to see interest growing in my work, but at this point the conversations were limited to why I sleep in slave quarters instead of focusing on slavery's lasting legacy. I was being recognized as an extreme researcher who's in the trenches. But I continued to resist any notion that I was attempting to reenact a moment in the life of an enslaved person. Instead, my simple act of sleeping in slave cabins is intended to draw attention to those places where enslaved people lived. Jodi Skipper latched on to that message when she heard my radio interview about the upcoming cabin stay in Anderson. After she earned a doctoral degree in anthropology from the University of Texas, Jodi entered a one-year postdoctorate fellowship at the Institute for Southern Studies at the University of South Carolina in Columbia. She arrived there about a month before my radio interview. She was so surprised to learn of my work that she called the National Trust for Historic Preservation and asked to be connected with me. As we spoke, Jodi was beginning to realize that my slave cabin project meshed with her plantation research. To earn a doctorate in anthropology, she uncovered the material representations of mostly enslaved communities in rural Florida, North Carolina, Georgia, and Mississippi. She found everyday items such as toys, animal bones carved into dominos, jewelry, clay pipes, and even lead shot that indicated enslaved people had weapons for hunting.

I invited Jodi to meet Terry and me in Anderson. She was among the group that greeted us at the slave dwellings on Morris Street. Being more familiar with rural slave dwellings, Jodi was surprised to see slave dwellings in Anderson's urban setting. But slave dwellings are sometimes hiding in plain sight in southern cities like

Charleston and New Orleans, east of her hometown of Lafayette, Louisiana. What attracted Jodi to my work was the mission to do what no one had done before. Historic preservationists typically focus on what they consider to be the most significant structures, usually properties tied to wealthy white families. Slave dwellings are usually affiliated with these larger projects where they are being preserved. But many other slave dwellings are privately owned and either neglected or in disrepair. A movement is emerging to memorialize these spaces, and Jodi credits me with contributing to that effort. As the sun was setting, Jodi and the others left Terry and me at the tiny house.

Meeting Jodi in Anderson lifted my spirits, knowing that someone with her academic credentials drove slightly more than two hours from Columbia to Anderson to meet me. Her interest gave me the fleeting notion that the Slave Cabin Project could go beyond just one year, but then I gave no more thought to the possibility of keeping the project alive into 2011. A film crew also came to interview me for a short documentary on the Palmetto Trust's effort to save historic dwellings, including the Morris Street houses. For the film, called *This Place Matters*, I wore my Civil War uniform.

The dwelling's urban setting didn't concern me as much as Hobcaw's isolation made my skin crawl. The contrast of plantation slavery, however, with slavery in Anderson's urban environment also shocked me. I blamed my surprise on my limited and faulty high school education. Since this was Terry's first cabin stay, he began to wonder what might happen on that hot humid night in a house filled with the stench of mildew. For years the house had been vacant, littered with trash and sealed with plywood. Terry thought Bedenbaugh would join us. But he made it clear he was not planning to sleep in the house. Besides, Bedenbaugh, who is white, felt that the story of sleeping in one of the houses was my story to tell. I was comfortable in Anderson with Terry despite the unpleasant odors. He also trusted that Bedenbaugh, a fellow preservationist, would not place us in an unsafe part of town. A night in a slave cabin, however, placed Terry on a renewed alert for the Confederate flag. Not everyone who flies that flag is a crazy quack, he said. But it is a sign of intimidation, a signal to Black people that they aren't welcomed.

Terry came with more than just the basic pillow and a sleeping bag. He had a camera, too. As a teenager he took pictures at family events, a hobby that led to a career. During the day, he took several pictures of the houses that for him didn't resemble a slave cabin. These structures lacked a brick chimney and long wooden siding typically seen on slave cabins. Instead, the exteriors of these light-yellow houses were covered with square asbestos tiles. As the sun fell, Terry stowed his camera away. It was too dark in the house for photography. Luckily, though, I had my new lantern.

Terry was settling in, anticipating a long conversation with me. We talked about reenacting and the recent Massachusetts Fifty-Fourth event on Morris Island. I told Terry of an upcoming cabin stay at Historic Brattonsville in York County, South Carolina, near Charlotte, North Carolina. Terry seemed excited about the idea of a future cabin stay, boosting my confidence I would not be alone for the remaining cabin stays in 2010. We talked as Latin music and other conversations in Spanish flowed from a nearby apartment building. We also overheard the chatter between people on the nearby sidewalk. I regretted that Terry's first cabin stay came at a house with bad smells, but his presence and commitment to join me on other cabin stays made our friendship even stronger. None of the distractions prevented me from falling to sleep, leaving Terry with no one to talk to during a night of restless slumber.

The following day I was still gleeful over meeting the people who welcomed me to Anderson. I was clearly establishing a fan base, and Jodi was the best among them. She pledged to be in touch with me, and she did that. She got me scheduled for a lecture before one hundred students and faculty at the University of South Carolina. That early recognition was significant, but it was made even more special because it was my first honorarium to talk about the Slave Cabin Project. My pledge to sleep in slave cabins was unexpectedly combining history, Black history, and my preservationist interest in using buildings to tell the story of enslaved people. The greeting in Anderson followed by a video-recorded interview inspired even more excitement for my next cabin stay. A month later, I saw the crumbling slave village at a plantation site on the Black River that stirred hometown memories of Kingstree.

FIVE

A Chapel for the Enslaved

Mansfield

Abbey Mishow enjoyed a golden childhood at the rice-growing Waterford Plantation on the Black River in Georgetown County, South Carolina. Her mother, an enslaved seamstress, died shortly after childbirth, leaving Mishow in the care of the white family who vowed to protect the Black child as their own. "I was raise just like a pet," Mishow recalled. "I don't know nothing about de [slave] street on de plantation, and what dey do dere, cause I ain't had no 'casion for go dere. I raise in de [big house] yard, I didn't wear de kind of clothes de field-hand chillen wear, and I get my dinner from de kitchen." Mishow shared her Waterford memories in the mid-1930s with a writer for the Federal Writers' Project who came to her home on Rose Lane in Charleston. Even then, decades later, the white-haired Mishow kept the dignity of a descendant of a house slave.

Shortly after the turn of the twentieth century, a similar but slightly different story emerged with the birth of Rebecca Golden at Mansfield Plantation, a former rice-growing enterprise also on the Black River. She was born in one of Mansfield's slave cabins, adjacent to a chapel where the enslaved community heard the gospel from the Reverend Alexander Glennie, who also ministered to the enslaved community at Hobcaw Barony. After owning the property for nearly two centuries, the Parker family sold Mansfield in 1912. But that didn't cut Golden's ties with the Parkers. She moved with them to Lake City, South Carolina, where she was the nanny for two generations of Parker children. John Rutledge Parker was one of them.

When Parker was in his sophomore year at The Citadel, South Carolina's military academy in Charleston, his mother called him to say Rebecca "Becky" Golden was dying. If he wanted to see her, he should come quick! After seven decades, life was leaving Golden. Under layers of blankets, she rested in a recliner when Cadet Parker entered her home. On the wall above her hung pictures of the Reverend Martin Luther King, John F. Kennedy, Parker, and his brother. "She loved us just like we loved her," Parker said as his voice cracked with emotion. "I looked at her brown eyes, and I said, 'Becky, I love you.' She said, 'Mr. John, I love you too. You are just like a child to me.' And I said, 'You're just like a mom to me.'" Three weeks later Rebecca Golden died. Six months later Parker's brother Arthur Middleton Parker II was killed in Vietnam.

John Parker paid $6.25 million in April 2004 to bring Mansfield back to his family. The following year he was diagnosed with Parkinson's disease, the same year he renovated the chapel and dedicated it to Rebecca Golden, whose grandparents had been enslaved at Mansfield. On September 25, 2010, Terry James and I spent the night there. John Parker greeted us at Mansfield with his slow-moving Labrador retriever, Henry, who snapped to attention like a Citadel cadet when he spotted a black-headed fox squirrel, providing just a glimpse of the abundant wildlife at Mansfield. A majority of the acreage is in a conservation easement to protect it from development.

The coffee-colored water of the Black River, stained by decaying swamp vegetation, hugs the contours of the 1,000-acre property and its 360 acres of former rice fields. The river had everything to do with my ancestors being enslaved in Williamsburg County. The waterway served as a transportation route for English colonizers upstream in the wilderness interior of South Carolina. It was there they saw a tree dubbed the King's Tree, a term that gave Kingstree its name. The river later provided a vital route for chattel slavery. It was the means of ferrying people and goods, produced by enslaved people, down to the port of Georgetown. Mansfield, about forty miles from Kingstree, is the closest I've come to Williamsburg County for an overnight stay in a slave cabin. Mansfield's nearness to my boyhood home rekindled memories of my grandparents.

In the 1970s, when I was an eighth grader at Kingstree Junior High School, I left my parents to live with my grandparents. It was my responsibility to give Grandma and Granddaddy the attention they needed and the respect they deserved. I was my grandmother's eyes. Diabetes took Ida Snowden's sight when she was young. I dished up her food and guided her to the dinner table, where she sat wrapped in her favorite housecoat. Before company came,

Grandma got her dentures and dressed up as if she was going to church. She took my arm for walks on the gravel driveway to the main highway. She and my grandfather, Samuel Snowden, lived in a small, plain, three-bedroom house near Kingstree. I enjoyed a room just for me at my grandparents' house. Living with them satisfied my sense of adventure in unfamiliar places. Later in life, that openness made it easy for me to sleep alone in extant slave dwellings.

Grandma and I talked often as we sat on the front porch, bare except for three metal chairs. One of them was a rocker wide enough for two. I sat with her, gently rocking us back and forth as she talked about her twelve children, six boys and six girls. My mother was one of them. Grandma was proud of them, especially her three daughters with college degrees. Most of her children had moved away, swept up in the Great Migration that steered Black people away from the tobacco fields for better wages up north. Diabetes eventually took Grandma's life when I was an eleventh grader at Kingstree Senior High and beginning to think about my future. She was buried in the Woodlawn Cemetery, a place where Black families by custom buried their dead, segregated from white cemeteries. I continued caring for Granddaddy. He needed me.

Tall, straight, and thin, Granddaddy towered over everyone in size and reputation. As a toddler I crawled around tobacco fields while he and other relatives were "putting in" the crop. As I grew older, I watched him pay the workers and mingle among them. People respected Granddaddy for his kindness and the work he provided. I was Granddaddy's sidekick on car trips. On one drive, I was nearly thrown out when he turned a sharp corner and the passenger-side door swung open. The door lock was broken, but he had improvised a way to secure it with an electric cable. I saw no need for the cable, so I removed it. That caused the door to suddenly fling open. Just as I was about to slide out of the car into a horrible fate, he quickly grabbed me by the arm in a fit of anger and desperation. He questioned me as to why I had removed the cable. Lesson learned: if Granddaddy did something, he did it for a reason.

After I moved in with my grandparents, Granddaddy showed me how to feed his hogs and do other chores. After Grandma passed away, my eldest sister, Lula Irene, also joined me to take care of Granddaddy and the house. Although he was elderly and frail, he insisted on continuing to raise hogs. That work fell entirely on me. I fed the pigs, caught those that escaped, and cut the grass.

Making money was not a problem if I was willing to work hard. I helped my Granddaddy and other farmers with the tobacco harvest. By the time I reached my senior year of high school, I drove a school bus. That money financed my first car, a blue-and-white 1971 Oldsmobile Cutlass. To drive the school bus, however, I had to live with my parents again. That's when my sister Lula moved in to care for our grandfather. The Cutlass cut me free. I drove to nearby towns to enjoy drive-in and walk-in movie theaters. Local dances and major attractions at Myrtle Beach, seventy miles away, were also on my busy social schedule. The car liberated me so much that I had two girlfriends at once. To further satisfy my ambitions and lust for travel beyond South Carolina, however, I prepared a plan to leave the state.

At seventeen, I started the process of joining the US Air Force, but I was not old enough to do it on my own. I needed my mother's signature. When she refused to sign, I stomped off with a long face.

"I don't want you to go," she said. I knew then that giving her eldest son permission to join the military was a difficult decision. After a week of my pouting, she relented, asking, "Are you sure this is what you want to do?"

Prostate cancer ravaged Granddaddy's body. He was not always aware of his surroundings, but nevertheless I told him of my plan to join the military. He didn't try to stop me. Two weeks after graduating from high school in 1979, I was off to Texas for basic training. I left on the day of my grandfather's funeral, so I was not able to attend his service. He was buried in Woodlawn, next to Grandma. My family knew I had to leave. Years later my departure exposed me to that unforgettable moment in the Anne Frank House in Amsterdam, where I learned that old buildings tell the story of the people who found shelter in them.

*   *   *

On my way into Mansfield, I had less of a feeling of the isolation that I experienced at Hobcaw Barony. Like Hobcaw Barony, the mile-and-a-half-long main road through Mansfield also passes through a dense pine forest, but it offers surprising roadside features. Beyond the brick columned gate, intermittent brick walls pop up along the dirt road. Brick guardrails also flank a bridge at a section of the road called The Valley. These brick structures hinted at the enslaver's flaunting the main house, still some distance away.

Before the road stops at the main house, however, it first passes through a slave village. I had expected that the slave cabins would have stood behind the big house. John Parker assured me that this did not suggest that in the early years of Mansfield before road travel the main house was oriented toward the Black River. The dilapidated cabins were larger than I've seen before, indicating they had been used into the twentieth century. A chapel stood among six slave cabins and a laundry house. Confronted with those rickety cabins, Terry and I decided to sleep in the chapel. Although it didn't qualify as a slave dwelling, I concluded I could sleep in the chapel because as a kid I would always fall asleep in church. Sleeping in the chapel required me to relax my rule of sleeping only in extant slave cabins that existed on the site where they were built by the hands of the people who lived in them.

Founded in 1741, Mansfield was one of the plantations on the state preservation office's list. Like many other sites, Mansfield Plantation, thanks to owner John Parker, was quick to agree to my stay. I was elated to meet Parker, a direct descendant of the Mansfield owners, whose sincerity was evident as he shared his commitment to preserve the chapel and cabins that stand on what he calls sacred ground. Parker sought to use my presence to help raise money to restore three cabins that were near collapse. Only one of them and the chapel had been saved. Parker's ambitions were right in line with the influence we hoped the Slave Cabin Project would have: Parker formed the Dr. Francis S. and Mary L. Parker Foundation—named for his great-great-great-grandparents—to guide the restoration of the buildings in Mansfield's thirteen-acre slave village. The parcel includes a five-acre cemetery with countless unmarked graves of enslaved people. Parker deeded the land for one dollar a year for one hundred years to the eight-member foundation. Baltimore, Maryland, resident Dwight Parker, an African American man, is the board's sole Black member. Dwight Parker's great-grandfather had been enslaved at Mansfield. John Parker remembers fondly another Black board member who made a huge contribution to its preservation. The Reverend Isaiah "Ike" Golden Jr., an AME minister, served on the Mansfield board of directors for a decade before his death in August 2020. The following month, his funeral was held at Mansfield, where his grandmother, Rebecca Golden, lived until she left Mansfield to live with the Parker family in Lake City, South Carolina. During Golden's tenure on the board, he and John Parker spoke nearly weekly. At board meetings, the Rev. Golden routinely delivered a short sermon in the dining room at the Mansfield main house. Ike Golden is buried at the base of a live oak at Mansfield.

"Everyone on the board truly loved Ike," John Parker said.

At Mansfield's white, one-story brick main house, built in the late 1700s, Terry and I joined Parker just before nightfall for dinner, a meal prepared by bed-and-breakfast innkeeper Catherine Green. Henry waited under the table for scraps. I found Parker's use of the property as a bed-and-breakfast that accommodates twenty-two people in nine bedrooms an appropriate business for a former plantation site as long as it didn't involve the sacred cabins. Even at dinner the chapel was on Terry's mind. He imagined what kind of songs might have been sung in the chapel. His thoughts always reverted to the people who were enslaved there regardless of what he heard or saw.

On our walk to the main house for dinner we passed other buildings, remnants of the bygone era of rice cultivation that depended heavily on enslaved labor. A winnowing house perched on stilts stands near an irrigation channel to the rice field. Workers thrashed the harvested rice on the hardened "rice floor," then pounded the grain in wooden mortars with pestles to separate the outer husk from the white kernel. Then they toted the mixture to the winnowing house, dropping it in through a grated floor. As the heavy rice kernels fell, the wind blew away the lighter chaff. The process was repeated until the rice was clean. Later a rice mill was constructed at Mansfield. The mill's machinery achieved the same results as the winnowing barn but required less labor. The mill was destroyed by fire in the late 1970s, but the towering chimney remains and is now a prominent feature alongside the modern Parker family home that was built on the mill's foundation.

Like other rice-growing plantations with steam- or water-powered rice mills, the large mill buildings with chimneys made the rice plantations more like factories than farms. This on-site process at Mansfield and at Hobcaw Barony added value to the rice before an enslaved boatman took the finished produce on the Black River down to market at Georgetown, once South Carolina's rice-growing capital.

After dinner, Terry and I laid our sleeping bags near the chapel's front door. Five long cypress benches extend the width of the squat, rectangular wooden structure also made of cypress and with a bell tower next to it. I only wanted to sleep in extant slave cabins, but the renovated chapel was by far the sturdiest structure along Mansfield's main entrance lined with live oaks, holly, and camellias. It would provide a different experience. I was beginning to see that I could break my rules for the right reasons.

Chapels for the enslaved at Hobcaw and Mansfield confounded me. Services might have given enslaved people something to look forward to: a day off, a time to bury the dead, baptize the young, and escape but for a moment the hardships of bondage. However, they were denied the full measure of their Indigenous beliefs. It is not clear if the enslaved people at Mansfield were able to use that unpretentious chapel to worship in the manner of their choosing away from the watchful eye of the Reverend Glennie. The chapel curiously bonded them to a hypocritical enslaver who professed to bring religion to the enslaved while using Christianity to justify slavery, thus violating all the rules of human decency.

Glennie's message set it all in motion. He instructed the enslaved to pattern their lives after an improvised savior to achieve the greatest reward of everlasting life. Glennie delivered this message at least once: "Masters are taught in the Bible how they must rule their servants, and servants how they must obey their masters." Mariah Heyward, enslaved on the Sunnyside Plantation at Murrells Inlet just north of the Waccamaw Neck, heard a similar message from Parson Glennie. "[He] come once a month to Sunnyside. Parson Glennie read, sing, pray. Tells us obey Miss Minna [the daughter of Duncan Alston, Sunnyside's owner]. Two of us 55 chillun! We'd fight. She knock me. I knock back! Wouldn't take a knock! [Miss Minna] say, 'I tell Parson Glennie! Lord won't bless you! You bad.' I say, 'You knock me. I knock you!'"

This message bolstered the planters' belief that control of an enslaved Black population required inducements such as part of a day off and extra rations in exchange for church attendance, where they'd hear that to obey God's law was to obey their master's law. Twelve years before Glennie was ordained in 1833, angry Africans at Mansfield killed a Black River planter. They fled to the swamp, where the state militia found them. During the Civil War, however, enslaved people became more rebellious as more of the white men left Georgetown to fight for the Confederacy. During the war, Parker's great-great-grandfather Dr. Francis Parker owned Mansfield, and he served as the local provost in charge of the militia. With the end of the war nearing and Union forces encroaching on Georgetown, it "exercised an unhappy influence" on enslaved people in Georgetown and on the nearby plantations. Dr. Parker appealed to the governor not to send his men to the front lines but rather to allow them to remain in Georgetown. He also outlined to the governor how he had punished enslaved people under his authority as provost marshal. "In the last three years, eleven [slaves] have accordingly been sentenced to suffer the extreme penalty for the law and have been executed, and others have been punished for offense committed against the peace and good order of the community."

We imagined how the enslaved at Mansfield might have worshipped before the chapel was built in the mid-1800s. Terry surmised they might have held clandestine nighttime spiritual gatherings in the forest under a hush harbor, also known as a bush arbor. Then we imagined a ringing chapel bell calling believers before a simple altar for the morning message followed by a baptism of a young child or an older convert. The Black River flows some distance from the chapel, so one of the irrigation canals that lattice the nearby rice field was the most likely place where sinners waited their turn to be dunked, then to rise as new believers. When Terry was a boy growing up in Florence County, South Carolina, his father and grandfather told him that men with long poles poked the sandy river bottom to frighten away snakes and gators before the pastor led baptism candidates clad in white calico down by the riverside.

The chapel's crude window shutters and doors were flung open to let in the breeze, but they also invited marauding mosquitoes to torment us all night. We bathed in mosquito repellent then slid into sleeping bags. The pests waited for us to come out for air before they attacked again, again, again, and again. The female mosquitoes craved our warm blood, a necessary protein for the production of their eggs. The fox's distant yelp, hooting owls, and buzzing needle-nosed insects were constant reminders of the pine forest and wetlands. It didn't take me long to fall asleep, but throughout the night I was awakened for another bout with the mosquitoes. Terry, however, struggled to sleep until finally he was able to rest around 3:00 a.m.

At sunrise, Terry grabbed his camera for the walk along the rice field dike to the Black River, about two-thirds of a mile from the main house. While he admired the beauty of the river's dark reflective waters, his thoughts again focused on the men, women, and maybe even the children and pregnant mothers who toiled in the rice field with trolling alligators and snakes. Then he thought about the chapel where we had spent the hot and humid night fighting mosquitoes. Anger grew within him knowing Mansfield's owner had built a chapel for the enslaved but ignored their desire to be free. A vexed Terry James found a way to vent his outrage when he joined me for another night in a slave cabin in York County, South Carolina.

SIX

Another State

Old Alabama Town

*This edited excerpt of an unpublished and undated composition writ-
ten by Episcopal archdeacon David Elred Holt is his conversation
with Uncle Louis, who explains why when he was enslaved, he hid on
an Alabama plantation to commune with nature and the spirits.*

* * *

Of course you know we always called the older Colored men
"Uncle" and the older Colored women "Aunt." It was proper
manners.

When Uncle Toby died, Uncle Louis became the oldest slave
on the plantation. He is what the slaves call a yard servant, and as
such, he picked up much of the talk of the white masters. He spoke
his version of their language. He could hunt with the best of them
because he understood the language of birds and beasts, too. He

claimed to have an intimate friendship with ghosts and spooks. Uncle Louis was a Guinea nigger. His ancestor had come direct from the Guinea coast of Africa. He looked just like them; heavy neck, thick lips, flat nose, and eyes like a hog.

Uncle Louis was a runaway nigger. Once every two to three years, he would run away at the end of the summer and come back just in time to help dig sweet potatoes. I was in the field one morning when he returned. After the field hands had knocked off work and Uncle Louis was sitting in front of his cabin, I went to him and asked, "Uncle Louis, what makes you run away? You don't get whipped or abused in any way."

The old slave scratched his grizzled head, puffed on his clay pipe, and pondered the subject for some time before he replied. "Marse Dave, I does cause de woods seems to call me. When de fall insec's is singin' in de grass an' the 'simmons is gettin' soft an' de leaves is beginnin' to turn, I jes natcherly haster go. De wild sloes, de red haws an' de crab apples is ripe. De walnuts an de hickory nuts an de beach mast drappin' an de blue smoke comes over de woods, and de woods birds an de yard birds goes souf wid de cranes and ducks and wil' geese and de blackbirds an de crows goes in droves—it seem lack all dat is jest callin' me."

"Where do you go?" I asked.

"Marse Davie, I never goes off de plantation. I always go to de woods back o' de past'er. Ole Master knows whar I is. Don't you know dat holler dat come down on de lef' han' side of de branch—de fus holler you comes to, not more dan two hundred yards in de woods."

"I know it well," I said.

"Don't you 'member a big green oak tree growin' on de right han' side of de holler bout a hundred yard up de path?

"Well, sir, dat tree is my home. I done toted some poles an some sedge gress up dar and made me a bed—but you can't see it from the groun'. When I gets up dar I can see all 'roun'. I seen you an Marse Joe de las' time you go fishin'. I lays dar all day and listens to de birds and critters talkin'. A chickadee tole me you was comin' long befor' I seen you. Den a jay bird caught a sight of you an' he tole me. Can't nobody come along widout de birds tellin' me. Dey pays no min' to a horse or a dog but when dey [spies] a man dey speaks. I done tame a squi'l so he comes see me ever'day."

The old man was wound up for an interminable talk on his favorite theme, the talk of critters, and to change the subject I asked: "Uncle Louis, ain't you afraid of ghosts?"

"Lor', chile, I ain't feared of no ghos' or spook, as I's seed lots of both. All a ghos' do is jes show hise'f. You never hear of one doin' nothin' to nobody. Dey is sociable an' wants to be near livin' people. When folks gets scared it hurts do ha'nt's feelin's an dey goes somewhere else. Dey has all de feelin's dey had when dey was livin'. You wouldn't stay by wid folks dats fear'd of you and want to run away from where you is."

* * *

Holt's proposition that it was "proper manners" to call older colored men and women "aunt" and "uncle" is jarring. Releasing them from chattel slavery so they could live "proper" lives would have been the "proper" thing to do. Nevertheless, this glimpse into the past offers a somewhat uplifting story of an enslaved man who took charge of his life at times to follow his instincts to stay connected to nature. Unlike Uncle Louis, however, when I sleep in slave cabins I am not in search of spirits. Uncle Louis had a relationship with them far beyond my desire and awareness.

Uncle Louis's narrative recalls the recollections of slavery I heard in Montgomery, Alabama, as I sat in the front pew of one of America's most historic Black churches, founded in 1877 on the site of a former slave pen. Alabama State University theater students performed slave narratives with so much authentic emotion that their portrayals gave life to the words of people like Uncle Louis who had been enslaved on Alabama plantations. The students went beyond a mere recitation. They embodied the enslaved through dialect, emotion, and movement. Their renditions conveyed the innate longing to be free, to be loved; so much so the performance brought tears to my eyes and to the eyes of those around me.

Those narratives and the presentation of them resonated even more perhaps because I was seated in the Dexter Avenue Baptist Church that birthed the modern civil rights movement led by a young pastor named Martin Luther King Jr. This sanctuary, King's church, was the heart of the Montgomery boycott in the mid-1950s that broke racial segregation on city buses. At first glance the church seems uncomfortably close to a building that had been the capital of the Confederacy beginning in February 1861 before it was moved four months later to Richmond, Virginia. Whites in the city hurled threats to force the church to move. But the congregation's defiance to remain on the site possibly prepared the church for the challenges to come in the civil rights era. These two buildings—one the seat of God's law and the other a place where men made unjust laws—represent opposing ideals.

Alabama is one of three states I visited during my travels with the National Trust. Elizabeth Brown, deputy state historic preservation officer at the Alabama Historical Commission, was a regular contact. Well aware of my travels to extant slave dwellings in South Carolina, Elizabeth harnessed the Slave Cabin Project's rising energy with her organization's clout to propel me beyond South Carolina. She arranged for me to spend a night in two slave dwellings in the Montgomery area. Elizabeth pushed me out of South Carolina on the heels of Eric Frazier's Hobcaw Barony story in the *Charlotte Observer* and my NPR interview. Both stories helped to lift my work toward a national stage. The overnight stays in Montgomery coincided too with the state preservation office's statewide convention. The slave narrative performance on October 6, 2010, served as a preconvention event. Elizabeth's invitation boosted my confidence and abruptly altered my plan to sleep only in slave cabins in South Carolina. With 2010 ending, I was seeing hints I'd be tempted to carry this crazy idea into a new year and maybe beyond.

When the students' performances ended, I stood before the altar where King preached. I wiped my eyes and apologized as I regained my ability to speak. I told the racially mixed audience of some seventy-five people that my work had begun in South Carolina as a one-year plan to sleep in slave dwellings in my home state. I had made several trips to Alabama to assist in preservation projects for the National Trust, but unlike previous visits I felt a growing uneasiness about being in Alabama. Unlike before, I was now preparing to sleep in two slave dwellings in the former capital of the old South. South Carolina has its own abysmal history with slavery, but the prospect of sleeping alone in Alabama slave dwellings tested my will to continue. South Carolina was familiar territory; Alabama was not. All of the negatives I'd heard about Alabama, beatings and lynchings, swirled in my mind. I resisted speeding away from Alabama when I realized I couldn't break my streak.

Elizabeth had arranged for me to sleep at Old Alabama Town, an outdoor museum consisting of fifty restored nineteenth- and early twentieth-century structures in a six-block area. After the program at the church I followed Elizabeth there, where I met the museum's curator Carole King. I was shocked to see where I would spend the night. Instead of a simple single-room slave dwelling, Carole showed me a two-story, redbrick, four-room slave quarter with two first-floor kitchens, each with a fireplace and a second-story balcony. If I had been enslaved, that dwelling would have been adequate given my circumstances. The slave dwelling and the main house next to it were built on the site. Other structures, under the threat of being torn down, were moved to Old Alabama Town. The slave dwelling where I'd sleep is one of the two buildings original to the location. Six other slave dwellings were moved there to rescue them from demolition.

This slave dwelling's story also shocked me. Carole told me that a dozen enslaved people lived and worked there and in the adjacent main house, both built in the 1840s. They were the property of Rebecca Mitchell, wife of cotton planter Julius Caesar Bonaparte Mitchell Jr. Mitchell had originally married Rebecca's older sister, but after she died, he proposed to Rebecca. Her mother insisted that Julius sign a prenuptial agreement to protect her daughter's dowry: the twelve enslaved people. To the union she brought Gilbert, fifty; Anthony, forty; Jerry, twenty-eight; Isaac, twenty-five; Frederick, sixteen; Peggy, thirty; Talitha, twenty-six; Charity, fourteen; Eliza, sixteen; Violett, fifteen; and an unnamed twenty-five-year-old woman.

This traveling troupe of enslaved domestic servants lived and worked in the two-story slave dwelling. They cared for Rebecca's needs while she was at the main house in Montgomery or on one of her husband's three plantations. Two of them were the same age as Rebecca and might have grown up with her. An older man might have been her driver. The Mitchells had several children. This large domestic staff no doubt was tasked to care for this large family.

The slave dwellings in an urban space immediately convinced me I must change the name of the Slave Cabin Project, an idea I first considered at the Heyward House in Bluffton, then later in Anderson. On the weekend college students passionately spoke the ancestors' words in the church that birthed the modern civil rights movement; the Slave Dwelling Project was born to embrace all structures that housed the enslaved, no matter the architecture or where I found them.

A courtyard with a covered well separates the slave dwelling from the main house. An exterior door off the courtyard leads to a steep, narrow staircase that divides the two second-story rooms. At the top of the staircase, I turned left to enter a room that held more surprises. A shaving kit, chamber pot, and framed bed adorned a space that seemed too luxurious for slave quarters. I felt the items were a disingenuous attempt to dress up slavery. I didn't mention my surprise to Carole. I was just happy to be there, and I didn't want to offend my gracious host.

Amid the urban sounds and distant train whistle I tried to focus on my surroundings, a nice building even if it had once housed enslaved people. That dilemma haunted me. If I had been enslaved here, I would have been comfortable. I struggled with that contradiction. Slave dwellings aren't supposed to be comfortable places. Slave dwellings were taking on a new dimension beyond my perception of them, based on my distorted history lessons in school. I didn't want to be physically comfortable in this space. I didn't want to sleep in the bed. I considered it as an artifact that should not be disturbed. Carole provided a sleeping bag. I placed it on the floor at the foot of the bed and near a door to the second-story balcony. I tossed and turned until I finally calmed my thoughts as the city sounds lulled me to sleep.

When the sun rose, Elizabeth led me just outside Montgomery to a former plantation on the Alabama River that has had two names. Like the two-story dwelling I had just slept in, this site's past was not the kind of lesson on slavery I had become accustomed to reading in South Carolina. Alabama was a new kid on the block when it came to slavery. The state of Alabama was established in 1819, a century and a half after the first enslaved Africans arrived in the British colony that became Charleston. In the late 1820s, white settlers moved to Alabama from Kentucky, Georgia, North Carolina, and South Carolina. They were the younger sons of plantation owners who were not in line to inherit their family's land. They went west to seek their fortunes.

RIVERVIEW

Mingo White was about five years old when slave speculators came to Chester, South Carolina, looking for people to buy. He stood on a stand as white people felt his arms, legs, and chest, and asked a lot of questions. "Before we slaves was took to de tradin' post Ol' Marsa Crawford [his owner] tol' us to tell eve'ybody what ast us if we'd ever been sick to tell 'em dat us'd never ben sick in our life. Us had to tell 'em all sorts of lies for our Marsa or else take a beatin'," he recalled. The enslavers picked Little Mingo up and put him in a wagon with other enslaved people bound for Burleson, Alabama. Mingo's dog Trailer wanted to go, too. Trailer stayed on the trail until the wagon reached Wilcox County, Alabama.

Cotton was king in Alabama's Black Belt. The region is named not for the Black people who picked the fluffy white fibers but for the rich black soil that anchored its roots. In the Black Belt, South Carolina historian Dale Rosengarten found an agricultural tool common to Lowcountry South Carolina. An Alabama woman showed Rosengarten a basket that had been in her family for generations. It was no typical basket. It was a coiled basket made with grass fibers consistent with the Lowcountry's coiled basket tradition brought to America by enslaved West Africans. The basket was an intricate "double basket" possibly used as a sewing basket to hold thread and needles. Rosengarten concluded that an enslaved person from South Carolina might have made the basket in South Carolina and traveled with it to Alabama. The basket also might have been made in Alabama with locally grown materials. The Lowcountry coiled baskets are now decorative art, but more than a century ago, coiled baskets were tools to clean and store rice.

Food crops and cotton were not grown on this land. Flamboyant businessman Jesse James Cox used this property, a large peninsula on the Alabama River, to quarter his steamboat crew; some were free, others enslaved, according to research done by Caius McWhirter, the son of the property's managing partner, Chris McWhirter. Before Cox acquired the property from his father, Wade Cox, it was called the Old Cox Place. Then, after the 1830s, it was labeled on maps as the J. Jesse James Cox Plantation.

Cox co-owned the Mobile-based steamship company that operated on the Alabama River at least seven steamers, considered to be some of the fastest and most luxurious boats on the river. Cox's steamships carried passengers and freight upriver to Montgomery and down to Mobile on the Gulf of Mexico. Cox fought in the Civil War with two local regiments. One of them, a sharpshooter unit, is credited with picking off Union officers. Cox left the fighting before the war ended. That decision didn't stop Union soldiers from seeking revenge. They burned Cox's ornate house fashioned like a steamboat.

A fenced-in pasture once used to corral livestock had been the lawn around Cox's house. The pasture is across the field from the cabin where I slept. Made of longleaf pine and cypress siding with a brick chimney at the rear, the cabin was large enough for one family. It was not the home of a typical family enslaved on a plantation. It is one of four remaining of some thirty dwellings that once dotted the property. Enslaved and free people lived in them when they weren't working on Cox's steamboats.

The cabin I slept in is raised about four feet off the ground, higher than the others. It sits on brick pillars because this land had a history of seasonal short-term flooding. That's what Chris McWhirter was told by the federally recognized Poarch Band of Creek Indians. McWhirter's extended family shares ownership in the property, but he's responsible for its upkeep.

The Poarch Band of Creek Indians are the descendants of the Creek Indians whose ancestors lived on this land before recorded time. Chris McWhirter's great-grandfather bought the land in 1890 from Cox's estate and named it Riverview. Around the time of my visit, archaeology students enrolled in archaeological field schools at the University of West Alabama and Troy University found evidence of Native American people living on the site one thousand years ago. On the high bluff overlooking the Alabama River, students and their professors scraped away the soil to reveal middens full of cooked shellfish caught in the river with pottery types known as the Hope Hull culture dating to between AD 900 and 1100. Native American history at this site goes back to 12,500 BC. University of Alabama (UA) and Auburn University have participated in digs for Native American artifacts at Riverview. Chris McWhirter said, "UA participated in antebellum digs in our main compound in the 1960s and early 1970s."

These early Hope Hull people are possibly the ancestors of today's Poarch Creek tribe, who were present when French and Spanish explorers arrived in the early 1500s. The story of the Poarch Creek's existence at Riverview is told by the faint signs in the soil of dwellings and a small earthen temple mound used for either worship or burials.

Elizabeth Brown knew that local archaeologist Teresa Paglione was involved in digs at Riverview. Elizabeth asked Teresa if she thought McWhirter would be open to having me sleep in one of the slave cabins. Because his family acquired the property after Emancipation, Chris McWhirter was not familiar with the enslaved people who once lived on the land before it was called Riverview. McWhirter's grandfather used the land as a dairy farm until World War II. The Black workers were the descendants of people enslaved there when Cox owned it.

McWhirter and his family divide their time between Riverview and Atlanta, where he once owned a high-performance Jaguar parts and repair shop. He and other family members bought out one side of his family to gain controlling interest in Riverview's one thousand wooded acres on a peninsula with a clearing of just 250 acres. Since then, McWhirter has invested time and a sizeable sum of money to restore some of the slave dwellings and outbuildings that were once part of the dairy farm. McWhirter and his sons, Caius and Rives, have spent enormous amounts of time and money preserving and improving the property. Rives McWhirter has worked for more than three years restoring the compound, according to his father. "Quite a bit of hot, dangerous, and physical work with no monetary compensation," the elder McWhirter said. "He receives great personal satisfaction on saving an extremely important part of American history."

After I followed the mile-long narrow road to the family's home built by McWhirter's grandparents, he greeted me there while cooking barbecue pork ribs on a hot grill. We sat outside on a deck across the field from the cabins. After the meal and conversation, he took me to them. At least two were used for storage. I chose one with an old mattress with exposed springs. It appeared to be a good place for my sleeping bag as long as I wasn't bothered by a nearby wasp nest. I was all by myself in Alabama. I fought against the idea of sleeping in the rental car parked near the only door to the cabin in case I needed to make a quick getaway. There were no overt threats. It was all in my head. I couldn't leave now after seeing slave dwellings outside South Carolina. I didn't want to offend my friends or my hosts or be called a coward. I needed to be true to my word.

* * *

A decade later I met one of Montgomery's most celebrated residents. Activist and author Bryan Stevenson is the founder and executive director of the Equal Justice Initiative (EJI), which operates the National Memorial for Peace and Justice, an outdoor space commonly called the Lynching Memorial. He came to Magnolia Plantation and Gardens, where he took the tour of four slave cabins, including the one where I spent the night in 2010 to launch my Slave Cabin Project. I didn't lead the tour he took, but after his tour was over I introduced myself to him.

"I am Joe McGill, founder of the Slave Dwelling Project."

"Yeah! They were trying to get us together," Stevenson said as we shook hands.

Our conversation was cut short because I was scheduled to give the next tour. I was envious of my coworker because he took the great Bryan Stevenson on a tour and sadly he had no clue who Stevenson was. I gave him my card as I was leaving. We've not spoken since.

In 2019, Stevenson was featured in a *Time* magazine interview with photographs by famed portrait photographer Annie Leibovitz. The story includes two pictures of Stevenson: one of him sitting on the edge of his desk, the other of him sitting on the steps in front of a slave cabin. Leibovitz said, "In this particular set of pictures, there are two pictures that create the person—there's a portrait of the person and then there's something else that is in their life. With Bryan Stevenson, his great-great-grandparents were slaves, and this other photo alongside his portrait is in a plantation outside of Montgomery, Alabama. You can see the slave quarters, and there's this tree, which you can draw your own conclusions on. It's a brief photo story."

Chris McWhirter confirmed that the slave cabin where Stevenson posed for Leibovitz's picture is at Riverview. It's next to the cabin where I slept on October 8, 2010. This is a chance encounter at the place Leibovitz said was the home of the enslaved ancestors of a living person who fights to correct the ills of slavery. What does this mean? Maybe the ancestors—Stevenson's ancestors, too—like the path I am on. Like Leibovitz said, you can draw your own conclusion.

SEVEN

Expanding My Horizon

HEN WALI CATHCART WAS A BOY, HE WALKED THE OLD ROAD that divides the abandoned Bratton Plantation his elders said was haunted. The big house, a brick slave cabin, and other forgotten structures straddled the two-lane road beyond overgrown brush and weeds. The eerie landscape held secrets his relatives didn't want to reveal. Eventually, through his mother, Cathcart learned his paternal great-grandmother Lila Bratton had been enslaved there. She birthed two children there—Daniel in 1861 and Matilda in 1864—fathered by the plantation owner's son, Dr. John Simpson Bratton Jr.

Lila Bratton was twenty-three years old when the Civil War ended, the year after Matilda was born. After Emancipation, Lila Bratton had two more children with a Black man, Larkin Crawford, who likely had been enslaved at another plantation. Lila and Larkin Crawford remained on the Bratton plantation as sharecroppers. Today, Cathcart's family is one of the Sacred Seven Families, an affectionate reference to the living descendants of people once enslaved at the Bratton plantation.* The property is now the restored Historic Brattonsville, which opened in 1977 as an eight-hundred-acre historic site in York County, South Carolina, on the border with Charlotte, North Carolina.†

The eighty-four-year-old Willie "Wali" Cathcart suspects his father, Ira, was ashamed of the nonconsensual relationship between his great-grandmother and Bratton, the second eldest of fourteen children, born in 1891 to Dr. John Simpson Bratton Sr. and his wife Harriet Rainey Bratton. "[Lila] was there [as his] possession," Cathcart said with a tone of resignation. Lila Bratton Crawford was among the more than 160 people who over two centuries were enslaved on the once-sprawling eight-thousand-acre cotton plantation established a decade before the American Revolution. "They owned them like they did the [livestock] or their other possessions," Cathcart said. He has wondered, too, whether his father blamed his grandmother for having children with Bratton. If it had not been for the persistence of Cathcart's mother, Jannie, and his grandmother Fannie Cathcart, Lila Crawford's fourth child, he would not have known of his great-grandmother's enslavement.

Fannie Cathcart shared other secrets too. As a boy, Cathcart was too timid to ask why so many light-skinned Black people in York County, who lived near the Bratton plantation, called his

---

* When Cathcart lived in New Jersey, he was a pitcher on a baseball team with Joe Black in the 1950s in the Negro Baseball League.

† Descendants of the Bratton family own the property, which is operated by the York County Culture and Heritage Commission. *The Patriot*, starring Mel Gibson, was filmed at Brattonsville in 1999.

grandmother Fannie "Cousin Fannie." She provided an answer. Her white grandfather, John Bratton Jr., and his brother, Rufus, had impregnated enslaved women, producing clandestine mixed-race branches of the Bratton family tree.* University of North Carolina at Charlotte historian Bertha Maxwell-Roddey explained the twisted relationships between enslaved women and their enslavers. Her research led her to find Bratton plantation descendants of enslaved families. Then, with her help, kinships aligned to bind the Sacred Seven Families, representing about one hundred people who identify with their ancestors named Bratton, Cathcart/Crawford, Feaster/Femster, Lowry, Moore, Smith, and Thompson. Not all of them are blood relatives to the Bratton boys. Some of them took the Bratton name after Emancipation.

I unexpectedly met four members of the Sacred Seven Families. That meeting came after I called Brattonsville to seek permission to sleep in the 1830s brick slave cabin a young Wali Cathcart walked past on his way to Mt. Zion Baptist Church, built on land the Brattons donated during the Civil War to their enslaved workers.

Brattonsville was on the list of former plantations I received from the state's historic preservation office. In most instances I asked the site manager for permission to sleep in a slave cabin, and then we would set a date for the overnight stay. Brattonsville broke from that routine, an unexpected glitch that raised my anxiety.

---

* During the Reconstruction period after the Civil War, Rufus Bratton, active with the Ku Klux Klan, was charged with the March 7, 1871, hanging of James Williams. Bratton fled York County, but charges against him were later dropped.

Brattonsville's site manager Kevin Lynch remembered me from his time in Charleston when I was a national park ranger at Fort Moultrie and Fort Sumter. In the late 1990s, Lynch was director of education and interpretation at Charles Towne Landing State Historic Site, a state park at the first permanent European settlement in South Carolina, established in 1670.

In 2003, Lynch became program director at Brattonsville, which features historic houses and structures built over three generations of the Bratton family and the enslaved community. The site covers more than eight hundred acres and includes farmland with heritage-breed animals, a Revolutionary War battlefield site, and a nature preserve. Three years after Lynch arrived at Brattonsville, the site began its outreach to descendants of enslaved people. His familiarity with me may have led to a conditional approval to spend a night in the last of twenty-two brick cabins at the site. My request also received early support from Nicole Moore, an interpreter of slavery at Brattonsville. Moore was shocked that my request was given initial approval. She thought my unusual ask would have been buried under layers of bureaucracy at the historic site that had not placed a high enough emphasis on the stories of the enslaved. That task, she said, was mostly left up to her and the late Kitty Wilson-Evans, another African American interpreter and storyteller who gained nationwide fame for her portrayal of Kissie, a fictional enslaved woman. They were assigned to the north side of Brattonsville Road, where the nineteenth-century history of slavery was presented. At a reproduction of a brick slave cabin, Moore tended a vegetable garden with okra, tomatoes, and beans to demonstrate what enslaved people grew to supplement their diets.

On the south side of the road, the presentation focused on Brattonsville's eighteenth-century and Revolutionary War history with little mention of slavery, she said. White interpreters told the story of Watt, an enslaved man who alerted the Brattons to approaching British troops, allowing them to flee. In Brattonsville's history, Watt is interpreted as being a loyal slave. It's a "good slave" narrative that white guides didn't hesitate to share with guests, she said. For his loyalty the Brattons placed a headstone on his grave, but he didn't die a free man.

Before the staff gave full support, they suggested I meet the Sacred Seven Families. The staff didn't want to make a decision without their consent. They also wanted to show the families I would not exploit their history.

Several weeks later, during a meeting at Brattonsville in late October 2010, Lynch and Moore introduced me to Cathcart and his cousins, Margaret Crawford Parson-Willins, Lisa Bratton, and Strauss (Bratton) Moore Shiple, Sacred Seven Families members who participated in events at Brattonsville.

Cathcart and Parson-Willins are the descendants of Lila Bratton Crawford, who married Larkin Crawford when she gained her freedom in 1865. Cathcart said he and Parson-Willins suspected they shared an enslaved ancestor from Brattonsville, but they didn't know the details until Brattonsville helped make the connection. "We didn't get any information about her [Lila] as I was growing up because of the subject of slavery," Parson-Willins said. "We African Americans were hush-mouthed about that. We didn't want to talk about it." In 2007, Cathcart and Parson-Willins joined the descendants' group.

Lisa Bratton's father, John Bratton, told her his grandparents Green and Malinda Bratton were enslaved at the Bratton plantation. In the 1950s, John Bratton left York County to live with his brothers and later got a job in the state's growing defense industry as a laborer in a shipyard at Ontario, California. Born in Vallejo, California, Lisa Bratton was six years old when she learned of her enslaved ancestors. She fully accepts she has the surname of the white family that enslaved Green and Malinda. It is her identity. She does not plan to change it.

Strauss Moore Shiple and I, in 2009, served together briefly on the board of the South Carolina African American Heritage Commission just as I was beginning the Slave Cabin Project. I didn't know then of her family's tie to the Bratton plantation. She lacks a conclusive connection to the plantation, but her aunt Virginia Bratton Anthony, who lived in Charlotte, said that her great-grandparents Boney and Minnie Bratton were enslaved on the plantation. When she was a child, Brattonsville was abandoned and her parents did not talk about it. Shiple became interested in Brattonsville after she returned to York County in the mid-1990s following college and eight years in the US Army. Shiple would not have visited Brattonsville had it not been for her position as a project manager for the Olde English District Tourism Commission, tourism promoters in a seven-county region that includes York County. During a visit to Brattonsville, she met Miss Kitty Wilson. Shiple told Miss Kitty about her great-grandparents Boney and Minnie Bratton. The usually mild-mannered Miss Kitty then urged Shiple at length of the absolute necessity to research her family's history. Miss Kitty continued to chastise Shiple when she sensed she was not serious about following her advice. Although Shiple never found proof her ancestors were enslaved at the Bratton plantation, she nonetheless feels their presence there.

As I sat with members of the Sacred Seven outside the staff's office on the eighteenth-century side of the property, the descendants asked about my intentions. In describing the Slave Dwelling Project, I told them of the other plantations I had visited as I stressed repeatedly that I did not want to sleep in the cabin to connect with ghosts. Although Lisa Bratton had not heard of my work, she was intrigued by the idea of sleeping in a slave dwelling to bring awareness to the importance of saving the structures. Shiple saw my request as an appropriate ask, especially since it came from a Black man. She would have been put off if the request had come from a white person.

Then I made a humble request to sleep in the cabin to honor their ancestors. When they agreed, I exhaled with the assurance I would have my tenth cabin stay completed before 2010 ended. I left the meeting most impressed that I had met descendants of people who had been enslaved at a plantation I was planning to visit. I had not made that kind of connection before. I was somewhat disappointed with myself that I had not considered connection to descendants of enslaved people as a necessary part of my work.

More than a month after I met members of the Sacred Seven Families, I traveled to Florence, South Carolina, on November 6, 2010, to meet Terry James for the drive to Brattonsville. After Terry and I spent the night in slave dwellings on Morris Street in Anderson and at Mansfield Plantation on the Black River in Georgetown County, he agreed to join me at another site. His presence said a lot about his commitment because the Morris Street and Mansfield buildings were not pleasant places to sleep. After hot nights in a former slave dwelling that reeked of mildew in Anderson and a mosquito-infested slave chapel at Mansfield, I was surprised Terry agreed to do another night. I invited my Civil War reenactment friends to join me at Brattonsville. Terry was the only one to respond. Terry's family history in Florence County was so similar to the Cathcarts' history at Brattonsville that I got the strangest feeling that the ancestors influenced his decision to join me.

Terry James is executive director of the Jamestown Foundation, whose seven-member board of trustees oversees 246 acres of heavily wooded James family land in Florence County, South Carolina.[*] The property could be as much as 276 acres, if the foundation updates the last land survey. The land sustained James's ancestors. Deer, wild hogs, wild turkey, rabbits, and squirrels provided an abundant source of food on a tract that gently slopes to the Pee Dee River Swamp. When flood waters receded, shallow pools held fish. The family grew tobacco, sugarcane, vegetables, and rice.

Between 1870 and 1945, about two hundred people resided in about twenty houses scattered around the self-sufficient Jamestown settlement. One remaining structure crumbling under the weight of its faded weather-beaten boards dominates a clearing near a three-acre family cemetery with the remains of four generations of James family descendants. Tony and Jane James were the last of Terry's relatives to live in the house. In 2013, when the foundation

---

[*] The Jamestown Foundation was established in 2013. For more information about the foundation's efforts to save the James family land, visit www.jamestownfoundation.com.

was established, it launched Come Celebrate Jamestown, an event that has grown into an annual celebration that attracts about two hundred James family members and others from around the country.

This land legacy would be a triumph for any South Carolina family. But what makes this story remarkable is that it started with 109 acres Terry's great-great-great-grandfather Ervin James bought from two slave owners six years after he gained his freedom. He paid $700 for the property at a time when Black men in the South found it difficult to buy or lease land from white people. The land sale in 1871 at Mars Bluff was an exception and a risky transaction for the buyer and sellers. James's legacy has been honored by federal, state, and local governments. South Carolina congressman James E. Clyburn in 2007 recognized James in the Congressional Record. Two years later, the South Carolina House of Representatives praised James with a concurrent resolution.[*]

Terry was about six years old when he began to hear the stories of his legendary grandfather. Decades later when he researched the family's history, he saw references to his grandfather in tax, land, and voting records. But he has not yet found proof that Ervin James was enslaved. He did find plantation records that show Nora James, Ervin's wife, was enslaved at George James's plantation, four miles west of Jamestown. The couple raised a dozen children at Jamestown.

When Terry and I arrived at Brattonsville, he was impressed that the site spilled over to both sides of the highway with more than

---

[*] Florence County Council signed a 2020 proclamation honoring Jamestown.

thirty historic structures dating from the 1760s to the late nine-teenth century. The site represents an evolution of Southern cul-ture and architecture in the Carolina Piedmont, settled beginning in the 1740s by Scots-Irish immigrants from Virginia who clashed with Indigenous people. The brick cabin where we would spend the night is the last original brick cabin that stood near the Brattons' main house, built on a ridge that parallels Brattonsville Road. Seven brick slave houses once flanked the main house with doors facing toward the main house, giving the Brattons a vantage to surveil the enslaved community. It is believed the people who lived in the brick cabins performed domestic tasks in the main house. The residents of the one-room brick slave houses might have felt an elevated sta-tus over the enslaved workers clustered in a dozen wooden slave cabins built closer to the cotton fields.

It is unknown who lived in the remaining brick cabin. Nicole Moore believes a spirit lives there. She can feel their presence and hear their movement. Outside the cabin, across the once-bustling plantation, she can sense the lingering energy of people who toiled there. Moore said Miss Kitty felt this too, and on occasion she would send special guests to the brick cabin. They'd return with astonished looks. So as not to upset the spirits in the cabin, Moore announced that she was there to tell their story. The day she entered the cabin to clean it in advance of my visit, she felt the presence of a fright-ened boy crouched in the corner. He seemed to be about eight years old. She later shared the experience with Brattonsville volunteer interpreter and storyteller Dontavius Williams. He had had a simi-lar experience with the little boy that led to the creation of "The Chronicles of Adam," the story of an enslaved boy sold away from his mother. But the most intense energy, she said, rises from the cellar in the brick house that served as a general store, stagecoach station, and polling place. Bad things happened in the basement's vault, she said empathically. Moore suspects it's where enslaved people were tortured and raped. Moore didn't share these thoughts with me until years after the cabin stay at Brattonsville because she didn't want me to think she was crazy. The only warning she gave me at that time was to be aware of a snake that crawled around the cabin. I was not concerned about the snake. I was more concerned about staying warm. The night of November 6, 2011, was below freezing, unusually cold for that time of year in the Carolina Piedmont.

The staff had cut firewood and stacked it near a stone fire ring outside the cabin. Soon Terry and I had a fire, but the modest blaze was no match for the swirling subfreezing wind. Our woolen Union soldier uniforms provided some relief but not enough for a substantial level of comfort. We sat at the fire until the cold forced us inside. The cabin was bare, unlike the cabins at Magnolia, Bluffton, and Montgomery's Old Alabama Town, which had been staged with period furniture. The staff considered the empty cabin a hallowed space. Placing furniture in it could detract from the people who lived in the cabin.

My earlier anxiety about sleeping in a cabin had eased now that I was on my tenth overnight stay. It was a quiet night except for the sounds rattling from Terry's sleeping bag. Terry and I arranged our sleeping bags side by side before a nonfunctioning brick fireplace. As we settled down, Terry revealed that he would use this cabin stay to simulate what a captured African endured during the ocean voyage to America. Terry brought two pairs of iron shackles. He would bind his wrists before he slid into his sleeping bag. He wanted to feel what they felt in slave ships. He also knew that at some point in his life, Ervin James, born in 1815, might have been shackled. He had acquired replicas of shackles from Danny Drain, a collector of slavery artifacts who managed a small museum in Walterboro, South Carolina, near Charleston. Drain had set up a display of slave artifacts at a Come Celebrate Jamestown event. Terry offered a pair to me. I declined. I only wanted to sleep in the places where enslaved people lived. I didn't want to be that dramatic.

When Terry removed the shackles from a camouflage book bag, the sight of those rust-colored, oversized handcuffs, joined by a short chain, jerked my thoughts toward enslaved people restrained for months on slave ships or maybe during detention at a plantation. The chains clanked throughout the night as Terry squirmed and tossed in a desperate hunt for a comfortable position. He could not spread his restrained hands wider than his body. His cold limbs felt like bare bones pressed hard against the wooden floor. The enslaved didn't have the option to walk away, so he didn't retreat. When he changed his position the clanking chains woke me up.

Although the night was uncomfortable and neither of us enjoyed sustained sleep, the experience was free of the stench, hunger, nakedness, and heat enslaved people endured in the cargo hold of a slave ship. With each clank of the chains, I pondered whether Terry was dedicated to honoring the ancestors or just crazy. By sunrise, I concluded he was just as dedicated as I am in telling the ancestors' stories. He just had a unique way of doing it.

I closed 2010 with that night in a brick slave cabin at Brattons-ville, my tenth and last cabin stay of my original plan of one year in South Carolina. Since I had traveled to two other sites in Alabama, however, I was no longer bound to remain in South Carolina, and the Slave Dwelling Project was set to extend into its second year. How much longer could it go on? And what other barriers might I break down along the way?

EIGHT

WHAT HISTORY TELLS US

EGYPT

The history of Mexico and Texas never appeared on the blackboard in my South Carolina classroom. It wasn't until adulthood that I learned Texas was once Mexican soil. Mexico's sparsely populated northern territory evolved into Mexico Texas, a colony of white Southerners who settled there with their Black slaves. When Mexico gained independence from Spain, the Mexican government welcomed American slaveholders. This Anglo-American migration led to a population boom, diluting the presence of people of Mexican descent. This influx of "American immigrants" also heightened growing concerns that an independent Mexico, unlike the United States, was gradually leaning toward abolishing slavery. Those concerns and other issues in the fall of 1835 sparked the Texas Revolution, a short war Texas colonists won the following spring. The victory led to an independent Republic of Texas with an army commanded by Sam Houston. A separate Texas still clashed with Mexican troops, requiring Texans to embrace their former country-men in the United States for protection. A decade later, the Repub-lic of Texas became the twenty-eighth state of the United States. Admitting Texas into the United States also maintained a momen-tary balance of political power between free and slaveholding states. Events eventually tipped the balance, however, in favor of free states, placing the country on a slippery path to civil war over the issue of slavery.

In the new slaveholding state of Texas, nearly a quarter of the estimated 125,000 people were enslaved. East Texas cotton fueled the demand for free labor. Most enslaved people came from the South, including South Carolina and as far away as Virginia. On one journey slave handlers passed through the Pee Dee region of north central South Carolina with six chained men snatched from Virginia to be sold in Texas.

Whipping became a common and acceptable form of punish-ment, although it was illegal for slave owners to kill or maim an enslaved person. But that law was certainly not always followed. George Washington Anderson, born in Charleston, South Caro-lina, in 1855, remembered hearing as a child stories of how slavery's brutality had touched his family. Four years after his birth, Ander-son's parents, Irvin and Eliza Anderson, were sold to Duncan Wood's East Texas plantation near Beaumont. "Dey tell me he had my gran' daddy beat to death. Dey never did beat me."

William Oliver, enslaved on a plantation in Horry County, South Carolina, near present-day Myrtle Beach, a popular ocean-side tourist destination, recalled stories of notoriously cruel Texas slave masters, though he had no firsthand experience with that oppression. "They tell me when your master . . . wanted to make you do your tasks they threatened to sell you to Texas." Work for the enslaved in Texas began before dawn in advance of the killing heat. The whip-wielding boss man shouted the order to work: a potential death sentence. "Heads up, you chop!" Women chopped until one of them dropped, dead. Texas was hell, Oliver said.

To escape the brutality, enslaved people took a lesser-known southern route of the Underground Railroad across the Rio Grande River to Mexico. In 1845, slave owner William Gudlow brought Felix Haywood's parents from Mississippi to Saint Hedwig, Texas, east of San Antonio. Shortly after they arrived, Haywood's mother birthed him. As a young man, Haywood tended cattle and sheep for ranchers near San Antonio. He was told of the northern route to freedom along the Underground Railroad, a network of people, Blacks and whites, who sheltered people fleeing the South from the late eighteenth century until 1865. "There wasn't no reason to run up north," Haywood explained. "All we had to do was to walk, but walk south, and we'd be free as soon as we crossed the Rio Grande. In Mexico, you could be free. They didn't care what color you was—black, white, yellow, or blue. Hundreds of slaves did go to Mexico and got on all right." Enslaved people who fled to Mexico faced working conditions similar to what they had experienced north of the border. However, they had the Mexican courts on their side in labor disputes, and they could sue an employer if they were mistreated.

Enslaved people sold to Texas plantations passed through New Orleans, a hub of the domestic slave trade after the United States abolished the importation of Africans in 1808, a year after England outlawed the slave trade in the British Empire. On December 8, 1852, slave traders in New Orleans stowed eighteen people on the steamship *Mexico* for a two-day journey to Galveston. Fifty-year-old Clarisa, a five-foot, seven-inch woman described as "yellow," was the eldest enslaved soul on the ship longing to be free. Three-year-old George was one of the youngest. The ship's slave manifest described the two-foot-tall child as "black." It is likely Clarisa fetched a higher auction price than George, who would not bring an immediate return on investment because of his tender age and lack of experience.

*   *   *

The Texas slavery legacy was not part of a National Trust for Historic Preservation conference I attended on October 27, 2010, in Austin, a few weeks before Terry James and I visited Brattonsville. Tanya Bowers, the Trust's director of diversity and one of my biggest fans, pushed me on the conference's big stage in the big state of Texas to talk about the Slave Dwelling Project and my travels through southern states. Tanya had also encouraged me to write blogs the Trust had published on its website, beginning with my first cabin stay at Magnolia Plantation and Gardens. The Slave Dwelling Project's popularity was on the rise following my interview in August 2010 on National Public Radio (NPR), early on when my work was still the Slave Cabin Project. I suspect the NPR interview and other media attention gave the Trust the trust to support my work with a quiet plan to share the national exposure with me. With this unspoken symbiotic relationship, I was imagining the

Trust might sponsor the Slave Dwelling Project, giving my work yet another level of prominence.

The Austin conference agenda did not include a discussion on slave dwellings. I was not surprised. I've always felt that historic preservationists focus too heavily on the slaveholders' architecturally significant buildings. I fill that gap. In a room packed with sixty-five people, some standing, I shared my experiences with a highly curious and intently focused audience that listened quietly as I recounted my travels to find hard wooden floors in century-old slave dwellings where I could lay my head. After my speech, conference attendees swarmed me with the often-asked question: "How many slave dwellings are there?" Each time I responded, "I don't know." They also asked whether I felt the spirits of wandering souls searching for the peace that eluded them in life. And, of course, many wanted to know if I was afraid to sleep alone in slave cabins.

Conference attendees traveled to Austin from Maryland, North Carolina, Louisiana, Virginia, and Pennsylvania. Historic preservationists from Maryland, North Carolina, and Texas invited me to their states. Texas was the first to make an invitation a reality. The Texas Historical Commission (THC) in Austin invited me to be the keynote speaker at its statewide conference on April 1, 2011.

I had planned to end the Slave Cabin Project in 2010, but the Trust's national conference kicked me into the next year with no end in sight. I had already broken the barrier of sleeping alone. Most of the people who had joined me were Black people. So far, no white person had asked to sleep in a cabin with me. Maybe they felt quiet moments in those sacred spaces should be reserved for people of African descent. I tended to agree.

Within a week of the THC conference, an idea emerged to combine my keynote address with two slave cabin sleepovers. The commission went into a higher gear. THC staff member Bryan McAuley was tasked to look for extant slave cabins where I could spend the night. I doubted he'd find any. I thought only a few cabins might have survived the harsh conditions in Texas. Surprisingly, McAuley's search led to two extant slave cabins: one at Egypt Plantation, established in 1835 as a sugar and cotton plantation on the Colorado River in Egypt, Texas, an hour's drive southwest of Houston; and the other at Seward Plantation, a cotton plantation a mile east of Independence, the hub of Stephen Austin's 1835 colony of three hundred white families who brought their slaves to Mexico Texas.

I was impressed and humbled that the commission found two slave cabins so quickly and obtained permission for me to sleep in them. This level of cooperation showed that my work had the potential to assist even more sites across the nation in the telling of their stories about slavery. The commission also recruited schoolteacher Naomi Carrier, an actress, historian, and CEO of the Texas Center for African American Living History, to be my guide to the Egypt and Seward plantations.

*　*　*

Eli Mercer and his wife, Ann, and their son, Elijah, left Mississippi in November 1829 to join the caravan of white settlers in Texas. That same year, Mercer established a plantation and ferry on the Colorado River on land that would become Wharton County west of Houston. The site originally called Mercer's Crossing was rechristened following a severe drought in 1827. When the fertile soil supplied corn for settlers, they began calling the area Egypt as a nod to the biblical account in Acts 7:11–12: "Now there came a dearth over all the land . . . and our fathers found no sustenance. But when Jacob heard that there was corn in Egypt, he sent out our fathers first." As citizen soldiers, Elijah and his father fought the Mexicans, and eventually Elijah Mercer and his regiment of Texas volunteers clashed with the Comanche Nation. William Jones Elliot Heard established the 2,222-acre Egypt Plantation in 1832. Seven years later Andrew Northington launched a stagecoach line that served Egypt. Northington later married Heard's daughter, Elizabeth. Today, Bud Northington, Andrew Northington's seventh-generation descendant, owns Egypt Plantation, the place where I'd spend my first night in a Texas slave cabin. McAuley and Naomi knew Northington. McAuley had worked for a nonprofit agency that assisted the THC in promoting history and tourism in a twenty-eight-county region. Before McAuley joined the THC, he had met Northington, who told him of his family's connection to Egypt Plantation and that the property had a slave cabin. Years later, when the THC assigned McAuley to find a cabin, he recalled that conversation with Northington and called him. Naomi knew Northington through mutual friends. She had led tour groups there several times, beginning around 2000. She also suggested Egypt as a site for me to visit. She and McAuley invited people to Egypt to meet me the day of the sleepover. The morning after the sleepover, a group of schoolchildren were invited for their first lesson on slavery at an authentic slave cabin.

Naomi greeted me at the Houston airport on March 30, 2011. We headed west to Wharton County, one of four counties along with Brazoria, Fort Bend, and Matagorda that are called the "Sugar Bowl" of Texas, where enslaved workers toiled in loose, fertile soil to grow sugarcane, a major cash crop before the Civil War. Sugar production continued after 1865, with leased convict laborers jailed on bogus charges then sent to sugar plantations that continued functioning after the war. Like the enslaved workers before them, they also suffered in blistering Texas temperatures, chopping tall tough stalks of cane with long razor-sharp knives. The back-breaking, hazardous work continued in sugar factories, where mechanized presses squeezed the juice from the cane but could also accidently break bones and rip flesh. The abuse ended in 1910, but the sugar tragedy soured even more when in 2018 the remains of ninety-five African Americans were found in a cemetery at a former prison farm that had become a Houston suburb.

Naomi said she suspected she and I had initially met years before in Atlanta during a conference of the Association for the Study of African American Life and History (ASALH) just before I launched the Slave Cabin Project in 2010.* But neither of us can remember the details of the meeting. The hour-long drive to Egypt in Wharton County gave Naomi time to also tell me what I could expect at Egypt, where three other people would join us for the sleepover, setting the stage for the largest gathering for a sleepover yet. At Egypt I met New Orleans artist Ted Ellis. He came with his easel, paints, brushes, and plans to create two paintings of Egypt's

---

* The Association for the Study of African American Life and History was founded in 1915 by historian Carter G. Woodson and others. Their efforts led to Black History Week, which was later expanded to Black History Month.

small red slave cabin with clapboard siding, covered porch, and a brick chimney rising on the building's narrow side. Geneva "Candi" Richardson Flora, a videographer, performer, and licensed practical nurse, who lives in Rosenburg near Houston, joined the group. Then I met McAuley after weeks of emails and phone calls. I was surprised so many people wanted to join me. Would there be room for all of us? Then McAuley, who is white, asked the inevitable question. He asked to sleep in the cabin with us. I hesitated. But then I realized if a white man was interested then other white people might also embrace the Slave Dwelling Project. I had seen this as a Black thing; now I was open to reconsidering my earlier ideas. Let us all sleep in these spaces together.

*   *   *

Egypt's owner Bud Northington and his wife, Mary Northington, and fifty other people greeted me. It was more than I had expected and larger than the reception at the Morris Street dwelling in Anderson, South Carolina. Naomi's elementary students at St. James School, an Episcopal school in Houston where she taught music, theater, and American and world history to middle schoolers, drew a welcome sign displayed on an old barn. "Welcome Joe McGill, Egypt Plantation, Slave Cabin Sleepover." The Northingtons treated us to a delicious vegetarian meal served in the main house, where they live. George Heard "Bud" Northington IV, a seventh-generation Texan, lives in Egypt's main house, built in 1857. When I asked for details about Egypt, he referred me to an entry in the Texas State Historical Association, an independent nonprofit established in 1897. The reference does not mention slavery at Egypt. Why the reference does not refer to slavery is unknown. But Northington said his ancestors didn't like the word "slave." Instead he called the cabin where we would sleep a "quarter cabin."

After dinner we stood outside the slave cabin just as a Texas-style "blue norther" swept through, rapidly plunging the temperature below freezing. The whistling wind, the howling dogs in the distance, and the blast of cold air convinced me to change my plans to sleep on the porch. We moved our conversations inside the tiny cabin until tired eyes closed well past midnight. Two beds filled the cramped cabin. I took one of them. Naomi took the other. After the mercury fell, Northington invited McAuley to spend the night in the main house with him and his wife. McAuley declined. He wanted to have the experience of sleeping in the cabin to add to his experiences of living history in the outdoors. He settled on the floor at the foot of Naomi's bed. At one point during the night, Ellis left us for the warmth of his car.

That left Flora the option of sharing the tiny bed with Naomi or sleeping on the floor. Unexpectedly, Flora had a plan for her night in a slave cabin similar to Terry James's night at Brattonsville. Flora also chose to sleep on the floor, but, unlike Terry, she bound her hands and feet with shackles. Flora didn't get much sleep that night with her wrists and ankles in tight shackles that weighed her down. She wanted to feel what an enslaved person felt both physically and emotionally.

The next morning, Bud and his wife prepared bacon, eggs, grits, toast, and jelly for breakfast, the kind of hearty meal I was accustomed to eating in South Carolina. Then we returned to the cabin to meet twenty elementary school students who stood in an authentic slave cabin and felt the weight of Flora's chains. The unusually cold weather didn't get better, surprising us all and especially the shivering students, who weren't dressed for the lower temperatures. When they huddled around me on the cabin's porch and I saw how uncomfortable many of them were, I brought them inside the tiny red cabin for a teachable moment. I asked how many had a bedroom the size of the cabin. Hands shot up. This space once held an entire family, I told them. They seemed stunned.

On the porch shaded by the cabin's extended roof, Naomi, dressed in a yellow Mexican poncho, raised her arms and led the children in song. "I am gonna jump down / turn around / pick a bale of cotton; I am gonna jump down / turn around / pick a bale a day." As she repeated those lines and the chorus, she jumped and turned around and soon the children mimicked her movements. As the conversation continued, Naomi noticed most of them had no knowledge of slavery in a state that had enslaved people of African descent before it joined the United States. Then Flora let the children hold her chains. If a parent was present and gave permission, she placed the shackles on their ankles and wrists. She wanted the children to experience being shackled so they'd know that slavery was not a joke.

SEWARD

On Christmas Eve 1833, Samuel Seward and his family along with Caroline, their slave, arrived in Texas at the Coles Settlement, where he bought 4,428 acres, or a league, of land. When Texas broke away from Mexico and gained US statehood in 1836, the

Coles Settlement was renamed Independence, a once-prosperous community that declined when the railroad passed it by. Between 1853 and 1855, enslaved workers erected the main house at the Seward Plantation. Family lore says the house, made of red cedar, originally had one story but was moved the year after it was completed. While this date can't be verified, it is known that the one-story house was placed on cottonwood logs and rolled for nearly three-quarters of a mile downhill to its current location, where a second floor was added along with multiple one-story rear additions. The enslaved craftsmen who built the house may have included Uncle Finn, a master mason who did the stonework and laid the stones for the chimneys. He also performed this craft throughout the Independence area, but his owner likely received the money for his skilled work.

The 1860 census lists three slave dwellings at Seward: two of them contained in a two-room duplex with one side made of logs and the other section constructed from stones, commonly called fieldstones, found just below the surface of the soil. The metal roof covers an older wooden split-shingle roof. According to Seward family tradition, Uncle Finn lived there. It is ironic that Naomi and I would spend the night in Uncle Finn's cabin with pecan logs and a cedar frame standing three feet off the ground. My father and his father were brick masons in Kingstree, South Carolina. The third dwelling at Seward for an enslaved worker became a shed used for storage. It was called "Aunt Caroline's house." It's possible this is the third slave house in the 1860 census.

During our drive to Seward Plantation, Naomi and I traveled along a scenic highway lined with bluebonnets, the Texas state flower. As she drove, Naomi delivered a lesson on Texas history and the resilience of Black women. She told me about Annie Mae Hunt, the grandchild of enslaved people near Brenham. Born in 1909 near Brenham, Hunt picked cotton for fifty cents a day in conditions she compared to "slavery times." She, her mother, and sister survived intimidation, beatings, and sexual assault by white and sometimes Black men. Even so, she declared, "A man never beat *me* up and got away with it!" In 1983, historian Ruthe Winegarten published Hunt's oral history, titled *I Am Annie Mae*. Winegarten and Naomi later transformed the book into a musical with eighteen songs Naomi composed. Initially the production, titled after the book, had a cast of fifteen actors, but it was later reduced to a one-woman play, featuring Naomi. Hunt became a grassroots political organizer who later traveled on the Greyhound bus from Dallas to Jimmy Carter's 1977 inauguration in Washington, DC. Although Naomi had done extensive research into Hunt's family life at Brenham, she was not aware of Seward Plantation.

Seward's owner Hank Ward told us stories of Caroline Seward, who continued to work as his family's maid after Emancipation until she died at age 91 in 1903. Ward respectfully refers to her as Aunt Caroline, even though "aunt" and "uncle" are paternalist terms white slave owners used to refer to their elderly enslaved people. LaSandra Sanders, however, does not refer to Carolina Seward as "aunt." To her she is a beloved ancestor who died at age 112.

Naomi and I slept in Uncle Finn's large, sturdy two-room cabin. One end was made with logs, the other half built with fieldstones. Each room has a chimney. That night a wind whipped through the door. Naomi didn't have a sleeping bag. Before daybreak she went to her car to warm up.

Ward had given us a tour of the property when we arrived, but just as we were poised to leave, he said, "I bet you don't know what this is." He pointed to what he called an auction block, where enslaved people were sold to the highest bidder. The block was made of two worn grist millstones stacked together with steps leading up to it. It served a dual purpose. White women could step out of a wagon onto the block and walk down the steps. Enslaved people could step up and stand with wrenching emotions, fearful of an unknown fate. Ward matter-of-factly said auctions were held at Seward because it was the center of activity for a self-sustaining community. Most people lived in log cabins, but in the mid-1850s, Seward's ten-thousand-square-foot main house dwarfed everything around it and served as a site for community meetings and funerals.

Ward invited us to stand on the auction block. Naomi was the first on it. She held her emotions in, but her face betrayed how she felt. As she stood there, she imagined how an enslaved person might have felt knowing they were on the brink of being sold away from family. Born in the Rio Grande valley, Naomi grew up near the Red River near Brownsville in the tiny village of San Benito, a Black settlement in the valley. She had spent decades investigating the history of slavery in Texas. She admits she does not know it all, but what she knows has driven her to tears. They were tears she didn't shed when she was on the auction block. She didn't want to let Ward see her cry. She suspects Ward didn't initially tell us about the auction block because he wasn't proud of it. Nevertheless, the experience elicited an emotional response that boiled within her. She's not ashamed of what enslaved people endured because they triumphed in spite of the trauma.

Before I took Naomi's place on the auction block, I braced myself so I would not cry. I didn't want the emotions to weigh heavy on me. I am already burdened with telling the ancestors' stories to give them the voices they didn't have when they were alive. This is emotionally consuming in a good way, but consuming nonetheless.

*   *   *

We left Seward for the one-hour drive to the THC conference in Austin. I was beginning to feel much more relevant in telling a national audience about slavery. I had reached unexpected milestones with the Slave Dwelling Project. I'd traveled farther west than I'd ever been before. I'd spent the night with people I'd just met for the first time. And the group at Egypt was the largest one to join me on a sleepover so far. I had no regrets. All of it showed me there was potential to have others join me, even if they were from a different race.

But just as I was feeling excited at the direction the Slave Dwelling Project was heading, the Trust dropped my blogs. They had the power to take it to the next level, and someone in the chain of command wanted to put the brakes on it. I suspect I was bringing forth a subject they were hearing about for the first time. I was filling a void in their understanding of slavery. When the Trust discontinued the blog, it felt like a divorce. I wasn't planning to do a blog because I didn't think this thing was going to go on this long. I wrote five hundred words, and people on the staff edited it and placed it on the Trust's website.

But just as one door closed, another opened. When I told Toni Carrier, founder of the Lowcountry Africana website, that the Trust booted me off their site, she took me in. She created a Slave Dwelling Project page on her website.* She got assistance from Corie Hipp, a marketing consultant in Charleston. I didn't miss a beat. Toni took me under her wing because she understood that what I was doing was soul work that does not always fit neatly into an institutional mold, and it needed a platform. She told me my work is important regardless of an institutional affiliation. It is important in its own right. Robin Foster, creator of the Saving Stories blog, also decided to carry my blog on her site.

*   *   *

My breakout year—2011—came early. With more out-of-state visits and offers of honoraria, the second year signaled that the Slave Dwelling Project could grow and sustain me, if I wanted it to. I felt increasingly relevant as the public became more enamored with my project. Were the ancestors making this happen? The more I traveled, the more I realized the "junk history" I was taught in high school distorted my view of slavery. Instead of delivering an accurate rendition of slavery, teachers repeated the "happy slave" narrative and ignored the reasons the country went to war during the era of slavery. That junk history and continuing media narratives portraying Africans and Native Americans as savages angered me.

---

* Toni Carrier launched Lowcountry Africana in 2007 as part of the University of South Florida's Africana Heritage Project. Magnolia Plantation and Gardens in Charleston, South Carolina, was one of its early funders.

Accurate history shows that enslaved Africans in America came from great civilizations before they were packed tightly in seagoing vessels for the largest forced migration in human times.

These swirling misconceptions of the ancestors angered and radicalized me. While I was still employed by the Trust, I remained guarded, but I became increasingly outspoken against the false idea that the great white male colonizers built America. Too many Americans who see this country as great don't see the crimes committed to achieve that greatness. In the process of proclaiming greatness, some paint others as inferior. As I spoke against this narrative, I felt empowered, knowing I was building trust nationwide.

The Palmetto Trust (now called Preservation South Carolina), which owns the slave dwellings on Morris Street in Anderson, invited me to Laurelwood Plantation, near Columbia, South Carolina, on April 15, 2011. The cabin was so rickety that I slept alone on the porch of the big house. A group of local high school students met me at the site the morning after my sleepover. A student called the big house a "beautiful eyesore." His poetic choice of words led me to see the beauty of slave dwellings, even the ones with dirt floors. The enslaved people made these basic cabins as sturdy as they could with the materials available. The cabins sustained life to allow the enslaved to pass their genes to us. Within those walls were perhaps the most peaceful times of their lives. The opportunity to be in that space gave it beauty.

As a result of my talk at the Trust's 2011 conference in Austin, I was invited to Bellamy Mansion in Wilmington, North Carolina; Sotterley Plantation in Hollywood, Maryland; and Evergreen Plantation in Edgard, Louisiana; and the following year Sweet Briar

College in Sweet Briar, Virginia, my first visit to a college campus. That year, I had eight cabin stays, most of them out of state and all of them by invitation.

I was beginning to see that slavery existed not just at former plantation sites in the South but also on land that became college campuses and state and federal parks, and at the homes of twelve US presidents elected prior to 1865. How were these sites interpreting slavery? How were they making amends for their participation in one of America's original sins?

NINE

HIGHER LEARNING

GREW UP WITH THE NOTION THAT COLLEGES AND UNIVERSITIES
are the cathedrals of liberal thought where we are all valued for
who we are. Of course, I was wrong. The founding of America's
higher education system is tightly intertwined with slavery. Historian
Craig Steven Wilder, author of *Ebony & Ivy*, succinctly chronicles
the abuses Africans endured at some of the nation's most prestigious
academic centers. He begins his indictment of slavery's link to higher
education with a stinging summation: "The slave economy and
higher education grew up together, each nurturing the other. Money
from the purchase and sale of human beings built the campuses,
stocked the libraries, and swelled the endowments of American colleges. Slaves waited on faculty and students; academic leaders
eagerly courted the support of slaveholders and slave traders."

The justification for the oppression of Africans began in the
1400s to support Portuguese slave-trading exploits along Africa's
west coast. Gomes Eanes de Zurara, the chief chronicler of Portugal

from 1454 to 1474, wrote that captured Africans had "lived like beasts, without any custom of reasonable beings ... [and] only knew how to live in bestial sloth." Their souls could be saved, and their lives improved once they were enslaved, he said. Thomas Jefferson carried this false notion further three centuries later as he wrote the foundational papers that underpin American democracy—the Declaration of Independence. He made it clear he was not referring to Black people when he wrote, "We hold these truths to be self-evident, that all men are created equal."

Jefferson also played an early and highly influential role in the establishment of pseudoscientific ideas about Black racial inferiority. A decade after he helped to write the Declaration of Independence, Jefferson published *Notes on the State of Virginia*, a comprehensive study of various subjects, including enslaved people. Jefferson used his influence to present the early false notions that Black people are inferior. Jefferson wrote, "In imagination they are dull [and] tasteless. . . . This unfortunate difference of colour, and perhaps of faculty, is a powerful obstacle to the emancipation of these people." Jefferson later founded the University of Virginia.

It is against this backdrop that slavery flourished on college and university campuses. Congregational minister Eleazar Wheelock, Dartmouth College's first president, relied on enslaved people when he established the college in 1769. Eight enslaved people— Brister, Exeter, Chloe, Caesar, Lavinia, Archelaus, Peggy, and a child—were with Wheelock when he set out with his family and eight students to survey the new campus at Hanover, New Hampshire. The incoming presidents of Harvard often arrived at Cambridge, Massachusetts, with Black people they owned. Titus, an enslaved man, lived with Harvard president Benjamin Wadsworth and his family. Two days before moving to the campus, Wadsworth wrote in October 1726, "I bought (on credit) a Negro Wench. . . . I paid no money down for her." In 1826, Washington College, now known as Washington and Lee, in Lexington, Virginia, advertised that it would hire out its "Negroes," consisting of twenty men, women, boys, and girls. Many of them were considered "very valuable."

Mars Hill University owes its existence to slavery. The campus at Mars Hill in western North Carolina was forced to find the money to complete the construction of a building after a contractor held one of the trustees' enslaved persons, Joe Anderson, as collateral. Anderson was seized in 1859 by the Buncombe County sheriff and jailed in Asheville until the contractor's $1,100 bill was satisfied. This is the only case known where a person—human flesh and blood—was locked up to force an institution to pay its bill. J. W. Anderson, one of the university's founders and secretary to the board of trustees, owned Anderson. He and ten other trustees collected the money among themselves and paid the contractor, after which Joe rejoined his wife, Jane Ray, and their children, Andy, Neal, and Cordelia. Joe Anderson's story attracted the attention of American and European newspapers.

Anderson's ordeal didn't divorce him or his family from Mars Hill. After Emancipation, Mars Hill established the Mars Hill Colored School. Anderson's granddaughter Effie Anderson taught there in 1901, and his nephew, Sam W. Anderson, was a faculty member on two occasions between 1905 and 1912. Joe Anderson also served on the Mars Hill Colored School Committee in 1907.

More than twenty of Anderson's descendants are buried in a cemetery adjacent to the campus. Camp Joe was the name given to the Depression-era Civilian Conservation Corps at Mars Hill opened in the 1930s by the federal Works Progress Administration to put men to work preserving forest land. Anderson died in 1910. He's buried on the Mars Hill campus along Joe Anderson Drive. A graveside granite marker bears the inscription: "In Memory of Joe." It notes his story is "one of the first known incidents of a monument erected to a person for going to jail."

To justify the buying and selling of Africans, Northern and Southern colleges and universities encouraged faculty to apply science to illustrate that "the Negro" was inferior. By doing so, the institutions could temper antislavery criticism in America and abroad. In some European quarters, the mingling of theology and science guided the moral currents and converged with the thought of ending slavery. "The abolition of domestic Slavery is not a Utopian Scheme," said Benjamin Rush, born in 1745 on a plantation near Philadelphia. He studied medicine in Scotland during the Scottish Enlightenment, which existed from the eighteenth to the early nineteenth century. During this period a flurry of liberal ideas shaped young minds like Rush's around moral doctrines of divine goodness and human freedom.

Rush returned to Pennsylvania, where he became a noted surgeon and a professor of medicine at the College of Philadelphia (University of Pennsylvania). He also was a signer of the Declaration of Independence, an advocate for the education of boys and girls, an abolitionist, and a supporter of Richard Allen, who founded the African Methodist Episcopal Church. Rush observed that human bondage was stressed under its own economic failings and rising public opposition, while theology had been exploited as a means to defend slavery. "A Christian Slave is a contradiction in terms," he said. Rush died in April 1813. Although he outwardly opposed slavery, his medical reputation earned him high praise two months after his death even in the cradle of slavery—Charleston. The Medical Society of South Carolina meeting at Circular Church in Charleston praised Rush, who had taught or mentored half of the society's members. It was a testament to him and the influence of the medical school in Pennsylvania and the cross-Atlantic reach of the science and medical faculties at Scottish universities. But in America, colleges and universities became increasingly reluctant to question slavery following an 1831 slave revolt in Southampton County, Virginia, led by Nat Turner. The debate over slavery ended at the South Carolina College (University of South Carolina) when the campus president, Thomas Cooper, insisted on a complete and positive defense of enslavement.

I first came to realize slavery's role in American higher education when I was invited for a sleepover at Sweet Briar College in Sweet Briar, Virginia, the first of eight Southern colleges I visited between 2012 and 2018. I was not surprised that the founders of American colleges and universities were enslavers, but colleges and universities, at that point in the Slave Dwelling Project, had not been on my agenda. I was very excited, however, by Sweet Briar's invitation. I was energized that a college had contacted me, sending me on a new path of discovery. Each first, like the first sleepover outside of South Carolina or the first visit to a more populated urban area, created a notable moment that gave me fodder for my blog and the will to continue. The gravity of what I was about to embark on at college campuses had not yet fully set in. That would come later.

Sweet Briar College

In October 2012, Lynn Rainville, the director of the Tusculum Institute for local history and historic preservation, invited me to Sweet Briar College, where she had done extensive research in documenting an African American graveyard on the campus. After my visit, she was named dean of the college, founded on a former plantation established by Elijah Fletcher, a Vermont businessman who moved to Virginia. He once called slavery "a curse on any country." However, by 1846 he was one of the area's ten major slaveholders. Embedded in Fletcher's narrative is the story of Martha Penn's unusual letter to Fletcher, dated February 16, 1854. Rainville includes this story in her 2019 book, *Invisible Founders: How Two Centuries of African American Families Transformed a Plantation into a College*. Fletcher owned more than one hundred Africans and Indigenous men, women, and children, who worked on his Amherst plantations, which included the Sweetbriar plantations.

Fletcher had been in the midst of settling the estate of another plantation where Martha Penn was enslaved when she wrote to him. The plantation where Martha Penn was enslaved was six miles away from Sweetbriar. The twenty-year-old Penn was held in a Lynchburg jail pending her sale to a buyer in the Deep South. In the letter she pleaded with him to buy her to prevent her from being separated from her sister Mary, who was enslaved at Fletcher's Sweetbriar plantation.

The 1989 movie *Glory*, which depicts Black men in the Union army during the Civil War inspired Joseph McGill to become a Civil War reenactor. He helped form the Massachusetts 54th Regiment, Company I. The group stands on Morris Island in July 2018 during a commemoration of the Union's assault on Battery Wagner. Ernest Parks, fourth from left, and James Brown, third from right, joined McGill for a sleepover at McLeod Plantation near Charleston, South Carolina.

Civil War reeenactor Terry James, left, and Joe McGill were among the historians at a living history program at Magnolia Plantation and Gardens in Charleston, South Carolina. James is a former member of the Slave Dwelling Project's board of directors, and he has spent the most nights in slave dwellings with McGill. During sleepovers, James binds himself in shackles to feel how an enslaved person felt when they were bound in chains during the voyage across the Atlantic Ocean from West Africa.

Charleston bricklayer Rodney Prioleau, a Civil War reenactor from James Island, South Carolina, demonstrates brickmaking during a living history program at Magnolia Plantation and Gardens in Charleston, South Carolina. McGill and Prioleau met when they were US Park Service employees at Fort Sumter National Monument.

Joseph McGill did not sleep on this replica of a bed in a slave cabin at the Heyward House in Bluffton, South Carolina. Instead, he rolled out his mat and sleeping blanket and laid his head on the floor as a hooting owl serenaded him to sleep. Enslaved craftsmen were the initial occupants of this cabin, about the size of a one-car garage, as they built the Heyward House.

Joseph McGill joined members of the Outdoor Afro network in Charleston, South Carolina, for a kayak tour of the Combahee River in Colleton County, South Carolina. The tour was held to honor Harriet Tubman, who led a Union navy raid on the river to free enslaved people from rice plantations that lined the Combahee. Outdoor Afro dispels the myth that Black people don't have a connection to nature.

This photo of Betsy Anderson, who was enslaved at Goodwill Plantation near Columbia, South Carolina, is one of the most prized possessions of Goodwill's current owner, Larry Faulkenberry. Anderson was among the enslaved people who were moved to Goodwill in the interior of South Carolina from the Combahee River on the coast after the start of the Civil War. Joseph McGill spent a night at Goodwill in 2010.

If *Charlotte Observer* reporter Eric Frazier had not joined Joseph McGill for a sleepover on July 24, 2010, McGill might not have made it through the night alone in this isolated cabin at Hobcaw Barony, on the sprawling Hobcaw Neck near Georgetown, South Carolina. Hobcaw was once a coastal rice empire that became the winter retreat for Wall Street financier Bernard M. Baruch.

Joseph McGill gave the inaugural lecture for the Williamsburg Historical Society's first Founder's Day Celebration on February 23, 2020, in his boyhood home of Kingstree, South Carolina. McGill holds a copy of Edward Ball's *Slaves in the Family*. After McGill launched the Slave Dwelling Project, Ball's book resonated with him. It helped him to understand the importance of connecting the descendants of enslaved people with the descendants of slave owners.

Joseph McGill was not afraid of the active wasp's nest in this slave cabin at Riverview Plantation near Montgomery, Alabama. McGill's visit to Riverview and Old Alabama Town in Montgomery, Alabama, in October 2010, was his first venture outside of South Carolina after launching the Slave Cabin Project in May 2010.

After Joseph McGill spent a night in this slave dwelling at Old Alabama Town in Montgomery, Alabama, he realized that slave dwellings were not confined to rural southern landscapes. That convinced him to change the name of his work from the Slave Cabin Project to the Slave Dwelling Project. Small cabins were not the only structures where enslaved people lived and raised their families.

One of Joseph McGill's most memorable moments came in April 2011, when he stood on an auction block at Seward Plantation in Brenham, Texas. He imagined how fearful it was for an enslaved person on the block as they faced the prospect of being separated from loved ones and their community.

Public historian Cheyney McKnight stands in the doorway of the hearth kitchen at Point of Honor Museum in Lynchburg, Virginia, on the James River, where she interpreted early cooking techniques during a living history program with Joseph McGill. Because of COVID-19 restrictions in July 2020, McGill and the living historians didn't spend the night in the kitchen building where enslaved people lived and worked on the former 750-acre plantation.

The day after Joseph McGill spent the night alone in this slave dwelling at Travellers Rest in Nashville, Tennessee, in May 2014, he got a compliment from an unlikely source. A woman who had attended his lecturer the day before the sleepover contacted him and said she was a descendant of Nathan Bedford Forrest, a Confederate army general during the Civil War and the first grand wizard of the Ku Klux Klan. The woman said that because of his lecture she was going to think differently about the real stories of enslaved people.

This long corridor on the second floor of this two-story slave dwelling at the Aiken Rhett House in Charleston, South Carolina, is one of the best examples of a slave dwelling in the city. Joseph McGill spent a night in the dwelling in May 2011. It was his first sleepover in a slave dwelling on the Charleston peninsula. Terry James, who joined McGill during the sleepover, slept in shackles.

This huge historic hearth at the Belle Grove Plantation in Middletown, Virginia, is one of the few places in the country that provides an opportunity to demonstrate how enslaved people prepared meals indoors. The size of this large hearth is a sign that the owners placed a high work demand on the enslaved cooks to prepare large meals for the white family and their guests.

The Black family reunion tradition rose after the Civil War as formerly enslaved people sought to reunite with lost loved ones. The Dickerson-Wood family carried on that tradition in August 2019 at Somerset Plantation in Creswell, North Carolina. Their ancestors were enslaved at Somerset. Joseph McGill joined them for their first reunion in nearly three decades.

As the story goes, Dinah, an enslaved woman at the James Logan Home in Philadelphia, also known as Stenton, saved the house from being burned during the American Revolution. Joseph McGill complimented Stenton's staff for remembering Dinah, but he encouraged them to also tell the stories of other people enslaved by Logan, the fourteenth mayor of Philadelphia.

Slavery required those held in bondage to become astute observers of the shifting moods and changing fortunes and misfortunes of slaveholders. The fluctuating financial circumstances or emotions of an enslaver could place a Black person at risk of a whipping or being sold away, severing ties with loved ones. In 1850, Martha Penn's owner died, leaving his estate in disarray. One of his heirs, who had moved from Virginia to Florida, was not interested in acquiring more enslaved people from Virginia. He decided to sell Martha to a local slave trader or "soul driver," whose occupation separated families by transporting Native Americans and people of African descent to buyers in the Deep South. Martha Penn was well aware of what could happen to her, so she made a desperate and risky plea to Fletcher, asking him to buy her. If the slave trader had discovered her plans, she could have been punished or beaten to death for meddling in his transaction.

"I write to you now for you to grant me a great favor which you will oblige me very much," Penn wrote. "Answer it as soon as you can and buy me if you please. I shall depend on you." Martha Penn likely dictated the letter while she was jailed in Lynchburg, where Fletcher had his office. Martha got her wish: Fletcher purchased her. It is likely she was assigned domestic duties at Sweetbriar. She also might have become a maid to Fletcher's eldest daughter, Indiana. Martha was born around 1833, a few years after Indiana's birth.

Fletcher died unexpectedly on February 13, 1858, nearly four years to the day after Martha's letter (February 16, 1854) requesting that he purchase her so she could remain close to her sister. Fletcher's will left Sweetbriar to his daughter, Indiana, who, in the fall of 1865, at the age of thirty-seven, married an Irish minister, the

Reverend James Henry Williams. Their only child, Daisy, was born a year after her parents were wed. The Williamses' hearts were broken when their sixteen-year-old Daisy died at a boarding school in New York in January 1884 of antitrypsin deficiency, which also had claimed her father. Sixteen years later Indiana succumbed to grief and illness. Her will transformed Sweetbriar plantation into Sweet Briar College, a place to educate women and honor the memory of her precocious Daisy. In that legal document, Indiana stipulated that the college could only admit white girls.

Sweet Briar College opened in 1906 with thirty-six students who lived and studied in ornately designed buildings on an appealing landscape hand-built by men whose ancestors had been enslaved there when it was Sweetbriar Plantation. Black men cleared the land, hauled the dirt, and molded the bricks from local soil to build a "temple of learning" closed to Black girls. Over time the college promoted itself as a place of "southern tradition," where its staff would cheerfully and obediently care for the white female student body. The college's marketing material distributed nationally included a picture of one of the surviving slave cabins with the caption "a picturesque old Negro cabin."

Sterling Jones was the last person to live in that cabin. Jones's father, Daniel Jones, was born in 1845, but it is unknown where or whether he had been enslaved. Sterling Jones's mother, Jemima "Minnie" Jones, and his father were married in 1871. Four years later, when Sterling Jones was born, the Joneses lived at Sweet Briar. The elder Jones was among the hundreds of Black men and women who lived and worked at Sweet Briar before and after the college opened. Many of them had been enslaved at Sweetbriar Plantation or were the children of people who had been enslaved there. Daniel Jones was one of the bricklayers who built some of the college's early buildings. Sterling carried water to the brick masons. When Daniel Jones died, he might have been assured that his son would have continuous work at Sweet Briar. And he did. During the next five decades, Sterling Jones was a laborer and janitor. He also raised and lowered the US flag at the college.

From 1898 to 1921, Jones's three marriages produced thirteen children. He and his first wife lived several miles away from the college, near present-day Monroe, Virginia. By the time of his third marriage in 1921, Jones had moved to the former slave cabin on the Sweet Briar campus with his third wife. Two of their children were born in the cabin: Louise in 1922 and Dorothy in 1924. Dorothy Jones Sales later worked in the college's bookstore. She worked at the college for more than fifty years. A year after her death in 2004, the college converted the bookstore to an academic building and named it in her honor.

When the eighty-two-year-old Sterling Jones retired from the college in 1957 after working there since he was a boy, he summarized his contributions to the college: "I've done pretty much of everything here at Sweet Briar." Later he developed Alzheimer's disease. He lived within walking distance of the college when on a snowy night in January 1959 he wandered away from home alone. Three days later his body was found buried under snow along the path he had taken for decades on his walk to the campus.

Sterling Jones's life and legacy at Sweet Briar had eluded his great-granddaughter Crystal Sterling Rosson until she heard a passing reference about him following the funeral of her grandfather

Sterling Jones Jr. Someone mentioned that her grandfather's older siblings had been born in a slave cabin on the Sweet Briar campus. A slave cabin on the Sweet Briar campus? She wondered where it was. Rosson had spent much of her life on the campus. She had attended preschool and kindergarten at Sweet Briar. She had participated in Girl Scout activities there and looked for Easter eggs hidden in the garden named for Indiana's only child, Daisy. Rosson was stunned to hear that revelation in the context of the college's legacy of slavery and her family's link to the campus after Emancipation.

For two weeks she searched the campus for the slave cabin. Surprisingly, she found it in the backyard of the president's residence that was once Sweetbriar's main house. The cabin is in view of where she attended school on the campus. She had seen the cabin, but she didn't know her family's connection to it. She's saddened that a stroke claimed her grandfather's life before she had an opportunity to learn from him about his father, Sterling Jones. Older members of her family likely had an inkling of the family's ties to the cabin and slavery, but they didn't talk about it. Rosson is Sterling Jones Jr.'s first grandchild. Her parents named her Crystal Sterling. On October 6, 2012, she joined me and seven others for the sleepover in the cabin.[*] Sterling Jones Sr.'s daughter Louise Jones was born in the cabin in 1922. She is now one hundred years old, and she lives in Maryland.

---

[*] A number of people joined me on the sleepover at Sweet Briar, including Toni Battle, a descendant of enslaved ancestors and a member of Coming to the Table; Crystal Rosson; Liz, a friend of Crystal's from Amherst; Lynn Rainville; Dave Griffith (then a Sweet Briar professor of English); and Michael Hayslett, the college naturalist.

COLLEGE OF CHARLESTON

Charleston's peninsula city rests on the bones of the dead. More than three centuries of successive burials have stitched together a subterranean skeletal fabric beneath the old city. It is not surprising then that one of the newest buildings at the College of Charleston is built on the remains of enslaved people entombed on an urban campus that likely benefited from chattel slavery. From 1794 to the 1930s, the site had been used to bury free Blacks and the enslaved. The Addlestone Library, the size of three stacked football fields, opened in January 2005. Three years later the college unveiled a monument commemorating people of African descent buried there. Four sets of human remains were found in 2001 during the library's construction. It is unknown whether the enslaved people interred there had a hand in building the college. Few details shed light on the role the enslaved played at the college founded in 1770. The American Revolution stalled the opening of classes until 1790. Today, the college boasts that it's the oldest educational institution south of Virginia.

A 1935 campus history lacks details about the college's connection to slavery, but the trustees' records offer the possibility that the college benefited from free labor in the renovation of a portion of the Revolutionary barracks, the campus's first building. Anglican priest Robert Smith, the college's first president, assigned the "negroes" from his plantation to repair the barracks. "This is the only conclusive evidence I have found so far of the use of slaves on the College of Charleston campus," wrote Jessica Farrell, author of "History, Memory, and Slavery at the College of Charleston,

1785–1810." In June 2021, faculty and students at the college unearthed a small, copper, diamond-shaped slave badge dating back to 1853 while excavating an area on campus. Inscribed with the word "servant," the badge also bore a date and registration number. The badge indicates that the enslaved person's owner had approved of that individual's working for someone else. The discovery of the badge on the campus, however, does not prove the enslaved person worked at the college. Slave badges have not been found in other US cities. Charleston may have been the only city that made a physical badge to identify an enslaved worker.

The college's early leaders, faculty, and supporters possibly had links to slavery. College slave-owning trustees included three signers of the Declaration of Independence—Edward Rutledge, Arthur Middleton, and Thomas Heyward Jr.—and three signers of the Constitution—John Rutledge, Charles Pinckney, and Charles Cotesworth Pinckney. They came to meetings infrequently. College backer and slave trader Miles Brewton left £2,000 sterling to establish the college. Farrell observed that the college often touts that its founders and supporters were influential Charlestonians, but college promotional materials fail to mention they also profited from human bondage.

To shed light on this untold story, College of Charleston professor Simon Lewis invited me to the campus.[*] Terry James and I spent

---

[*] My visit at the College of Charleston was part of the campus's Jubilee Project, which commemorates Emancipation in 1863, educational access, and the end of segregated schools in South Carolina, beginning in 1963. I spoke to students about the Slave Dwelling Project as part of a panel that also included discussion of Maj. Gen. John C. Frémont. During the Civil War, in August 1863, as commander of the Western Department for the

the night in a house the college owns at 16½ Glebe Street, built before 1855 for the Episcopal Church. The house sits on a narrow, long lot that prior to 1861 would have been owned by the vestry and wardens of St. Philip's Protestant Episcopal Church. When I saw 16½ Glebe Street on August 30, 2013,* I knew immediately it was a slave dwelling. The two-story brick building sits behind a much larger two-and-a-half-story structure that faces Glebe Street, a one-block-long street in the historic core of the College of Charleston. The college uses both structures as guesthouses. I am willing to wager that most of the guests are also unaware of this history. Presently, the dwelling does not have a chimney, but I have concluded it once served as a kitchen and living quarters for the enslaved domestic servants who either worked in the larger adjacent house or were part of the enslaved workforce that serviced the college.

To function as a guesthouse, the dwelling has been updated with a fully equipped kitchen, living room, and downstairs half bath tucked neatly under the stairway to the second level, which offers a bedroom and full bathroom. A flat-screen television mounted in the living room and a Wi-Fi router are unique contemporary features that surprised me. None of the forty-six former slave dwellings I have seen can compare with 16½ Glebe Street. Although I was surrounded by comforts, I couldn't resist a stroll through the streets of historic Charleston. During the walk, I reflected on the enslaved

---

Union army, Frémont issued a contested de facto emancipation proclamation in the state of Missouri that he was later forced to rescind.

* The weekend Terry James and I visited the College of Charleston we also spent a night at 25 Longitude Lane. At that time, it was the home of Susan E. Heape. The Longitude Lane sleepover is described in Chapter 16.

people who made the bricks for the antebellum buildings along my route and the slave tags that hung around their necks to identify them by craft, number, and the year the tag was issued.

When I returned to 16½ Glebe Street, the modern adornments made it difficult for me to imagine the lives of the enslaved people who lived there. The Wi-Fi connection gave me a unique and impromptu opportunity to post photographs of the dwelling on my Facebook page. The comments poured in hot and heavy. This spur-of-the-moment experience gave my Facebook followers one of the best opportunities yet to interact with me in real time during a sleepover.

Terry also marveled at the dwelling's amenities. Prior to the college, Terry was with me at the Old Charleston Jail, where we slept on concrete floors, and at a former slave cabin in Simpsonville, South Carolina, where we slept on dirt floors. The college's 16½ Glebe Street was a big improvement. Terry took the couch downstairs. I went to the second-floor bedroom. As expected, he slept with his hands in shackles.

The next morning, Terry impressed me with his discerning eye for former slave dwellings. We both noticed that 16½ Glebe Street was the only slave dwelling left behind the houses facing Glebe Street. An 1884 map of the area shows smaller buildings behind the homes fronting St. Philip Street on the other side of the block. But the college's massive cafeteria now occupies that space on St. Philip Street. The absence of slave dwellings on the other side of the block is part of the building trend that has eliminated many of the structures where the enslaved lived. All colleges and universities in urban settings are guilty of expanding their footprints at the expense of eliminating historic buildings. If tearing down an architecturally significant building is acceptable, then there is no incentive to preserve the backyard structures where the enslaved lived. Doing so presents a double whammy for historic preservation and our interpretation of old buildings. If the main house is lost, so is the opportunity to interpret the stolen energy and talent embodied in that structure. Likewise, eliminating the places inhabited by the enslaved prevents the telling of a full and accurate history of the enslaved ancestors.

University of Virginia

In the glow of flaming tiki torches, hundreds of clean-cut young educated white men dressed in polo shirts and khaki pants formed a nighttime processional across the University of Virginia campus in Charlottesville, Virginia. Outwardly the gathering appeared to be a harmless fraternity initiation. Their words and symbols, however, revealed a hateful intent. An alliance of far-right-wing groups carried Confederate and neo-Nazi flags with other incendiary images as they chanted "Jews will not replace us." This Unite the Right rally on August 11, 2017, continued into a second day to protest the removal of a statue of Confederate general Robert E. Lee. As a counterprotest gathered the next day, a white supremacist rammed his car into the crowd, injuring thirty-five people and killing Charlottesville native Heather Heyer.

Early in the Slave Dwelling Project, I had been warned to be aware of white supremacists who might want to harm me. Those concerns never stopped me from sleeping in extant slave dwellings.

But as the nation watched the events in Charlottesville and Rich-mond, I considered whether I should cancel an upcoming October 2017 sleepover at the University of Virginia (UVA). The sleepover would be part of a joint gathering with UVA's conference on Uni-versities, Slavery, Public Memory, and the Built Landscape, along with the fifth Annual Slave Dwelling Conference. The UVA event focused on the university's connection to slavery during the cam-pus's bicentennial.

That UVA conversation grew from a study Brown University conducted in 2006 on its role in human bondage. Money that sup-ported Brown's founding and expansion came directly and indi-rectly from slavery. Brown's oldest building, University Hall (formerly the College Edifice), was constructed in the 1770s, likely with slave labor. Donors pledged the labor of their enslaved work-ers, including Pero, a sixty-two-year-old African, and Job, a Native American. Mingow, apparently a free African, was also enlisted for the work crew. The college's endowment campaign begun in the mid-1760s received pledges from rice planters in Charleston, including Henry Laurens, who steered North America's largest slave-trading operation.

In 1764, when the College of Rhode Island was founded, the slave ship *Sally* sailed to West Africa. Nicholas Brown and Com-pany owned the ship in partnership with his brothers, John, Joseph, and Moses, prominent Providence merchants. The brothers were also major college benefactors. Following a substantial gift to the college from Nicholas's son, Nicholas Jr., the college was renamed Brown University and was moved in 1804 from Warren, Rhode Island, to Providence. Before the slave trade was outlawed in 1808,

Rhode Island had been the home port for more than one thousand slave ship voyages. One of the *Sally*'s Atlantic crossings would end in an epic tragedy. On the return to America, 196 captured Africans purchased on behalf of the Brown brothers were stowed on the *Sally*, but at least 109 of them died. Some were killed in a failed insurrection. Others perished from disease, suicide, and starvation.

The memory of the *Sally* weighed on Moses Brown's conscience as he threw himself into an aggressive antislavery campaign. In a 1783 letter to two Providence merchants who allegedly were planning to fund another slave ship voyage to Africa, Brown cautioned against it. If the *Sally* had not sailed to Africa, he pleaded, "I should have been preserved from an Evil, which has given me the most uneasiness, and has left the greatest impression and stain upon my own mind of any, if not all my other Conduct in life." The merchants ignored his advice; the ship left for Africa in 1784.

In 2003, Brown University president Ruth J. Simmons appointed the Steering Committee on Slavery and Justice to examine Brown's link to slavery. Three years later, the president's charge led to the "Report of the Brown University Steering Committee on Slavery and Justice," the first study of its kind at an American university. The comprehensive 107-page report has become higher education's "gold standard" for understanding slavery's legacy. Soon more than one hundred colleges and universities across the United States and some foreign countries followed Brown's example as they joined the President's Commission on Race and Slavery based at UVA. (The list also includes some historically Black colleges and universities.) I was invited to participate in the group's first symposium in 2017 at UVA, two months after the Unite the Right rally.

By the Slave Dwelling Project's third anniversary, I had traveled to twenty-seven extant slave dwellings in nine states. The Slave Dwelling Project had become so popular that I was encouraged to form a nonprofit organization in 2014 that would give me the opportunity to accelerate my work with foundation and donor contributions. That same year, with the help of supporters, we staged the first Slave Dwelling Conference in Savannah, Georgia, and in 2015 in North Charleston. This conference proved to be a milestone event that opened the door for the Slave Dwelling Project to get an endorsement from the University of Virginia.

Inspired by the Brown report, UVA's Kirt von Daacke and Marcus Martin began in 2013 to shape the slavery commission and assemble an advisory board that included grassroots participants and other experts who might not be part of the UVA community. Two years later, I met von Daacke, Martin, and other UVA faculty at the 2015 Slave Dwelling Conference in North Charleston. They called their presentation "Slave Dwellings at the University of Virginia: Acknowledgement, Preservation, and Memorialization." They had asked Matthew Reeves, director of archaeology at Montpelier, James Madison's home, to join the slavery commission's advisory board. Then Reeves and Daniel Pitti, a UVA faculty member in the Institute for Advanced Technology in the Humanities, recommended that von Daacke and Martin contact me. UVA invited the Slave Dwelling Project to hold our conference in conjunction with a 2017 conference on the built landscape at UVA designed by Jefferson after he left the White House. During his lifetime, Jefferson, the third US president, enslaved more than six hundred people.

* * *

Beginning in the early 1800s, brothers William Holmes and Alexander Hamilton McGuffey edited a series of textbooks for first- through sixth-grade students. The series was highly popular among educators from the mid-nineteenth to the early twentieth century. Readers purchased about 120 million copies between 1836 and 1960, placing the textbook's sales on par with the Bible and Webster's Dictionary. The series remains in use today in some private schools and by homeschooled children. The "Eclectic Readers" came to be widely known as the "McGuffey Readers." William McGuffey was a UVA professor, who, like many of his colleagues, enslaved people of African descent.

McGuffey had left the Ohio frontier, where he was born in 1800, to become UVA's second professor of moral philosophy at the age of forty-five. In Ohio, he had been a college professor and president, and in 1829 he was ordained a Presbyterian minister. McGuffey lived on the UVA campus with his wife and three children. His wife died in 1850. He remarried and continued to live on the campus until his death in 1873.

As a college professor, one account notes that McGuffey could not have afforded to own slaves but instead rented enslaved people as house servants. The 1850 census lists McGuffey as owning two enslaved women, ages twenty-eight and forty-four, and one enslaved man, age thirty. A decade later the census shows he owned one enslaved woman, age fifty. McGuffey's daughter Henrietta, age twenty-one in 1853, said her mother, Harriet, had been reluctant about raising her two daughters in the South, where enslaved people did domestic work. "My Mother was never very happy after she went to Virginia[;] she had been born and had lived in Ohio all her life and she could not become accustomed to the ways of society in Va. They were so entirely different from what she had be use[d] to and she disliked the idea of her daughters growing up and not being able to learn any thing about housework. We had plenty of good servants to do our work so there was no necessity for our working. Indeed no ladies at the University did any work I mean housework."

Although William McGuffey was not believed to be an abolitionist, he helped enslaved people and free Black men. He also preached to Black congregations and contributed to the construction of a Black church in Charlottesville. By one account, McGuffey's daughter, Mary, taught William Gibbons, an enslaved man her father rented to work as the family's butler, to read and write. It is possible that Gibbons was a body servant for a university student before he joined the McGuffey household. If so, Gibbons might have used whatever social capital he gained from his constant interaction with the white student who owned him and the student's friends to advance his own education.

Gibbons did not live with the McGuffey family, but he lived on campus. The early instruction Gibbons gained enabled him to continue his education. He became a Presbyterian minister in Washington, DC. Gibbons on occasion visited McGuffey, who entertained him in the family's home, much to the displeasure of some on the faculty. McGuffey and his family lived in a faculty dwelling on the UVA campus. It was one of five two-story brick dwellings on the campus that were built for the faculty members and their families. Enslaved workers or one family may have lived in an adjacent plain, one-story brick cottage built in 1850. Although the cottage has one chimney, it once had two exterior doors. One of them is bricked over from the inside. The structure is now called McGuffey Cottage. I spent the night in the cottage with eight other people.

When Jefferson designed the campus, he didn't take into consideration the necessity to accommodate enslaved people, von Daacke said. In 1817, the Board of Visitors of Central College approved Jefferson's design. Two years later the Virginia General Assembly established the University of Virginia, and Central College became UVA. It opened in March 1825 with five professors and forty students nearly a year and a half before Jefferson's death. Jefferson designed a twenty-eight-acre Academical Village with a rotunda, classrooms, and a library as a focal point at the north end of the U-shaped complex of buildings on an elevated site that gradually slopes toward the south with a view of the Southwest Mountains of Virginia. Beyond it sits Monticello, Jefferson's home, which I had visited before I arrived at the UVA campus. Five pavilions line the east and west sides of the campus lawn. Each pavilion, designated with Roman numerals, served as faculty housing and classrooms with student dormitories interspersed among them. McGuffey Cottage stands at the southern end of the west side of the lawn as part of Pavilion IX, where McGuffey lived.

It is estimated that four thousand enslaved people, including William Gibbons, lived or worked at UVA between 1817 and 1865, von Daacke said. That number includes people who were rented to university staff for a few days. So far, the university has named 658 of them. Researchers have identified specific persons who lived in a specific dwelling on campus. As professors moved in and brought enslaved people with them, the campus landscape changed dramatically. Kitchens were moved out of basements and into external buildings. Attics were added, and some of them were used by the enslaved.

The joint UVA and Slave Dwelling Project's conference created an incredible buzz. Five hundred people came, and another 350 names were placed on a wait list. A white tent erected near the rotunda on the north end of the historic core of the campus served as an event space. Von Daacke had invited the Slave Dwelling Project to the multidisciplinary conference. He wanted presenters, many of them nonacademics like me, to speak to the heart and not the head. Unlike in the past, when I was alone in an extant slave dwelling, I now needed to think beyond just my safety. My advisors and I considered canceling my participation in the conference because of the Unite the Right rally. Donald Trump had awakened those sleeper cells of racists who were threatening Jewish people, but we all knew that people of color were also in their sights. Since McGuffey Cottage could only hold nine people, more than twenty others slept under the tent near the rotunda. For our safety, the university hired a security guard to patrol the area that night. After the daytime conference events, I and others retreated to the warmth of the cottage, where I thought often about Heather Heyer and her tragic death.

TEN

PRESIDENTIAL SLAVEHOLDERS

ᴠIRGINIA ᴘLANTER JOHN CUSTIS ᴅEEDED 275 ᴀCRES ɪN NEW Kent County, Virginia, to his son, Daniel Parke Custis. By the time the younger Custis had reached his midtwenties, he had settled into a comfortable bachelor's existence surrounded by one hundred enslaved people at his White House plantation. Daniel's landholdings soared in 1749 to nearly 18,000 acres and two hundred more slaves when his father died. A year after his father's death, thirty-seven-year-old Daniel married seventeen-year-old Martha Dandridge, daughter of another local planter. Martha gave birth to four children, but only one of them, her second son, John Parke Custis, lived to adulthood. Mysteriously, John and his father became ill on July 4, 1757, possibly from a throat infection. The younger Custis survived; but the illness killed Daniel, leaving Martha Dandridge Custis as one of the wealthiest slave-owning young widows in Virginia.

Augustine Washington, a leading Virginia planter in Westmoreland County and a justice of the county court, became a widower when his first wife, Jane Butler, died in 1729, leaving him with two sons and a daughter. He later married Mary Bell, and the first of their six children, George, was born on February 22, 1732, at the family's plantation. The Washingtons moved in 1734 up the Potomac River to another family property that was later renamed Mount Vernon. George spent most of his youth, however, at another family property in Virginia near Fredericksburg. When Augustine Washington died, eleven-year-old George inherited ten slaves. George Washington went on to a successful military career, ending with the stunning achievement of leading the Continental army's victory over the British during the Revolutionary War. Washington later married Martha Dandridge Custis. When Washington was elected the nation's first president, he and Martha owned nearly three hundred slaves, the majority of which she brought to the union.

As a child, I accepted what my teachers taught me, but none of them told me George Washington was a slave owner. In the US military, I defended the Constitution and respected the presidency. Studying US history as a National Park Service ranger, however, I found truths I didn't hear in school or the military. Twelve US presidents, including Washington, enslaved people of African descent during their lifetimes, and many of them continued to do so after they were elected to the nation's highest public office. That shattered my view of the commander in chief. Systematically and deceitfully, the most powerful men in the world at that time owned people who looked like me. The education system excluded my ancestors and chose instead to tell one-sided stories devoid of slavery's atrocities.

If I had known America's true history, maybe I would not have been so surprised that US presidents bought and sold people. Two presidents, Washington and James Madison, were delegates to the convention in Philadelphia that laid the foundation for American systems that perpetuated slavery. Washington, Madison, and other wig-wearing wealthy white men debated the US Constitution for four months in 1787 until they ultimately extended for two more decades the nation's participation in the international slave trade. Some convention delegates had spoken out strongly against slavery, but they knew that to stop it they'd lose the Southern colonies' support. A compromise was reached to delay ending participation in the trans-Atlantic slave trade until 1808. The driving need for the Constitution grew out of economic necessity to give a central government the authority to decide issues of trade, tariffs, debts, and currency. By extension, slavery, and the property rights associated with it, was a key economic issue.

Convention delegate Gouverneur Morris from Philadelphia, a strong opponent of slavery, crowned the Constitution with "We the People," definitively declaring that government power rests with the people and not the states.* If delegates had heeded Morris and other slavery opponents, an end to the importation of Africans could have come sooner, if the Southerners had agreed to it. It might not have brought an immediate end to slavery, but it certainly would have saved generations of Africans from the shipboard horrors of the Atlantic crossings and could have secured the civil rights of their descendants in America decades sooner.

---

* James Madison is often called the father of the US Constitution, but it was Gouverneur Morris and Pennsylvania's James Wilson, delegates to the Constitutional Convention, who gave the constitution's preamble the memorable phrase, "We the People."

In March 2014, the Slave Dwelling Project began to shine a light on slaveholding presidents. That year I went to James Madison's Montpelier near Orange, Virginia, and I returned there on several more occasions. I've also slept at Andrew Jackson's Hermitage in Nashville, Tennessee, in 2014 and again five years later. Thomas Jefferson's Monticello near Charlottesville, Virginia, was on my schedule in 2015 and 2016. In more recent times, I've visited James K. Polk's Home and Museum at Pineville, North Carolina, in 2017 and 2019, and George Washington's Mount Vernon in Mount Vernon, Virginia, in 2019.

I hold the homes of US presidents in the highest esteem. Jefferson wrote, "All men are created equal," the opening to the Declaration of Independence. Madison, called the father of the Constitution, guided the debate and helped draft the document during the Constitutional Convention. Incidentally, Jefferson did not attend the convention. He had left the country in 1784 for a three-year mission as America's minister to France, returning to the colonies two months after the Philadelphia convention. In their lifetimes, these five men and seven other US presidents owned 1,364 people, with Jefferson enslaving nearly half of them by himself.

The staff at these presidential homes invited me. My presence demonstrated a commitment to accept the past; even though these place-names don't include the word "plantation," that's what they were. Most people will likely say they have not visited a plantation. But many of them have visited Washington's Mount Vernon, Madison's Montpelier, Jefferson's Monticello, and the homes of other early US presidents. These places are the homes of slave-owning presidents, and as such they are former plantations where that legacy of slavery has sometimes been minimized. However, Montpelier and Monticello are among the presidential sites that are expanding the narrative to include the enslaved. If these sites can do so, then others with extant slave dwellings should follow their examples. As they improve their interpretations of the enslaved, more of the little-known stories of the ancestors will be revealed to show these presidents were morally flawed and do not deserve unconditional reverence.

MONTPELIER

The young girl often sneaked away from her village in Ghana to play in the ocean, the ocean she called her own. She gazed at the hilltop, where a large gnarly tree with twisted branches spied on her village and the ocean. Her world changed suddenly one night at the ocean when black hands grabbed her and turned her over to white men who chained her to a shipload of strangers. "I didn't know the word for slave back then, but I knew I had no chance to be free again. No home. No mother and father, no big sister and baby brother, no dances and drums, no lessons from the village elders, no friends to laugh with, no grinding grain with the women and other girls, no chickens clucking at my feet, no big, twisted tree. No cool, mighty ocean," the girl would tell her family years later. She was sold into slavery in America and named Mandy. On the boat the white men raped the women, boys, and girls. Somehow, she was not raped then. But at a Virginia tobacco plantation her master, James Madison Sr., fathered her child—Coreen.

In the Madisons' kitchen, Coreen was a fine cook, but James Sr.'s son noticed Coreen for more than her excellent apple pies.

Like her mother, Coreen was raped. She gave birth around 1792 to a boy named Jim. James Madison Jr., the future US president, was his father. About that time, Dolley Madison's sister-in-law died, leaving as orphans her two daughters. One of them, Victoria, was an infant. Dolley took in both girls and assigned Coreen to be Victoria's wet nurse. Coreen fed the white baby on one breast and her Black son, Jim, on the other. They were raised as twins, and eventually in their teen years they fell in love. Their flirtations continued beyond the War of 1812, when Coreen and Jim were among the Madisons' slaves at the White House. After the war, Dolley insisted that Jim had to go when the encounters with her niece did not stop. Eventually, Jim was sold away. The future president's Black son ended up at a Tennessee plantation.

An enslaved person's proximity to powerful white men gave them privileges that were not available to enslaved people owned by ordinary white people. Paul Jennings exemplifies an enslaved man who, in spite of his status, witnessed some of the nation's early history during Madison's time at the White House and his central Virginia home. Jennings was born at Montpelier in 1799, the year George Washington died and five years after Madison married Dolley Payne Todd. Jennings and his mother were among the one hundred people Madison enslaved. Little is known about his mother other than that at least one of her grandparents was a Native American. Although Jennings's father, Benjamin Jennings, was a white British merchant, the younger Jennings was still classified as a slave, assigned to household duties. Being so close to the Madisons, he eventually became Madison's manservant. Jennings attained some independence, and later was taught to read and write. After Madison was elected president, a ten-year-old Jennings went to the White House with the nation's fourth president. Madison was inaugurated in 1809, a year after the United States officially suspended its role in international slave trading, but the smuggling of captured people lasted until 1865. In the White House, Jennings was a ringside observer to a young nation's history as he prepared the table for formal meals. He was in the White House during the War of 1812. Accounts of that time are told in Jennings's 1865 book, A *Colored Man's Reminiscences of James Madison*. It is considered to be the first memoir about life at the White House. In it Jennings reports on the evacuation of the White House as British troops approached. "About sundown I walked over to the Georgetown ferry, and found the President and all hands . . . waiting for the boat," Jennings wrote. As he left a burning Washington, Jennings observed a fire deliberately set to destroy the Navy Yard so it would not fall into enemy hands.

Dolley Madison is credited with saving Washington's eight-foot portrait from the White House before the British could burn it. She gave the painting to two New York art dealers, who secured it before the British arrived. She said, "Our kind friend, Mr. (Charles) Carroll, has come to hasten my departure, and is in a very bad humor with me because I insist on waiting until the large picture of Gen. Washington is secured, and it requires to be unscrewed from the wall. This process was found to be too tedious for these perilous moments; I have ordered the frame to be broken, and the canvass taken out it is done, and the precious portrait placed in the hands of two gentlemen of New York for safe keeping."

In his book, however, Jennings offered a different version of that event. Jennings wrote that "when Mrs. Madison escaped from the White House, she cut out from the frame the large portrait of Washington . . . and carried it off. This is totally false. She had no time for doing it. It would have required a ladder to get it down. All she carried off was the silver in her reticule [small handbag], as the British were . . . expected every moment." White House staff members John Sioussat, a steward, and Thomas McGraw, a gardener, removed the canvas "and sent it off on a wagon, with some large silver urns and such other valuables as could be hastily got hold of." Dolley Madison owned Jennings for over a decade after her husband's death in 1836; then she sold him for $200. Jennings's new owner then sold him for $120 to statesman Daniel Webster. Jennings worked for Webster as a house servant. He was required to pay him eight dollars a week for his freedom.

The dwelling at Montpelier where Jennings and his mother lived has been lost to time along with three other slave cabins. The Montpelier archaeology department found the location of six slave dwellings, including Granny Milly's log cabin. She was 104 when the Marquis de Lafayette, a French aristocrat and military leader, visited Montpelier in 1825 and met her, her daughter, and her nearly seventy-year-old granddaughter. Lafayette, who commanded American soldiers during the Revolutionary War, opposed slavery, and as a friend to Madison and Jefferson, he urged them both to free their slaves. It is likely Granny Milly was born around 1720, but it is unknown where. It is believed she arrived at Montpelier sometime after 1732 as a teenager or an adult. Her name is listed on James Madison Sr.'s personal property tax records from 1782 through 1784. Sometimes her name is spelled "Milley" from 1782 to 1784 or "Milly" from 1785 to 1786.

A second person named Milly appears once in the 1782 personal property tax list.

The younger Milly was in her midteens when she was given to James Madison Sr.'s daughter as a wedding gift. It is unknown if the two Millys were related. Two very different kinds of documentary sources give evidence of Granny Milly's presence at Montpelier: tax records that offer a cold and impersonal statement, and a personal memoir that sanitizes and sentimentalizes slavery's realities. Granny Milly's presences in Montpelier tax records lack insight into her humanity, noted Hilarie M. Hicks, Montpelier's senior research historian. "Did Milly feel relieved to be allowed to spend her last years with a daughter and a granddaughter? Was she resentful of— or reconciled to—any separations from other family members that she had experienced? . . . How did she feel about being placed on display for guests like Lafayette?"

Because I could not sleep in an extant slave dwelling at Montpelier, I was among fifteen volunteers who, during a five-day field school, built a hand-hewn partial replica of Granny Milly's cabin at Montpelier now owned by my former employer, the National Trust for Historic Preservation. The replica, called a ghost structure, has exposed roof rafters. Matthew Reeves, director of archaeology and landscape restoration, told us Montpelier did not have the funds to build a full version of the cabin, but a partial structure returns a representation of it to the landscape. I joined the other rookie builders for a briefing on how to use the antique hand tools. We built the replica in a parking lot that had been cleared of ankle-deep snow. We worked in the frigid temperatures within view of Montpelier's main house, which served as a looming reminder of how well the

Madisons lived as compared to those they enslaved. By the second day, I saw the outline of the log cabin begin to appear. By the fourth day, it was my turn to use a hand tool to shape a pine log. I began to slice the log, but I trimmed the wrong side. The crew couldn't use it; I didn't get a second chance.

During breaks we toured the main house on the sprawling 2,650-acre estate at the northeast end of the Southwest Mountains, a small range of highland in eastern Virginia. Fifty miles to the south is another presidential site, Jefferson's Monticello. I looked closely at the exterior bricks for the fingerprints of the enslaved children who had pressed the moist soil into wooden molds to form the bricks. We also toured the site where four slave cabins and two smokehouses once stood.* After we built the ghost cabin, a professional crew disassembled it, moved the pieces from the parking lot, and rebuilt it at the site of the original structure. They put all the pieces back together after the archaeology work at the original site was done. The dig unearthed many artifacts, but I became fixated on a piece of fine china. We all speculated how the enslaved obtained it. The field school experience also gave me an appreciation for the hard work the enslaved ancestors performed to build their shelter.

In the enslaved community, Old Sawney was Granny Milly's neighbor. At his house, Sawney raised his favorite vegetables, cabbage and sweet potatoes. Granny Milly had a garden too, and others

---

* Because Montpelier does not have an extant slave dwelling, I slept in the postbellum Gilmore cabin and the Arlington House, an antebellum structure enslaved people built in 1848 on the Newman Plantation, which is now part of the Montpelier property.

in the enslaved community tended it for her. Sawney also raised chickens and eggs he sold to "Miss Dolley." Sawney had a unique status in the enslaved community. He was the enslaved overseer, one of two enslaved overseers on the Madisons' property. (The other two overseers were white men.) Sawney and the other Black overseer, Ralph, appear in references in Madison's correspondence many more times than other individuals, such as enslaved field workers. Instead of mentioning them by name, Madison referred to "the laborers" collectively. Sawney was likely born at Montpelier, where he learned how to operate the farm while he gained the trust of the Madisons and the enslaved community. After Emancipation, Sawney is referred to as Sawney A. Early Sr. His descendant Sherry Williams of Chicago has said her family tree reflects "the information gleaned from census reports, death records, and oral histories passed down generations. Close to twenty people (both Black and white) are tied intimately to Sawney A. Early, Sr. The family . . . is a testament of thirty-plus years of research that ties close to sixty folks."

When the plane landed in Richmond, Virginia, on April 17, 2015, I rushed to get a rental car for the half-hour drive to Montpelier, Virginia. I was in a hurry to be on time for lunch with descendants of the enslaved families at Montpelier.* After the meal I would have a sleepover in the roofless replica of Grammy Milly's cabin. On my first visit to Madison's home, Terry James and I rode in a rental car from South Carolina. But on this second trip, I was on my own. I set the navigation app in my cell phone for Montpelier,

---

* The lunch also was a reunion of the Black and the white Early family descendants.

Virginia. During the drive I relished the idea of being invited back to Montpelier. It was another stamp of approval for the Slave Dwelling Project and another confidence builder that further strengthened my resolve to continue my search for extant slave dwellings. I cruised along the rolling highway lined with horse farms and wheat fields with my eyes peeled for the Montpelier sign. When I saw it, that was my first clue I was in the wrong town. James Madison's Montpelier is in Orange, Virginia. I was nearly fifty miles off course. I was late for the lunch!

Descendants of the enslaved had participated in an archaeology field school at Montpelier's South Yard, where their ancestors lived. Chicago residents Sherry Williams and Cyndi Hinton were among the descendants who attended the lunch. Arriving just as it was ending, I expressed deepest regrets that I was late. I was assured that I wasn't the first visitor to confuse Montpelier the town with Montpelier, Madison's home. Meeting Williams and Hinton was the second time I'd met ancestors of enslaved people. The first time was at Historic Brattonsville in York County, South Carolina. Since then I had not made it a priority to communicate with descendant families. I was not yet wise enough in my slave dwelling experiences to understand the importance of meeting them so I could hear the stories of their ancestors and honor them. I've grown since then.

After the lunch Williams and Hinton joined me and others at Granny Milly's cabin. They requested permission from the eldest person in the cabin before they entered. Since I was the elder, I granted it. With a smoldering bundle of sage to appease the ancestors, they blessed the cabin's four corners as smoke scented the air. Then we acknowledged the ancestors' contributions to Montpelier and the great migration of African Americans from Southern to Northern states before six sets of heavy eyes gave way to sleep.* Williams and Hinton left the cabin before the snoring began.

I commend the Montpelier staff for telling the stories of the enslaved and working with the descendants to honor their ancestors. In June 2021, the majority white sixteen-member Montpelier Foundation board said it would give equal representation on the foundation's board to members of the nonprofit Montpelier Descendants Committee. The agreement was initially called a stellar example of how historic sites where Black people were enslaved could share equally in the oversight of the properties. When details of the agreement were revealed, however, members of the descendants committee called it a "power grab" by the white board members. Eventually, an agreement was reached that led to more Black representatives seated on the board in the spring of 2022.

MONTICELLO

On April 17, 2015, astronomers predicted a meteor shower in the night sky over Virginia. After sunset I sat around a campfire with twenty people at Thomas Jefferson's Monticello home. Some of them included descendants of the people Jefferson enslaved. It was my second sleepover on the Monticello mountaintop in as many years. Some in the group saw meteors, but I did not. Instead, my fireworks display hovered at eye level. I stepped between two angry

---

* Matthews Reeves, Carol Richardson, and Terry Brock were among the six people who joined Joe for this sleepover.

Black men who nearly came to blows over the question of whether Jefferson's relationship with Sally Hemings, an enslaved woman, was consensual or rape.

When Sarah was born in 1773, she was likely called Sally, the often-used diminutive version for that name. Sally was the last child born to Elizabeth Hemings, a bright "mulatto" enslaved woman, and John Wayles, who died shortly after her birth. Elizabeth and Wayles had five other children together. Wayles's white daughter from his earlier marriage, Martha Wayles Skelton, a widow, married Thomas Jefferson in September 1772. She died a decade later from the strain of bearing six children. After his wife's death, Jefferson had six more children with Sally, one of his slaves and his wife's half-sister. Sally's "mighty near white" skin and long straight hair distinguished her from the other enslaved people when she arrived at Monticello as a toddler to live there with her family. Then at a young age, Sally became a nursemaid for Maria, Jefferson's youngest daughter.

On July 5, 1784, three years before the start of the Constitutional Convention, Jefferson sailed to France with his oldest daughter, twelve-year-old Martha, to promote America's interests in France and the rest of Europe. Three years later, in May 1787, a fourteen-year-old Sally Hemings traveled to Europe with Jefferson's nine-year-old daughter, Maria. During the journey, Sally served as Maria's caregiver. After two weeks in London with Abigail and John Adams, the nation's future first lady and second president, Sally and Maria accompanied Jefferson's butler to Paris, where Sally may have lived with the Jeffersons on the famed Champs-Élysées. While in France, Sally enjoyed freedom. Enslaved people brought into France could use a complicated process that often led to emancipation.

While in Paris, Jefferson took Sally as his concubine. Initially, she refused to return to Monticello, but she did so after striking a deal with him. The then-sixteen-year-old agreed to return only if she gained "extraordinary privileges" for herself and freedom for her future children. Just as she began to speak French fluently, Sally returned to Monticello with the Jeffersons two days before Christmas Eve in 1789.

The spark that ignited the heated debate around the campfire centered on whether Sally was free or enslaved, and if she was free, whether she enjoyed favors not afforded to other enslaved people at Monticello. Sally moved to Charlottesville in 1827, a year after Jefferson, the nation's third president, died on July 4, 1826. She lived with two of her sons, Madison and Eston, who were freed in Jefferson's will, which did not emancipate their mother. The 1830 census, however, suggested she was a free white person, but in a special 1833 special census, taken following the 1831 Nat Turner Rebellion, Sally appears as a free person of color.

At Monticello, nearly all of the domestic servants were Hemingses. Sally, her mother, and her sisters did not have to endure the summer heat in the fields. She and the other house servants wore finer clothing, including tight-fitting knitted cotton stockings rather than the saggy stockings issued to other enslaved people. Freedom came for Hemings's children at age twenty-one. "Though enslaved, Sally Hemings helped shape her life and the lives of her children, who got an almost fifty-year head start on emancipation, escaping the system that had engulfed their ancestors and millions of others. Whatever we may feel about it today, this was important to her," said historian Annette Gordon-Reed.

Sally Hemings's descendant Diana Redman, a retired government worker in Gahanna, Ohio, said her ancestor was "in an untenable position. Today we would be looking at sexual harassment. She was not in a position to change her environment or to refuse. . . . That was the system for many Black women in the United States who were slaves. Even if they were not slaves in today's terms we'd talk about that as sexual harassment. I can't imagine myself in that position, not knowing what happened to your children, not having a say over where those children lived. . . . It is inconceivable."

Although Monticello now showcases Sally Hemings, it was not so long ago that her legacy was literally being spoiled. Her living quarters—fourteen feet, eight inches wide, and thirteen feet long—were near Jefferson's bedroom in Monticello's South Wing. The space, built in 1809, was converted in 1941 to a men's restroom after being neglected for decades. In 2017, archaeologists uncovered the space. Finding Hemings's quarters means that over time, the artifacts recovered there might shed even more light on her life and her connection to Jefferson. The unsettled question of whether she was Jefferson's consensual lover or convenience for lustful pleasure might finally be settled. In the meantime, I am not surprised that her living space was being used as a restroom, a shameful and disrespectful choice. I've seen it done before in Georgia at Hofwyl-Broadfield Plantation on the Altamaha River between Darien and Brunswick.

On a cool night around the campfire on Monticello's mountaintop setting, I had my second experience at Jefferson's home, the cream of the crop of presidential sites. I had twice reached this presidential pinnacle, giving yet another boost to my already secure confidence that the Slave Dwelling Project had earned a solid reputation. The evolution of my work had arrived at a point where I did not need a list of plantations to call. Historic sites called me, and some that I had been to before asked me to return. My blogs were getting attention from readers who were impressed with the project's longevity. Social media views were garnering clicks from people who wanted to hang out with me on a sleepover. As I expanded the narrative of our ancestors, more historic sites called for my advice. The staff at Andrew Jackson's Hermitage near Nashville, Tennessee, was among them. I joined a workshop to examine their interpretation. I also participated in a three-day workshop in February 2018 with sixty historians and site managers to develop a plan to show historic properties how to engage with the descendants of their enslaved communities. At Montpelier that plan inspired the formation of the Montpelier Descendants Committee. For those sites that do not have extant slave dwellings, I stressed that this was not an excuse to avoid focusing on the contributions of the enslaved. The evidence of their existence could sometimes be as simple as their finger-shaped impressions baked into the brown bricks of the slave masters' big house.

ELEVEN

LIVING HISTORY IN OUR FEDERAL, STATE, AND COUNTY PARKS

I AM OFTEN ASKED IF THERE WERE GOOD SLAVE OWNERS. THE question is ridiculous and insensitive. No privilege extended to an enslaved person can blunt the crime of slavery and its harsh reality. Anna Kingsley, however, might be that theoretical model of a benevolent slave owner. The latitude she extended to the people she enslaved may have been due to the laws that controlled her society and her own enslavement.

In the Kingdom of Djolof, in what is now Senegal on Africa's west coast, Anta Madjiguène Ndiaye is remembered as a happy, pampered, and proud princess whose royal lineage extended to both sides of her parentage. She was the favorite child of her father, the ruler of the Kingdom of Djolof. Then, around 1806, she suddenly disappeared. The teenage princess was snared in slavery's net and placed on a ship at the slave depot on Gorée Island, and after surviving an ocean voyage, she arrived at Havana, Cuba. Slave ship captain and the forty-one-year-old owner of an East Florida plantation Zephaniah Kingsley bought the thirteen-year-old princess, then made her his wife. In Spanish Florida, the African princess became Anna Madgigine Jai Kingsley. In a St. Augustine court four years after she had been purchased by Kingsley, an English Quaker, he granted freedom to her and their three "mulatto" children. That court decision came in the Spanish settlement of St. Augustine, founded in 1565, half a century before the English colonized Jamestown, Virginia, in 1619.

Before she was freed and before she gave birth to her first child, however, Anna Kingsley managed Kingsley's household at his twenty-six-hundred-acre Laurel Grove Plantation on the St. Johns River that is now present-day Orange Park, south of Jacksonville. Anna was not the only enslaved woman Kingsley took as his wife and who bore him children, but she was his principal wife. After she gained her freedom, Kingsley and her children moved to the other side of the river to establish a twenty-acre farm with twelve slaves: two men, three women, and seven children. But a so-called patriot rebellion covertly supported by President James Madison in 1812 sent US troops and civilian marauders from South Carolina and Georgia into the region to overthrow the Spanish government and grab property, forcing Kingsley to abandon Laurel Grove and Anna Kingsley to leave her newly established farm. Seminole Indians, who had traded with Kingsley, attacked Laurel Grove after the "patriots" used it as their headquarters. The Kingsleys, their children, and their enslaved workers settled on Fort George Island on Florida's Atlantic coast, at the entrance to the St. Johns River. The land would become Kingsley Plantation, a site where I spent a night in June 2018 with Anna Kingsley's descendant Peri Frances of Atlanta.

Under Spanish law, the courts upheld the rights of enslaved people. They could marry, obtain freedom for notable achievement, own property (including people), and work an extra job to earn money to buy their way out of bondage. As late as 1860, the strong-willed Anna Kingsley continued to hold her slaves after her husband's death, but she carried on his rule that allowed them to pay one-half of their value to gain their freedom. Enslaved and free people worked together; enslaved people labored until 2:00 p.m. and then were free to do other work or tend a garden.

Kingsley Plantation is now owned by my former employer, the National Park Service. It is one of fifteen former plantation sites owned by federal, state, and local governments that I've visited. I have gained access to five state parks in North Carolina; four state parks in South Carolina; state parks in Arkansas, Minnesota, and Maryland; and national parks in Louisiana, Virginia, and Florida. Most of them contacted me. In my experience, these government-owned parks are the most difficult sites to access because of bureaucracy. These sites, created through federal and state laws, are mandated to provide spaces for recreation on lands that just happened to be former plantations.

In most cases slavery was not initially the reason these parks were created. Governments at all levels acquired these sites to tell the story of the white male enslaver and not the story of the people they enslaved. However, by preserving the extant slave dwellings at these sites, the government gave me the opportunity to counter the "happy slave" and "benevolent slave-owner" narratives. My presence has helped to change that. Redcliffe Plantation, a state-owned park in Aiken County, South Carolina, is an example of that. Redcliffe was on the list of former plantation sites I received in 2010 from the state preservation office. It was the first site to tell me no. Redcliffe's decision came at a time, however, when a rejection didn't faze me. I already had a long list of positive responses that were strengthening my desire to follow my crazy idea of sleeping alone in slave cabins in South Carolina.

Five years after rejecting me in 2009, Redcliffe asked me to attend a meeting at the site. Redcliffe already had embarked on its plan to fully interpret the contributions of the enslaved, but I suspect they were pleased with the progress I was making in telling the stories of the ancestors. Shortly after the Redcliffe meeting, I was granted the approval to conduct a sleepover there. I am convinced the work I had done up to that point proved to Redcliffe's managers I was legitimate. I don't blame them for rejecting my initial request. When I approached them, I had no track record. The bureaucracy of a government-owned site meant managers were understandably cautious, which often delayed the timing of my sleepovers, as it did at Kingsley Plantation near Jacksonville, Florida.

Kingsley

MaVynee Oshun Betsch walked American Beach on Amelia Island, Florida, with her seven-foot-long thick locks draped over her slender arms or trailing in the sand. She moved with a passion to preserve the beach's ecology and history stemming from a time when

American Beach was a sun-soaked segregated haven in the Jim Crow South that drew the full spectrum of Black society. That passion followed a decade-long career as an opera singer in Germany. After she gave up the European spotlight, she returned home to live on the beach as a free spirit, resting at times on a chaise longue. As time passed, she became known as the Beach Lady.

Peri Frances had heard the American Beach stories before. But by the time she reached her early twenties, she began to bond with her aunt, MaVynee. Frances had not been to Kingsley Plantation when her aunt repeatedly told her, "We are Kingsleys." She didn't know what that meant, and she didn't understand its significance. Then during a series of conversations, MaV explained their family is related to Anna Kingsley, the African princess and mistress of a Fort George Island plantation, just south of American Beach.

MaV repeatedly told Frances of three people she needed to meet. She referred her to Kingsley park superintendent Roger Clark; his wife, Carol S. Clark, a park ranger; and university historian Daniel Shafer, who later authored *Anna Madginine Jai Kingsley: African Princess, Florida Slave, Plantation Slaveowner*. The book is the culmination of nearly half a century of Shafer's research into the Kingsleys. Since then Frances has embraced not only her lineage but also the former plantation site where her seventh-generation grandmother owned land and slaves in the Florida wilderness. She has traveled to Senegal, where her family there has welcomed her and shared their oral history of the thirteen-year-old princess who was stolen by slave traders.

In 2017, when Shafer guided a second group of Senegalese visitors to Jacksonville and the Kingsley Plantation, the site's superintendent, Barbara Goodman, and a staff member called Frances with an urgent request that she come to Jacksonville to meet her kinfolk. Frances rushed to Jacksonville for her first meeting with her great-uncle Medoune Ndiaye. In the lobby of a Jacksonville hotel, he took her hand and said in French, *"Maintenant, je peux mourir heureux,"* which means "Now I can die happy." In the hotel room, he gave Frances an unexpected history lesson; the names of each of Anna Kingsley's relatives dating back to the Djolof Empire, which ruled the region of Senegal between the Senegal and Gambia Rivers from 1350 to 1549. Although he is not the community's griot or storyteller, he is the family's historian and has retained a verbatim recall of the family's lineage going back to long before Europeans arrived. With his detailed recitation of her family tree in Senegal, goosebumps rose on Frances's arms and tears welled in her eyes.

I was a National Park Service (NPS) employee at historic sites in Charleston, but I was not aware of this history at Kingsley Plantation in 2010 as I was beginning the Slave Cabin Project. Mike Allen, my NPS colleague in Charleston and my distant cousin who steered me to an NPS internship in Charleston, knew the Anna Kingsley story. He suggested that I place Kingsley on my list of plantations to visit. He volunteered to contact the Kingsley staff and Barbara Goodman, the site's superintendent. My request was denied then, but eight years later another door opened at Kingsley. The Florida Trust for Historic Preservation asked me to be the keynote speaker and participate on a panel during its fortieth anniversary conference in Jacksonville. Something else more intriguing came with the offer: a night in one of two extant slave cabins at

Kingsley near the planter's home, built in 1798, making it the oldest standing plantation house in Florida. Conference organizer Adrienne Burke, who handled the details to make the sleepover possible, invited Frances to join a small group that would spend a night in the Kingsley cabin, made of an extremely hard concrete-like mix of shells, stones, and lime called tabby, a coarse building material used on the sea islands along the southeast coast.

Spending time with Frances after the panel discussion and around a campfire near the tabby cabin gave me insight into why Barbara Goodman might have rejected my request to visit Kingsley. Goodman considered Kingsley to be sacred grounds. She was an NPS leader in "nature's army" charged with protecting the park. In Frances's view, the NPS, like the military, is a highly bureaucratic institution. Instead of going to war, they protect nature and historic sites. My presence at Kingsley ran counter to that mission.

Frances also helped me understand and appreciate Anna Kingsley's complicated life. White people often tell me Africans also enslaved Africans and sold them to slave traders. I view those comments from white people as feeble attempts to absolve their ancestors of chattel slavery. Anna Kingsley was a Black slave owner, so on this sleepover I would not only spend my first night at a historic site in Florida, but Kingsley Plantation would be my first sleepover at a site once owned by a Black female enslaver. By the time I met Frances, she had had two decades to ponder her ancestor's relationship with her white husband (Zephaniah Kingsley, a Quaker from England), the people they enslaved, and the life she had lived in a slaveholding African society before she too was sold into slavery in America.

Frances imagines that her seventh-generation grandmother's relationship with the people she owned in Florida may have been an extended family-like community more than the typical slave-master arrangement. Anna and Zephaniah Kingsley permitted the people they enslaved to pursue trades. Most of the enslaved men kept their African names, but most of the women were given Anglicized names. The enslaved people lived together as a family unit and were free to practice their African rituals. As long as the plantation functioned, an enslaved person on a Kingsley plantation could enjoy weekend entertainment and free time. Allowing the Africans to express their cultural tradition created harmony in the enslaved community. In spite of those conditions, they couldn't return to their African homes. The best of any abhorrent system is still slavery. If Anna Kingsley had remained in her African society, she likely would have been married and bearing children in her early teens. She also would have had enslaved people assigned to her as a member of the ruling class. But in that African society, enslaved people were afforded a level of humanity that was not present in the Americas.

Initially, Frances didn't consider Zephaniah as her grandfather. As a Southern-born African American descendant of an African princess, however, she had wondered why she has green eyes and freckles with a fair complexion. Finally, she accepted her connection to Zephaniah Kingsley. Initially, she viewed him as a lecherous and exploitative old man. But then she recognized that for better or worse, Anna Kingsley and their children were his family, and they looked like the other Africans he enslaved, including Anna's co-wives, who altogether bore him eleven children. Zephaniah lived in the African culture of all of his wives. He never married a

European woman. Frances also grappled with decisions made by Anna Kingsley, an emancipated woman who owned other people at a time when there were few economic options available. Frances settles on the reality that life is not black and white, and real-life issues from more than two hundred years ago must not be viewed entirely from a twenty-first-century perspective.

Finding the name of an African ancestor is rare, but what's even rarer is the knowledge of an enslaved African ancestor who became a slave owner. Frances has carried this story within her for more than two decades. Now it is difficult for her to remember how it has changed her. Since learning this family history, she has walked through the tabby cabins at Kingsley Plantation to thank the ancestors and tell them she loves them.

Anna Kingsley is not the only person enslaved by Zephaniah Kingsley whose name history remembers. History buffs in Charleston will immediately recognize the name Gullah Jack and know of his association with Denmark Vesey, leader of a failed 1822 slave revolt in Charleston. Vesey and Gullah Jack were among the thirty-five people hanged for their roles in the plot. Kingsley "imported" Gullah Jack in 1806 from Mozambique to Charleston. Gullah Jack, a skilled wood carver, became a carpenter in Charleston, where Vesey, a free man, also worked as a carpenter. It is possible that Kingsley sold Gullah Jack to Paul Pritchard, a Charleston planter and shipbuilder on the Wando River.

As the fire grew dim, the time came for us to find our places in the cabin. Peri Frances had a special delivery to aid in her comfort. Her gift also saved me from sleeping in the dirt. Her friend Yuwnus Asami, curator of the American Beach Museum, brought her a sleeping bag and a two-person tent, which she erected inside the cabin's sturdy tabby walls. The delivery included a portable massage table. I slept on it. An approaching tropical depression brought threatening rain and cooler temperatures that along with a smoky campfire did little to completely control the mosquitoes. Nevertheless, we endured a night with the haunting call of distant birds in the surrounding nature sanctuary mixed with squealing pet peacocks at nearby private homes. In those somewhat quiet moments, however, Frances had her own thoughts that eventually gave way to sleep. Did the enslaved on the island have an opportunity to leave briefly, and if so, where did they go? How did Anna Kingsley, her children, and the other free people of color in Florida face the threat of being enslaved again in the 1830s following a rise in racial tensions in northeast Florida? It must have been emotionally gripping to again fear the auction block. Those are the threats that forced people to make hard decisions about where to live or when to leave. Zephaniah Kingsley made that decision when he moved his principal wife, Anna Kingsley, his three other wives, their children, and others on the plantation to Haiti to live in a colony free from the threats of enslavement. Anna Kingsley eventually returned to Florida to win her claim to Kingsley Plantation.

STAGVILLE STATE HISTORIC SITE

Thomas and Judith Stagg's tavern on sixty-six acres provided the core for Stagville Plantation in eastern Durham County, North Carolina. Following Thomas Stagg's death, Virginia-born merchant Richard Bennehan purchased the property in 1787 from Judith

Stagg. Bennehan built a store and a dwelling as a home for himself and his wife, Mary, and their children, Rebecca and Thomas. By the end of the eighteenth century, Bennehan had acquired nearly four thousand acres and forty-two enslaved workers, who grew tobacco and cereal grains and tended to livestock. In 1803, Rebecca Bennehan married lawyer and planter Duncan Cameron. They settled on a plantation near her father's Stagville house. Rebecca's brother, Thomas, never married. When he died in 1847, Stagville was passed to the Cameron family under the ownership of Duncan and Rebecca's son, Paul Cameron. By 1860, Paul Cameron had expanded the property to the largest plantation in North Carolina, which covered thirty thousand acres with more than one thousand enslaved people.

When Union soldiers marched through Stagville in 1865, they told the enslaved people they were free. That jubilant news did not convince Doc Edwards, who was born in 1853 at Stagville, to leave Paul Cameron. "When de Yankees come day didn' do so much harm, only dey tole us we was free niggers," the eighty-four-year-old Edwards recalled. "But I always feel like I belong to Marse Paul, an' I still live at Stagville on de ole plantation. I has a little garden an' does what I can to earn a little something. . . . I will get a little pension, an' I'll stay right on in dat little house 'til de good Lawd calls me home, den I will see Marse Paul once more."

Cyrus "Cy" Hart lived and worked at Snow Hill farm on the vast Stagville Plantation complex. Hart also recalled when the Yankees arrived and chased off Confederate soldiers who had searched for Cameron's silver. They killed a couple of the rebels, and the rest of them fled. Union soldiers took ham from Cameron's meat house and told Hart's mother, Nellie, to fry it. After they ate most of the ham, along with hot bread and freshly brewed coffee, she got the leftovers and some money too with a declaration from the Yankee captain. "He tole her dat she wuz free, dat we didn' belong to Marse Paul no longer," Hart, seventy-eight, said. But Hart and his mother didn't leave, and he stayed with Cameron until he died. Before Cameron died he "selected eight of us niggers to tote his coffin to de chapel. . . . We didn't make any fuss while sittin' dere on de floor, but we sho was full of grief to see our dear ole Marse Paul lying dere dead."

I am not surprised Doc Edwards and Cy Hart shared fond boyhood recollections of their enslaver, Paul Cameron, with a writer from the Works Progress Administration's (WPA) Federal Writers' Project. WPA writers documented the experiences of enslaved people across the country. Edwards and Hart grew up at Stagville among more than one thousand enslaved people and an enslaver who didn't know them all by name. Slavery was likely not as harsh for them as it was for their parents and other older enslaved people. Edwards and Hart may have become content in a system that met their daily needs but did not extend to them the benefit of their free labor. It is also likely that as older formerly enslaved men of African descent, they told WPA writer Daisy Whaley, a white woman who interviewed them on August 6, 1937, what she wanted to hear: a romanticized version of their enslavement. Some Black historians have shied away from using the WPA narratives because they are tainted with the racist intent to stereotype the elderly informants as loyal to their former masters.

Historic Stagville is managed by the North Carolina Historic Sites, a state agency that manages twenty-five historic sites. In

addition to Stagville, I've visited three other North Carolina properties, including the home of President James K. Polk in Pineville,
North Carolina. The state has afforded me unprecedented access to
these properties as a result of the strong support I've received from
Michelle Lanier, executive director of the North Carolina Division
of State Historic Sites.

When I arrived at Stagville in May 2015 for my second
sleepover, I participated in Freedom 150, a program that commem-
orated the end of the Civil War and the emancipation of enslaved
people at Stagville and elsewhere across the South.* The end of the
war led to the rise of Black churches and the Southern sharecropping system that kept newly freed families trapped in poverty and
threatened retaliation if they complained. At Stagville, many of the
families remained on the land to till the soil as sharecroppers until
the 1950s. The Freedom 150 program surprised me. More than two
hundred people came to the event, which included storytellers at
the slave cabins, United States Colored Troops encampment and
interpretation, live music, and an outdoor cooking demonstration. I
hung out with the Civil War reenactors. African American reenactors are rare, so I knew them all. As usual the visitors were enamored
by their cannon. The other living historians included Nicole Moore
of Interpreting Slave Life and Dontavius Williams, on staff at Historic Brattonsville in York County, South Carolina, who helped
Jerome Bias, a Stagville staff member, prepare a meal of Hoppin'
John and hoecakes over an open fire. After sunset, Dontavius stood
in the distance and began to sing "Steal Away" as he approached

---

* My first visit to Stagville was in October 2013.

with a sack slung over his shoulder. He then told the story of Adam, a young enslaved boy sold away from his mother, who never saw him again. Dontavius's poignant and simple words held me from start to finish. Many of us wept.[*]

The Freedom 150 audience was the most diverse gathering at a former plantation site I had seen in the five years since I began sleeping in slave cabins. It is a challenge to convince African Americans who know of an enslaved ancestor to visit former plantation sites. But Stagville has a different relationship with the descendants of enslaved people who live in the Durham community. Many of them came to the program.

To improve the health of the enslaved workers, Cameron built four two-story dwellings for them in the early 1850s. Enslaved people had lived in poorly constructed, leaky, dirt-floor cabins. The new structures were erected in a row at Horton Grove on the Stagville property. The four identical rectangular dwellings were positioned in a row between a green meadow and dense forest. Born at Stagville in 1832, Abner Jordan lived in one of the new structures warmed in the winter by fires in chimneys at each end of the buildings. Each of the four rooms was assigned to a family. That one-room allocation of space meant Jordan lived in extremely overcrowded conditions with his parents, Ovid and Ellen, and ten brothers and sisters. In 1844, Jordan and his father were among the forty-four people who worked in the Camerons' house. Vera

---

[*] The living historians during Freedom 150 gave me the idea to create my own traveling troupe of living historians I called "Inalienable Rights: Living History Through the Eyes of the Enslaved." I formed the group in 2016 with a grant from the SC Humanities Council. Since then, we have presented programs in six southern states.

Cecelski, Stagville's site manager, said it is unknown how many dwellings housed the enslaved community. Clusters of houses were likely placed around the property near the fields where the enslaved people worked. Stagville was the largest plantation in the complex, consisting of about twenty-six enslaved people.

I spent the night in the Holman House at Horton Grove. It is named for George and Janie Holman, the children of enslaved people. They were born free after the Civil War but worked at Stagville as sharecroppers. They lived next to the Hart House, named for Cy Hart, whose descendants also remained at Stagville as sharecroppers. The four structures, including two other dwellings named for sharecropping families Umstead and Cameron/ Justice, stand across the meadow from a tobacco barn reminiscent of the barn I worked in as a boy in Williamsburg County, South Carolina.

Before we found places to sleep in the Holman House, Jerome cooked pork jambalaya, succotash, and pumpkin custard on a campfire while public radio journalist Leoneda Inge interviewed me and others. Civil War reenactor Terry James also joined me at Stagville along with three graduate students from North Carolina Central University and Prinny Anderson, a member of the board of directors of the nonprofit Slave Dwelling Project.

After dinner we stretched out in the lower level of the dwelling to talk for as long as possible. We covered race relations, the Underground Railroad, and the 2013 movie *The Butler*, the story of a Black butler in the White House. We finally tossed, turned, and snored until the roosters crowed and the sun peeped through an open space that serves as a window.

None of us had a good night's sleep, including Terry, who struggled with shackled hands. "My hips are sore and my back is sore," he said. "I'd still do it to pay tribute to those people who came over and suffered and died."

MARIETTA HOUSE

Legal scholar Andrew T. Fede of Hackensack, New Jersey, suggested that Supreme Court Associate Justice Gabriel Duvall, considered by some historians as the most insignificant justice to serve on the nation's highest court, deserved reconsideration based on his 1813 dissenting opinion that placed the right to freedom over the right to property. Duvall believed that one of the court's rulings that denied an enslaved family their freedom would block "reasonable protection" to people of African descent.

In this case, the court rejected the appeal of Mima Queen and her minor daughter, Louisa, who sought their freedom because Mima Queen's great-grandmother, Mary Queen, had the reputation as a free woman of color who had been illegally enslaved. Mima Queen's lawyer, Francis Scott Key, lyricist of "The Star-Spangled Banner," based the appeal on a lower court's refusal to follow a previously accepted rule to admit hearsay evidence to establish an enslaved person's freedom. Mary Queen was a free woman, and therefore, her descendants should also be free, Key argued, based on the hearsay rule of evidence. Courts had followed the hearsay rule before, especially in cases involving manumission lawsuits. When Duvall was a lawyer in Maryland between 1778 and 1796, he had represented enslaved people who sought freedom by presenting hearsay evidence that they had non-African or free Black maternal ancestors. But in this case, Chief Justice John Marshall declined to make an exception for the Queens. The Queens were no strangers to Duvall. He had represented members of the family in a petition for freedom in the 1790s in a lower court in Maryland before President James Madison appointed him in 1811 to the Supreme Court.

During his near twenty-three years on the Supreme Court, Duvall wrote a scant fifteen opinions. He came to the court at age sixty and later was so deaf he could not hear court testimony. By this measure, historian Ernest Sutherland Bates in the 1930s considered Duvall of no major consequence. But historian Irving Dilliard argued that Duvall's legacy should be given renewed consideration in light of the historical context of his refusal to not join the court's majority in denying the Queens their freedom. It was one of those rare moments when Duvall wrote a dissenting opinion. Fede maintained time is the measure of a dissenting opinion's strength. Duvall's interpretation of the hearsay rule eventually was included in the Federal Rules of Evidence.[*]

As a Maryland lawyer from 1778 until 1796, Duvall won the overwhelming majority of the antislavery lawsuits he filed for enslaved people. His trial lawyer experience and his opinion in the Queen appeal, however, are in stark contrast to his private life. In 1783, Duvall enslaved at least nine people. During his lifetime, he owned more than one hundred people at Marietta, his Maryland

---

[*] Gabriel Duvall, former president Barack Obama, and former vice president Dick Cheney have genetic ties to Mareen Duvall, a 1650 Huguenot immigrant from France and a Maryland slave owner.

tobacco plantation. When he died in 1844 in Prince George's County, his estate included thirty-six enslaved individuals. He was typical of the hypocritical white men of his day. He defended enslaved people in court, but in his home he enslaved people to reap the financial gains of that sinful institution. They knew it was morally wrong because they wrestled with it publicly, but they acquiesced privately for selfish reasons.

After years of representing enslaved people, Supreme Court Associate Justice Gabriel Duvall was summoned to Maryland state court to respond to a freedom petition filed by one of his enslaved families. Georgetown barkeeper John Dales (or Dells) transported Tom and Sarah Butler and their three daughters from Maryland to Virginia and then to the District of Columbia, where he hired them out to a Georgetown grocer. Between 1803 and 1805, Dales then sold away two of the Butlers' daughters, Jane and Lydia, to a buyer in Virginia, leaving the Butlers with their infant daughter, Sally. In the summer of 1805, Dales sold the Butlers and their child to Duvall, who at that time was the first US comptroller of the Treasury. The Butlers didn't stay long at Duvall's home in the District of Columbia before they and other people Duvall had purchased were moved to Marietta, Duvall's tobacco plantation in Prince George's County in Maryland.

This was an abrupt shift for the Butlers, accustomed to working in urban shops but now suddenly thrown into hard labor on a tobacco plantation. For the next twenty-six years, the Butlers toiled on Duvall's tobacco fields while he expanded his fortunes. Between 1812 and 1815, Duvall built Marietta House, a two-and-a-half-story brick mansion, as a home for himself and his wife, Jane. After they settled at Marietta House, Duvall's plantation grew from 150 acres to about 700 acres.

As Duvall expanded his wealth, the Butlers charted a legal course to freedom. As enslaved people who once worked in an urban community, they had witnessed how other enslaved people used the courts to their advantage. The time had come for them to do the same for themselves. They turned to Duvall's friend Francis Scott Key for help. The Butlers filed a freedom petition on June 2, 1828, in the DC court where Duvall had purchased them. They sought freedom for themselves and their children Sally, Airy, Matilda, and Rezin, and two granddaughters, Lydie and Eliza. They maintained that as "persons of colour," they were entitled to their freedom. In May 1831, the court agreed. The court ruled the Butlers had been illegally purchased in the District of Columbia and then transported to Prince George's County, a violation of importation laws. The Butlers strategically filed their suit in the Washington, DC, courts where the case had a higher chance of success than in Prince George's County, where Duvall lived at Marietta.

The staff at the Marietta House Museum, now owned by the Maryland-National Capital Park and Planning Commission (MNCPPC), uses this slavery-freedom paradox to present a compelling narrative for visitors who want to learn more about Duvall and the people he enslaved. Julia Rose, Marietta's historic house manager, said although Duvall was an enslaver, he followed a strict interpretation of the law when he came to an individual's freedom. He genuinely believed his former clients, the Queens, were free. As an attorney, he had represented more than twenty-two members of the Queen family in freedom lawsuits. It was not a question of him favoring one race or another, nor was he taking an abolitionist's position, she said, but he truly believed their ancestor was free; therefore, they too should be free. However, he viewed the Butlers as his property, she said. They did not have a legacy of family freedom; therefore, they were deemed to be chattel.

Marietta is one of the three MNCPPC sites I've visited.* Their invitations to these sites in Prince George's County convince me they are doing the right thing to tell the real story of these properties. Commercial and residential development over time has reduced Marietta to twenty-five acres. None of the slave dwellings have survived. The likely location of one of them, within fifty yards of the main house, has recently been found and is set to be explored. As I ascended the staircase with Rose in September 2021, we arrived at a tiny second-floor bedroom adjacent to Duvall's bedroom, where I would sleep. I said, "Oh, that looks good," when I saw a bed in the room. Rose said that Duvall family letters from the 1850s through the 1860s do not indicate that enslaved people lived in the house. It is likely that during the periods when a Duvall family member was ill, an enslaved person slept on the floor nearby.

Sleepover veteran Lynda Davis, currently a racial justice organizer from Linthicum, Maryland, agreed to take the floor in the nearby children's parlor, a room directly below Duvall's granddaughter's bedroom upstairs. In that bedroom, an enslaved caregiver, Rachel, slept on the floor steps away from the baby's crib.

---

* I've had sleepovers at Montpelier House Museum in Laurel, Maryland (2020), and Mount Calvert Historical and Archaeological Park in Upper Marlboro, Maryland, in 2019.

Marietta was Lynda's fifteenth sleepover. I met her during a September 2015 symposium titled "How Do We Get Americans to Talk Honestly About Slavery?" at George Washington University in Washington, DC. After the event, she asked me whether I had made progress on finding a place to stay during an upcoming National Preservation Conference in the DC area. I had put that request out on Facebook. When I told her no, she spent weeks searching for a place that would allow a sleepover and then connected me with Gunston Hall in Lorton, Virginia. The property is associated with one of America's founding fathers, George Mason. On November 3, 2015, I stayed in their re-created laundry room with Anne McWhirt and Lynda; it was her first sleepover.

Conversations that Lynda had with Stephanie Sperling, the senior archaeologist in the Archaeology Office at the Natural and Historic Resources Division, Department of Parks and Recreation, Prince George's County, spurred the creation of the "Echoes of the Enslaved" program, which has been staged each year since 2019. The Marietta House Museum was the host site for the 2021 program. The Slave Dwelling Project is a partner in this program, which features compelling and thought-provoking conversations around a campfire.

Earlier in the day of the Marietta sleepover, I was part of a panel discussion that included Dr. Will Thomas, author of *A Question of Freedom: The Families Who Challenged Slavery from the Nation's Founding to the Civil War*. He said that resistance against slavery was not exceptional. Enslaved people pressed for freedom at every moment. Lynda had learned that her white ancestors had been enslavers. Thomas's words came to her as she struggled to find a comfortable position on the floor where an enslaved person had once slept. She thought about that person's life and how they slept on a pallet in a room with no heat and were at the beck and call of the enslaver's family. Thomas's comments made Lynda think about her enslaver ancestors who abused the people they enslaved. She also thought about her own complicity with oppressive systems. Her truth-seeking moved her from the sidelines to the front lines of the movement for racial and economic justice.

TWELVE

ABOVE THE MASON-DIXON LINE

A COMET BLAZED ACROSS THE SKY AS COLONIAL AMERICA USHERED in a new year: 1760. Weeks later, at 2:00 a.m. on February 14, an enslaved woman gave birth to her fourth child. She named him Richard. She and her infant, her husband, and her other children belonged to a white attorney. Richard spent his early years in a bustling city where shackled men, women, and children were bought and sold at public auction, a commercial activity that surely severed kinship ties forever. A similar fate finally fell on Richard's family around 1768 when their owner sold them to a farmer. Eventually, the farmer sold Richard's mother and three of his siblings to pay debts. At age twenty-three, after arduous years of cutting wood and hauling bricks, Richard bought his and his brother's freedom. Negro Richard was then set on a path to perhaps fulfill the comet's prophecy. He took the name Richard Allen and became America's first Black bishop of the African Methodist Episcopal Church, which now has 2.5 million members worldwide.

Allen's inspiring tenacity to work his way out of bondage to establish the antislavery AME denomination didn't unfold in an urban Southern city or rural plantation in the South. Allen was possibly born into slavery in Delaware but likely in Philadelphia, the Northern "City of Brotherly Love" when it was entrenched in the British Empire. At birth, Richard Allen and his family were owned by Philadelphia legal scholar Benjamin Chew, a member of the Quaker society, which was divided over the issue of slavery. I had my first northern state sleepover on June 23, 2011, at Chew's Cliveden House in Philadelphia.* Like universities and presidential residences, sites in northern states presented another path to expand the Slave Dwelling Project. Later, I traveled to slave dwellings and spaces where enslaved people lived and worked in Connecticut, Delaware, Massachusetts, New York, Rhode Island, and Washington, DC. I often received pushback from whites in the North when I mentioned my sleepovers in northern cities.

Less than a year after my visit to Cliveden, the Reverend David Pettee, a Unitarian minister who grew up near Boston, joined me and two other persons at a sleepover in the attic at the Bush-Holley House in Connecticut. David said:

> Northerners have inherited a powerful historical amnesia when it comes to the memory of slavery. But don't worry. We haven't forgotten our history. We still worship the stories of the Sons of Liberty. We still teach "the midnight ride of Paul Revere" to our school kids. "Listen my children and

---

* I returned to Cliveden in November 2015.

you shall hear . . ." Every third Monday in April is Patriot's Day, when we commemorate again that first shot fired on Lexington Green that was heard 'round the world.

I live in Massachusetts. Our license plates remind us that we are the "Spirit of America." We are the good guys. In 1754, the [British] Crown requested that every city and town in Massachusetts report the number of slaves over the age of sixteen. [In Massachusetts] 114 communities responded to the census; 109 recorded at least one slave. The town fathers of Boston dutifully recorded 989 slaves, representing nearly nine percent of the population.

[Did they say] 989 slaves? In Boston? How come I had to discover this fact by accident? Within walking distance of where I work in downtown Boston, there are numerous buildings and sites that pay homage to Boston's storied colonial past. Every day on my way to work, I pass the Robert Gould Shaw 54th Regiment Memorial on Beacon [Street]. Directly across the street from the memorial is the Massachusetts State House, built on property once owned by John Hancock. We all know John Hancock. Or do we? The plaque that mentions where his house once stood conveniently neglects to mention that Hancock was also a slaveholder.

Today, Bay Staters (a native or resident of Massachusetts) are very proud of our abolitionist past. We forget that in 1835, William Lloyd Garrison, editor of the *Liberator*, was nearly murdered by an angry mob on the streets of Boston. In the 1960s, in the name of urban renewal, the office where the [abolitionist] newspaper was published fell unceremoniously to the wrecking ball. At the base of Beacon Hill in the Boston Public Gardens stands a statue of Charles Sumner, widely considered the most radical abolitionist in the United State Senate before the Civil War. In 1856, after Sumner was nearly caned to death in the Senate chambers by South Carolina Representative Preston Brooks, hundreds of people sent money to Brooks so he could buy a new cane. It is quite understandable that many Massachusetts citizens were outraged! Few, however, questioned Sumner's outlandish claim made two years before, when he thundered on the Senate floor that "no person was ever born a slave on the soil of Massachusetts."

Other notable Northern slaveholders included Ben Franklin and William Penn, and Quakers enslaved Africans. These facts shock some white people, especially northerners, because in their misinformed minds chattel slavery was strictly a Southern problem. It took the Civil War and the Thirteenth Amendment to the US Constitution to end slavery in Southern states. In the North, the process began after the American Revolution. Following the North's abolition of slavery, however, Northerners remained complicit in the slave trade through the ownership of insurance companies, banks, ships, and the factories that added value to cotton picked by enslaved people. One did not have to touch or even be around enslaved people to enable the continued existence of their bondage or benefit from their stolen labor. One must wonder if Northern enslavers freed their enslaved people when the law required them to do so, or did they sell them down South to recoup their investments?

By 1804, fifty-seven years before the first shot of the Civil War, Northern states had legislatively abolished slavery. New Jersey was the last Northern state to pass a gradual end to slavery. Connecticut in 1784 declared that enslaved children born after the law was approved would be freed at age twenty-five. New England is the only region where slavery ended rather quickly. In other areas of the North and West, slavery continued until just before the Civil War. During the colonial period, 41 percent of New York City's households held slaves, often as domestic servants and laborers. The last enslaved people were freed by 1827 in the state of New York.

Southerners cheer when I bring attention to slavery in Northern states. They want it known that slavery is not an exclusively Southern sin. Confederate reenactors are perhaps the most vocal. In countless conversations with them, I've heard the refrain: "If you are against the Confederate flag because of slavery, you should be against the American flag, too, because slavery existed under that flag." Northerners, however, are surprisingly shocked to learn slavery existed above the Mason-Dixon Line, the pre–Civil War boundary between free Northern states and Southern slaveholding states. I was also once misinformed about slavery. When I launched the Slave Cabin Project in 2010, I thought slavery was confined to the South. My ignorance was due to the public schools I attended in Kingstree, South Carolina, where I was taught the "happy slave" narrative.

The elegantly renovated Cliveden House, owned by the National Trust for Historic Preservation, was the site of the 1777

Revolutionary War Battle of Germantown, one year after the home's completion. Before the war, Chew owned between forty and sixty enslaved workers on a farm in Kent County, Delaware, and a second home in Philadelphia. Pennsylvania was the first colony during the Revolution that agreed to a gradual end to slavery. Cliveden did not fit the mold of any of my previous stays. Cliveden is the epitome of the house on the hill. It is in contrast to the adjacent two-tier slave dwelling, a two-story carriage house, and four other outbuildings.

On my first visit to Cliveden in June 2011, I slept in the slave dwelling. On my second visit in 2015, I slept in a room over the kitchen at Cliveden House that was used by an enslaved person. During that first visit, I sat for two media interviews, attended a Germantown Historical Preservation Association reception, and dined with others at a local tavern. I altered my presentation to include slave dwellings whose owners stayed connected with the descendants of the enslaved. The presentation proved appropriate for Cliveden's goal to tell more stories of the people who were once enslaved there. The staff said the crowd was the largest ever for the Cliveden Conversations.

The staff provided me with padding, a sleeping bag, and a pillow. But they had given me much more than that. Their gift to me emerged during the National Trust for Historic Preservation's conference on October 27, 2010, in Austin, Texas, where I spoke before a standing-room-only audience. After my talk, Rick Fink, Cliveden's education director, invited me to the property. The next day, I unknowingly sat beside David Young, Cliveden's executive director, on the bus ride to a conference event. He confirmed the invitation. What Rick and David did was what so many others have done. They kicked me out of my comfort zone and my original one-year plan. But they and so many others set me on a different path. Rick and David gave me my first sleepover in a northern state. The ancestors were apparently now leading my work. What must be, will be. The ancestors also made it so with this opportunity at Cliveden to tell more stories of enslaved people. Going to a northern state also presented me with a crash course on slavery in the North. As I drifted off to sleep at Cliveden, I expected to hear sirens and other city noises, but the evening was peaceful. The next morning the soothing sound of falling rain on the trees was quickly interrupted with the squeal of the house security alarm. I set it off when I went to the restroom. As fear of a Rodney King–style whipping ran through my mind, I parked myself in one spot to wait for staff or the police. Luckily, the staff arrived first.

The Cliveden experience prepared me to take on the never-ending stream of people who consistently shove slavery into the southern narrative. I am determined to show that every state east of the Mississippi, many in the Midwest, and some in the Pacific Northwest have ties to slavery.

BUSH-HOLLEY HOUSE

Pouring a liquid on the ground is a libation ritual performed before a sleepover to acknowledge the African ancestors and the millions of them brought to America and their American-born children who built this country. The libation ceremony at the Bush-Holley House in Greenwich, Connecticut, in March 2012 was an unusual moment.

I stood in the damp night air under a budding cherry tree in the garden near the slave dwelling with New Jersey writer Dionne Ford, an African American descendant of an enslaved person and an enslaver. Two northern white men, Canadian biographer Grant Hayter-Menzies and Unitarian minister Reverend David Pettee from Boston, whose ancestors were slave owners, joined the circle. As we held hands, Grant described the moment as a remembrance for the ancestors who lived in all the slave quarters along the Eastern Seaboard and across the South and a blessing for those extant slave dwellings waiting for me to step inside. "*Ase.*"*

At Civil War reenactments, the Confederate actors quickly offered that their ancestors did not enslave people, as if to say the Civil War was not about slavery. I have read my signed copy of Edward Ball's *Slaves in the Family.* None of that fully resonated with me until I attended my first meeting of Coming to the Table (CTTT) in 2011, where I met Dionne, Grant, and David Pettee, three people whose white ancestors owned people of African descent. Coming to the Table connects people to the past, present, and future to find solutions to issues that divide Americans and to foster national healing. Housed at the Eastern Mennonite University's Center for Justice and Peacebuilding in Harrisonburg, Virginia, CTTT was launched in 2006 to connect people with an enslaved-enslaver relationship to help them realize they have shared untold stories about the past and the promise of our collective futures.

---

* "Ase" is Okun language for "amen"—a concept and term shared by most nations, cultures, and religions.

Grant was the reason we held hands and prepared to spend the night together in a slave dwelling at Bush-Holley House, the centerpiece of the Greenwich Historical Society's site on Cos Cob Harbor, three miles east of the Connecticut–New York State line. The preserved Bush-Holley House, built in the 1730s, features architectural elements added during the nineteenth and twentieth centuries. Today, the landscaped gardens are a visual reminder of when the house was used as an artist colony.

Grant's Deep South ancestors had enslaved Black people from the first years of the nineteenth century until Emancipation. Then he learned that his New England ancestors from a century earlier also had been enslavers. Grant's ancestor Captain Benajah Bushnell sold Guy Drock of Norwich, Connecticut, in 1752 to a white woman who wanted to marry Drock. This story was only uncovered through years of research, not only by Drock's descendants but also by the diligence and personal passion of Norwich historian Dale Plummer.

Grant volunteered to contact the Greenwich Historical Society (GHS) and ask them if he could bring the Slave Dwelling Project to the attic room over the Bush-Holley House kitchen. GHS president Debra Mecky agreed. Then Grant asked if he could join the sleepover. He knew that Black people and white people had participated in sleepovers, but he didn't know if I had shared a dwelling with a descendant of an enslaver. I agreed. Grant wondered if I would think of his desire to sleep on the hard floor as a penance to absolve him of "white guilt." He candidly admitted he was ashamed of his slaveholding ancestors but realized that he can't expiate his ancestors' past sins.

Dionne was once only interested in the stories of her enslaved ancestors, but to find them, she had to explore the enslavers' documents. This quest began when her daughter, at five, proclaimed she was white like her father and not Black like Dionne. In a Mississippi bayou cemetery, one of her white ancestors lay atop a hill above the people he enslaved. She wants her daughter to accept her family's ancestry, even her mixed-race great-grandmother, Josephine, and her slave and master parents.

David is related to dozens of New England enslavers, including one branch he shares with Grant, the Leffingwell family of Norwich. He stumbled onto that side of his family in 2006 when he upgraded his Ancestry.com subscription. It led him to the 1774 Rhode Island census that showed that his ancestor Edward Simmons owned four slaves in Newport, Rhode Island. The next day he drove to Newport to fix what he thought was an error. Instead, he found eleven more Newport ancestors who enslaved Africans. Since then he has discovered thirty additional slaveholding ancestors and one ancestor who captained at least five slave ship voyages. All of these newly found slaveholding relatives lived in New England and not the South.

After we poured the libation, genealogist Toni Carrier, curator of the website Lowcountry Africana, where my blogs are posted, helped me open an online chat room on her site. The text messages came fast and furious. I kept up as fast as my Blackberry would allow. I was thankful for those who found the Slave Dwelling Project compelling enough to engage in the live chat room. It also proved I had to improve my technology to communicate with my followers if I wanted to continue offering them an opportunity to participate in sleepovers via a live chat room. The questions also forced me to think more about the spaces for sleepovers and the people who once occupied those spaces. After the live chat, Dionne, Grant, David, and I talked about the challenges ten enslaved people had sharing a twenty-five-by-twenty-foot attic that also served as a storage area. We were in a room above the kitchen. Maneuvering in the space was a challenge. It was set up to be viewed from an adjacent observation area. Allowing us to sleep there was the site curator's worst nightmare. The space was filled with artifacts and replicas that depicted the living quarters of an enslaved family. Because of its cramped size, Grant and I slept there. Allowing too many people in the space would compromise its structural integrity. David and Dionne shared the adjoining observation area, where visitors stood to observe the living quarters. Luckily, we were only separated by a three-foot-high sheet of plexiglass. The kitchen was once separate from the main house, but David Bush in 1777 attached it to the house. We reminisced about how Coming to the Table brought us together. Soon sleep silenced the conversation, but it didn't stop the swirling thoughts and deep emotions within us.

Grant entered the dwelling acknowledging the hearts, souls, and dreams of people who, despite centuries of enslavement, still knew the beauty of being free. He honored them in that chilly, creaking space with the ratatat just over our heads of rapid raindrops bouncing off the shingled roof. On the unforgiving hard floorboards, he panicked briefly for not fully comprehending life in that space for an enslaved family. In their quarters they lacked privacy from slaveholders' ears, forcing them to constantly speak in hushed tones. Unable to change their situation, they endured the summer's heat and winter's cold. They silently rose with the sun to renew their work, knowing that if they stopped, the repercussions could be degrading threats to their dignity or personal safety.

Before Dionne quieted her mind for sleep, she sent a "good night" cell phone message to her family and noticed a genealogy buddy's message. Her friend's ancestors are from Dionne's hometown, Ocean Springs, Mississippi. Their enslaved ancestors are buried in the same Mississippi cemetery as her family, raising the possibility they may even be distant cousins. Her friend asked her to touch the wall and whisper her ancestor's name. Dionne whispered "Johanna" into the still Connecticut air.

The camping pad under David's sleeping bag didn't soften the unforgiving planks. He thought about me and Dionne, on either side of him, and wondered what it was like for us as Black people to share the attic with two descendants of slaveholders. The rain's pitter-patter was a timeless sound that helped him finally fall asleep. Startled by snoring at 4:00 a.m., he awoke suddenly, twisted in his sleeping bag, feeling hot, clammy, and disoriented. In 1750, the people who lived in that attic were probably already in the hot kitchen below baking bread by 4:00 a.m., preparing breakfast for their masters.

By 6:30 a.m. we were awake. I was happy to learn that no one accused me of talking in my sleep—snoring, yes, but not talking. The libation ceremony, the live text chat, and sharing the space with descendants of slave owners had the potential to give me the words I'd mumble in a sleep monologue. The group conversation did continue from the previous night when I blatantly asked David and Grant, "Do you feel like outcasts for revealing the history of the slave owning by your ancestors?" Neither of them retreated. They've accepted their family ties to slaveholders and are handling it in their own ways.

JOSEPH LLOYD MANOR

Salvation comes by Christ alone,
The only Son of God;
Redemption now to every one,
That love his holy Word.

Dear Jesus, we would fly to Thee,
And leave off every Sin,
Thy tender Mercy well agree;
Salvation from our King.

Salvation comes now from the Lord,
Our victorious King.
His holy Name be well ador'd,
Salvation surely bring.

Dear Jesus, give thy Spirit now,
Thy Grace to every Nation,
That han't the Lord to whom we bow,
The Author of Salvation.

Dear Jesus, unto Thee we cry,
Give us the Preparation;

Turn not away thy tender Eye;
We seek thy true Salvation.

These opening stanzas to Jupiter Hammon's poem "An Evening Thought: Salvation by Christ, with Penitential Cries," published on Christmas Day in 1760, reflects his Christian faith and the conditions of his life. Before Hammon penned this poem, he learned to read and write and later worked as a bookkeeper. The Great Awakening, a religious revival that influenced colonial America during the 1730s and 1740s, guided Hammon. During that period Protestant ministers emphasized good behavior and individual faith over secular rationalism. The movement solidified his faith.

Hammon's use of "salvation" and "redemption" are references to his circumstances. Hammon was born into slavery near Lloyd Manor in Lloyd Harbor on New York's Long Island, where he lived his life in bondage from 1711 to about 1806 as the property of Henry Lloyd and later the property of Henry Lloyd's son, Joseph, who moved Hammon to Connecticut. Henry Lloyd supported Hammon's schooling and placed him in the family's business as a bookkeeper and negotiator. With his poem in 1760, Hammon was the first Black poet published in the United Colonies, sixteen years before the United States of America declared independence. Eighteen years after his first published poem, he released "An Address to Miss Phillis Wheatley," the most prominent Black poet and abolitionist of that time. "A Poem for Children with Thoughts on Death" was released in 1782. Hammon's literary portfolio includes at least six poems and three essays published during his lifetime. In 1786 at Joseph Lloyd Manor, he wrote "An Address to the Negroes of the State of New-York" and "An Essay on Slavery." In October 2020, Joseph Lloyd Manor was designated a Literary Landmark in Hammon's honor.

In spite of his enslavement, Hammon's poem "An Evening Thought: Salvation by Christ, with Penitential Cries" makes it clear the master of his life is Jesus Christ and Him alone, wrote blogger Hannah Brown:

> It is amazing how slave owners while understanding the threat that teaching a slave to read and write . . . did not have the foresight to see the even greater threat that slaves believing in God possessed. By allowing slaves to identify with a Creator, the slave masters had unwittingly allowed themselves to become dispossessed of their power and identification as master. The slave once learning of their Creator understood that their true ownership was that of God Himself. Understanding the [slave's] identification with God, Jupiter Hammon's work becomes a silent protest, an insertion of dissent, a break in the slave mentality.

Imagine if Africans of his time had had the privilege of Jupiter Hammon's education. Imagine an America where the Africans' innate creativity was allowed to blossom like Jupiter Hammon's. Imagine what America could have become. Would America have emerged as a society free of the inequities that divide the impoverished descendants of those enslaved and the privileged descendants of the enslavers?

I heard a National Public Radio story on Jupiter Hammon. Months later, in October 2014, I met Jason Crowley, preservation director at the Society for the Preservation of Long Island Antiquities, at the National Preservation Conference in Savannah, Georgia. He brought up the idea of a sleepover. We talked about me coming for a sleepover at the Joseph Lloyd Manor House, a site under their stewardship. Jason was employed at Magnolia Plantation and Gardens in Charleston, South Carolina, before I joined Magnolia as a part-time slave dwelling interpreter while I served as a program officer with the National Trust for Historic Preservation. That conversation led to an August 2015 sleepover at the eighteenth-century Joseph Lloyd Manor on Long Island, New York, which overlooks the scenic Lloyd Harbor. Lloyd Manor is thought to have served as barracks during the American Revolution for Loyalists stationed at the nearby Fort Franklin. The Loyalists repulsed a 1781 attack by French and American troops. In addition to being Jupiter Hammon's home, the house was home to Charles and Anne Morrow Lindbergh during the years leading up to World War II.

Jason connected me with two other historic properties—Sylvester Manor and Thomas Halsey Homestead—also along the stretch of pricey homes on posh Long Island. At Joseph Lloyd Manor, I slept in the room where it was believed Hammon had slept. The second-floor room held the trappings that could easily classify Hammon as an "uppity Negro." It had a bed, fireplace, and two functional large windows with glass. A period-reproduction rope bed with a goose-feather mattress would surely provide me with a comfortable place to lay my head. Langston Hughes once described Hammon as a "privileged slave." It was easy to see how this less stressful living condition could satisfy and support his demand to write.

Before the sleepover, I attended a reception at the house. The audience was impressively diverse. Some had attended a prior lunch with me, and some were visiting the manor for the first time. In a series of one-on-one and group conversations, I engaged the audience of about fifty people regarding the Slave Dwelling Project. Many of them expressed that they would have wanted to spend the night had the invitation been extended with enough notice. I was alone on this night. The house was equipped with Wi-Fi, so I had ample time to communicate on social media and to begin my Joseph Lloyd blog entry.

In 1703, 40 percent of New Yorkers owned slaves. This stay was an example of how slavery in some Northern states was much more intimate because most enslaved people lived in the attic or basement of their owner's home. These homes have been saved not because they served as the living quarters of the enslaved who served the white men who owned them. These homes remain because they've been deemed more important than the enslaved humans who lived in them.

THIRTEEN

RESISTANCE

RESISTANCE CAME LOOKING FOR ME, AND IT FOUND ME. IT FOUND me at the start of the Slave Dwelling Project's third year in 2012. Resistance had not revealed itself to me before, but I am certain enslaved people knew it. They knew it when they stole food and valuables, sabotaged machinery, or ran away. Resistance shoved them before a judge to demand their independence, arguing that their owners reneged on promises of freedom, that they had a free ancestor, or that they had traveled through a free region. Resistance spoke another tongue too, much louder than the others: rebellion! Resistance helped me realize I can raise my voice to tell how the ancestors fought back!

Jennifer Hurst and Elizabeth Kostelny traveled four hundred miles from Richmond, Virginia, to Charleston in early 2012 to invite me to one of the nation's early epicenters of resistance— Bacon's Castle. Hurst was the statewide education coordinator and Kostelny was the executive director at Preservation Virginia, a

123-year-old landmark preservationist group. Preservation Virginia had been awarded a Jessie Ball duPont Fund grant to visit locations around the country to speak to site managers engaged in cutting-edge historic interpretation. They had heard about the Slave Dwelling Project. As we sat and talked in a conference room at the National Trust's office in Charleston, I told them that I wanted to do more than just sleep in a slave dwelling at Bacon's Castle. I told them I also would meet with students and community groups before and after the sleepover. They liked that idea. While in Charleston, Hurst and Kostelny visited the Aiken-Rhett House, once the property of South Carolina governor William Aiken Jr., that has maintained its 1850s slave quarters, and Drayton Hall, a plantation on the Ashley River next door to Magnolia Plantation and Gardens. They also visited other historic sites around the country, but I was the only person they invited to Bacon's Castle. Built in 1665, it is the oldest brick building in North America, where Africans and whites rebelled against Virginia's colonial government. It spurred laws that separated the races.

The Arthur Allen family built a mammoth dwelling as a symbol of extravagant wealth in Virginia's backcountry. Originally, it was called Allen's Brick House. The design of the two-and-a-half-story house with a prominent triple diamond-set chimney distinguished it from the homes of common farmers. The research of genealogist Peighton Young, a graduate teaching assistant at the College of William & Mary, shows that between 1673 and 1774, the Allen family owned as many as one hundred people. Peter and Bess, along with their children Rose, Peter, and Sue, were part of the enslaved community. Around 1673 the Allen family acquired

Simon, Emmanuel, Tony, Stephen, Mingo, and Mathew. Young later learned that Mingo gained his freedom sometime after 1673. "He went on to marry a woman named Charity and fathered a daughter named Jane Mingo," she reported. "The Mingo family line continued to expand in Norfolk and Southampton County well into the 1830s."

Nathaniel Bacon, born in Suffolk, England, arrived in Virginia in 1674 at age twenty-seven. Supported by his father, Bacon acquired a plantation above Jamestown, Virginia's colonial capital, and another plantation at the present site of Richmond. His social position, wealth, kinship ties, and family relationship through marriage with colonial governor William Berkeley led to his quick appointment to the governor's council. Personality clashes between the two ambitious and strong-willed white men, however, severed their cordial relationship.

Bacon and his followers charged that colonial leaders failed to protect them from Native Americans and guarantee ownership of land in the colonial frontier. The Bacon Rebellion was a biracial movement uniting enslaved Africans and indentured Europeans to destroy Jamestown. The uprising alarmed white planters when Black people joined Bacon's movement. "Soon after Bacon's Rebellion they increasingly distinguished between people of African descent and people of European descent. They enact laws which say that people of African descent are hereditary slaves. And they increasingly give some power to independent white farmers and land holders," historian Ira Berlin said. "Now what is interesting about this is that we normally say that slavery and freedom are opposite things—that they are diametrically opposed. But what we see here in Virginia in the late seventeenth century, around Bacon's Rebellion, is that freedom and slavery are created at the same moment."

Before Virginia crushed the uprising, Bacon's followers used Allen's Brick House as a base of operations. Since then, Allen's Brick House has been called Bacon's Castle. Many of Bacon's followers were subsequently executed, but not Bacon. He died in October 1676, reportedly from dysentery. The rebellion collapsed with his death. Virginia hanged twenty-three people for their roles in the rebellion. An investigating committee arrived from England. Following its report to King Charles II, Berkeley was removed as governor and sent back to England, where he died nearly one year after Bacon's death.

A few months after Preservation Virginia came to see me, I was with fifteen people who spent the night in a two-story white clapboard structure with opposing twin chimneys built in 1829 and enlarged in 1849 to house enslaved families at Bacon's Castle. The group included history buffs from California, North Carolina, and Texas, as well as the community from surrounding Surry County. Some people even pitched tents outside the dwelling. It is the last of the eighteen slave houses, built around 1829, remaining at Bacon's Castle. Vacant slave quarters were often left to deteriorate or were demolished after the war to avoid paying property taxes. It is believed that as many as three hundred people were enslaved there at the start of the Civil War. This was the first of my two visits to Surry County, Virginia.

A year after Bacon's death, Bacon's Castle had four enslaved workers. By 1700 the enslaved community had grown to thirteen people. In the early years, enslaved people lived in the garret of the main house. Camilla Pierce's descendants were among a dozen people who joined me for the first Bacon's Castle sleepover. Curled up on a portable chair in the slave quarters, Surry County resident Barbara Anderson wondered aloud if Pierce, her great-great-grandmother, might once have slept under the same roof. She wondered too if she had gone to the field of fluffy white cotton near the musty dwelling to pick cotton, which served as a lucrative crop before the Civil War. "It's an honor to walk over these grounds where my great-great-grandmother once walked," she said. "But the chance to stay in [the] same house where she may have once laid her head—that is just amazing." Barbara Anderson came with her sister, Judy Anderson. She called the event a "once-in-a-lifetime experience." In 2008, the Anderson sisters learned that when Camilla Pierce was born in 1830, she joined a community of seventy-six enslaved people at Bacon's Castle. Most of their information about her came from researching census records and court documents. Their family has scarce oral history about Pierce.

Peighton Young's research into Bacon's Castle's African community extended into the nineteenth century to uncover more acts of resistance, including the 1831 Nat Turner Rebellion in Southampton. Turner's insurrection shocked whites across the South and stiffened laws to control enslaved people. It even led to concern as far away as northeast Florida among free people of color. Plantation owner Zephaniah Kingsley moved his African-born wife Anna Kingsley, his other African wives, and their children to Haiti for fear they'd be enslaved. At Bacon's Castle, John, also known as John Claiborne, was convicted in the Nat Turner uprising. He was possibly sold to a buyer in Alabama or Mississippi. During the Civil War, Black people who ran away obtained weapons and fought slave owners. Several of them liberated enslaved people at Bacon's Castle, including Gilly and his grandchild, who were freed in December 1864.

Students of history are familiar with Nat Turner. Unfortunately for me, growing up in South Carolina, my history books cast Turner as a criminal and terrorist and left no room for discussion. During my second visit at Bacon's Castle in June 2015, a student from Marquette University High School in Milwaukee, Wisconsin, asked me, "If you were enslaved during the period that this nation allowed the practice of slavery, would you acquiesce? If not, whose method would you have followed to obtain your freedom?"

Prior to this sleepover, I would have easily answered abolitionist and orator Frederick Douglass, who was once enslaved. But after my experience at Bacon's Castle, I began to lean toward rebel Nat Turner. That opinion did not sit well with everyone, but that is the power of having profound, frank, and uncomfortable discussions in a place that once housed the enslaved. My opinion of Turner was influenced during a nearby tour earlier that day of the location where Turner led the raid.

It would be the first of many uncomfortable talks. I've developed a style of interjecting questions to stimulate thought. I've moderated conversations that have evolved to topics beyond preserving slave dwellings—especially when descendants of the enslavers join in. Many of those conversations spark intense and sometimes angry reactions. I've learned to treat angry people, whites and Blacks, like people, to engage with them, and eventually tempers cool.

At the historic Beauregard-Keyes House in the New Orleans French Quarter, for instance, I stepped in when a white man's views on slavery offended others, nearly sparking a fistfight. He had suggested slavery was not the theft of labor, arguing that enslaved people got free housing, were fed, and were given clothing—so the labor wasn't "free." At Thomas Jefferson's Monticello, I had intervened during the contentious debate regarding Jefferson's relationship with Sally Hemings that nearly led to an altercation. Weddings at former plantation sites are another issue that evokes strong emotions among people who consider nuptials at plantations an offense to the ancestors. When the topic is mentioned, white people consistently do not object to weddings at plantations. But Black people feel differently. While I have become a conversation starter, I am sometimes forced to act as referee.

Fort Snelling

I could not sleep. Too many buzzing mosquitoes. I slid under the blanket, but when I came up for air the menacing little devils attacked like dive-bombers. Maybe if I opened the windows the summer breeze from the Mississippi River would blow them off course. I struggled to again think about why I was in this place, a sturdy building poised on a high bluff overlooking the river. It was a re-creation of the original 1800s structure with gray stone walls and a brown brick floor. This is what it looked like when an enslaved couple, Dred Scott and his wife, Harriett, lived here 150 years ago.

I wanted to sleep in this space because of what this fort and the Scotts represent to American history. The Scotts' struggle redefined

American citizenship. This is not a Deep South slave dwelling on the Mississippi. This sleepover brought me to Fort Snelling, a former United States Army post in the midwestern city of St. Paul, Minnesota, at the confluence of the Mississippi and Minnesota Rivers. Sleeping here on August 14, 2018, illustrated that people of African descent were enslaved even in the free territory that later became the state of Minnesota, "the Star of the North."

Southern slaveholders had invested in Minnesota, including William Aiken Jr., South Carolina governor from 1844 to 1846. In the summer of 1857, Aiken loaned between $10,000 and $20,000 to the struggling University of Minnesota. As the owner of more than seven hundred enslaved workers, Aiken was flush with money to invest. When Aiken arrived in Minnesota, likely traveling up the Mississippi on a steamboat, the campus had been closed for three years. His loan briefly reopened the university in 1858, but accumulated debts before the end of the year forced it to close again.

Manifest Destiny and the Louisiana Purchase created the need for forts like Snelling west of the Mississippi. Manifest Destiny was the nineteenth-century notion that America was destined by God to expand across North America. The Louisiana Purchase in 1803 bolstered a belief in Manifest Destiny. The land deal with France added more than five million acres to the United States, nearly doubling the size of the country and eventually opening space for fifteen new states, including Minnesota. Removing Native Americans was the next step before white settlers pushed westward. Troops garrisoned at Fort Snelling purged Native people. Between the late 1820s and the early 1850s, more than one hundred enslaved workers built and operated the fort. It's often said that America's original sin was slavery. America's original sin was the forced removal of Indigenous people from their land.

As states organized within the new territory, the status of slavery became a contentious debate in the United States Congress. Southern states wanted slavery extended west, but Northern states just as strongly opposed admitting new states as slave states. The 1820 Missouri Compromise attempted to balance the interest of free states and slave states.

With the help of antislavery lawyers, Dred Scott petitioned the St. Louis Circuit Court in 1846 to seek his freedom. Scott argued that following his time in portions of the new territories that disallowed slavery, he considered himself to be free. Scott had traveled with his owner, army surgeon John Emerson, from Missouri, a slave state, to Illinois, a free state, and then to Wisconsin, a free territory. Eventually, Emerson took Scott to Fort Snelling, where he served as the fort's surgeon from 1836 to 1840. At Fort Snelling, Scott married Harriet Robinson in either 1836 or 1837. Emerson later became a medical officer in Florida during the Seminole War. The Scotts then moved to St. Louis, Missouri, with Emerson's wife, Irene, until John Emerson left the military in 1842, a year before he died. Four years later, Dred and Harriet Scott filed separate lawsuits to obtain their freedom.

After Dr. Emerson's death in 1843, the Scotts had become Irene Emerson's property. After waiting for just over a decade, the Scotts got an answer. The Supreme Court ruled seven to two in March 1857 that all Black people, enslaved and free, were not and could not become US citizens and the court didn't have the power to exclude slavery from the territories. Therefore, the court ruled, the Missouri Compromise was unconstitutional. The stunning decision set the nation on the path to civil war to settle the question of slavery. When Dred Scott's legal struggle failed, it prolonged slavery in the United States territories, including parts of Minnesota created through the Louisiana Purchase. The year after the Dred Scott decision, Minnesota was admitted as a free state. The Supreme Court's opinion stood until 1866, when the Congress enacted the Fourteenth Amendment to the US Constitution, granting citizenship to all persons born or naturalized in the United States, including former slaves.

Following my visit to Fort Snelling, I've vowed to look for more historic figures like Dred Scott. So far, I've visited the Harriet Tubman Museum and Educational Center in Cambridge, Maryland, not far from where she was born in Dorchester County, Maryland. I didn't sleep there on that trip, but I'd like to return for a sleepover. As a Civil War reenactor, I find Tubman's time with Black Civil War soldiers in Beaufort County, South Carolina, and Folly Island near Charleston before the Massachusetts Fifty-Fourth's attack on Battery Wagner to be vital in telling the story of the Black man's fight for freedom. I also want to sleep in Frederick Douglass's home. I am determined to see these places and others like them.

Managers of historic sites have depended on archaeology to re-create buildings that are no longer on the landscape. James Madison's Montpelier and Thomas Jefferson's Monticello have used this method of re-creating buildings. The building where I slept at Fort Snelling was built on the footprint of the old structure.

The Minnesota Historical Society invited me to Fort Snelling. It was a risky decision. Matthew Cassady, the fort's program specialist, was very familiar with my work, but he was not convinced that the Twin Cities community would be excited to hear what I had to say. He felt most Minnesotans believe the history of enslavement was a Southern issue, not realizing that its reach extended north and that Minnesota was also complicit in supporting slavery during the first half of the 1800s. Would anyone be interested in hearing this story that is at odds with the stereotype of "Minnesota nice"? He planned two programs for the day: a free public lecture about the Slave Dwelling Project and my work and a special ticketed after-hours tour of the site to explore the stories of enslaved people at Fort Snelling.

As an admitted worrier, he made frequent checks with the box office to monitor ticket sales. Two days before the event, only three out of forty tickets had been reserved. If few people were interested in the tour, how many would come for the presentation? In this time of divisiveness, Cassady wondered whether the topic was too difficult for people to handle. He was afraid that low attendance would embarrass the society.

On the day of the event, Cassady picked me up at the airport for a meeting with the fort's staff and tour of the grounds. But all the while he was distracted by a gnawing worry that no one would come to the events. But to his surprise, when the time came for the afternoon presentation, the auditorium was packed with a diverse group of guests of all ages. Many in the audience were people of color, a group the site had traditionally underserved with its programs and events, Cassady told me. What was meant to be an hour-long program became a two-hour discussion with dozens of people who stayed to ask me additional questions. People crowded the ticket desk to inquire about the sold-out evening tour. The response was more than Cassady could have imagined. For many of the people in the audience, it was their first visit to Fort Snelling. Several had never felt the fort had anything to offer them, but now they were connected to its history. Cassady was pleased that guests also talked and laughed among themselves as they explored a painful history together. In doing so, they created a sense of community inclusive of people of different ages and cultural backgrounds.

* * *

The fire of resistance burned in Nat Turner and Dred Scott. Like John Brown and Frederick Douglass and Martin Luther King Jr. and Malcolm X, they chose different ideological paths from their contemporaries to express their anger. Turner and Scott, however, share Southampton County, Virginia, as the place of their births. Scott and Turner were born in Southampton at the turn of the nineteenth century in 1799 and 1800, respectively. Each also has been bestowed with historic markers to memorialize their existence. The markers stand along Southampton County highways in southeastern Virginia.

FOURTEEN

GARDEN CLUBS

BEFORE JEFFERSON DAVIS WAS ELECTED PRESIDENT OF THE Confederacy, he owned seven hundred slaves. James Lucas was one of them. Lucas's pregnant mother, Silvey, was picking cotton on October 11, 1833, when the infant she would name James decided to leave her womb. Women in the field "fixed my maw up so she didn' lose no time," Lucas said. "She sho'e was healthy." Silvey's mother came to America on a "big boat." The other Africans called her "O Betty." She spoke a "gibberish" people called "gulluh-talk." Lucas had two owners before Davis bought him. By the time he was an adult, his next master was "Jefferson Davis, hisself," Lucas told an interviewer in the mid-1930s. At the time of the interview, Lucas said he was 104 years old. Davis was good to him, Lucas said, adding that Davis's wife, Varina Howell Davis, was better. The Davises were married in Natchez. "I . . . de only livin' person whose eyes eber seed 'em bofe," Lucas boasted about his odd place in history. By the time Lucas was an adult with a wife and two children, "de wah broke out" and the Davises left Natchez.

Natchez has not forgotten the wedding of Jefferson and Varina, his second wife, when she was seventeen years old and eighteen years his junior. The nuptials are remembered during the annual Natchez Pilgrimage, which began in 1932 as the Natchez Garden Club's monthlong spring spree to open stunning privately owned antebellum mansions to tourists hungry for Southern nostalgia and that tired lost-cause narrative. Since then the event has evolved into biannual spring and fall pageants of hoopskirted debs paired with beaux in Southern garb. The Natchez pageantry stacks millions of dollars in local cash drawers. King cotton once covered Mississippi, and the cash crop spawned in Natchez nearly as many millionaires as New York City. In the first half of the nineteenth century, the state was the center of global cotton production. With that kind of wealth, Natchez businessmen built grand homes and bought coffles of slaves at Forks of the Road, the South's second-busiest slave market after New Orleans. The historic home tours may have saved the city during the Depression, but they also "served as a celebration of the Confederacy with people praising that time period without acknowledging how those homes were built and cared for and how that wealth came to be," said Roscoe Barnes III, cultural heritage and tourism manager at Visit Natchez.

Slavery's harsh legacy in Natchez likely explains why I've failed to gain access to the slave dwellings behind the city's big houses. The local garden clubs hold access to these slave dwellings, and they aren't buying what I am selling. In Richard Grant's *The Deepest South of All: True Stories from Natchez, Mississippi*, Natchez resident and nationally known chef Regina Charboneau and her husband, Doug, shared some garden club insight. She is the executive chef at King's Tavern, a business she co-owns with Doug. She professed that "the garden clubs don't do any gardening, although we do appreciate flowers." Doug added, "The garden clubs are about raising money, social prestige, tourism, and the historic preservation of antebellum buildings. They're run by women, and they have a lot of power. Natchez is probably the closest thing to a matriarchy that you're going to find in America."

The mission statement on the Natchez Garden Club's website states, "The Natchez Garden Club's community service projects include maintaining the antique rose garden at the James Andrews House/Lawyer's Lodge, and our work at the historic Natchez City Cemetery Camellia Project. We also supply food for the Stewpot and much-needed supplies to the Guardian Shelter." Founded in 1927, the club perpetuates "the history of Natchez, and [aims] to keep the memory of the lives, traditions, and accomplishments of the people who made that history; To sponsor the Natchez Pilgrimage and support other community projects and endeavors." I wonder if any of that includes people who look like me.

The Historic Natchez Foundation submitted my request to sleep in an extant slave dwelling behind one of the city's mansions. The foundation's efforts didn't produce results. Although the old-guard garden club stands in the way, fate intervened. I have spent three nights in two homes where enslaved people lived in Natchez and in a nearby community. Jessica Fleming Crawford, archaeologist and southeast regional director at the Archaeological Conservancy based in Albuquerque, New Mexico, found another path for me to follow. Through her efforts I spent one night in the big house at Prospect Hill Plantation, a conservancy property founded in the early 1800s east of Natchez in Jefferson County. Prospect Hill's owner, Isaac Ross, a South Carolina planter and Revolutionary War veteran, instructed in his will that money from the sale of his property should be used to send people he enslaved to Liberia, a colony in West Africa. Those who made the journey in 1838 named their colony Mississippi. Ross is in a long line of enslavers whose emancipation actions came after they died. I am wondering if they thought their after-the-fact-of-death decisions would grant them admission to Heaven. Jessica also booked me into the Concord Quarters, a former slave dwelling at the Concord Plantation in Natchez. The dwelling is now a bed-and-breakfast owned by an African American couple, Gregory and Deborah Cosey. Concord Quarters is one of those rare cases where the big house is no longer on the landscape, but the dwelling for the enslaved survived.

My uphill battle in Natchez compares to convincing the United Daughters of the Confederacy to yank Confederate monuments from the southern landscape. Garden clubs in the South cherish the built environment of the treasonous part of their history, but they shun the people their ancestors enslaved. The Slave Dwelling Project is a correction to let the public know these beautiful homes are not the entire story. Stolen labor built them.

Natchez and Holly Springs, Mississippi, is a tale of two cities. I've had more success with garden clubs in Holly Springs, once a trading post for cotton plantations just south of Memphis, Tennessee. Black history buffs will likely know immediately that Holly Springs is the birthplace of journalist and anti-lynching activist Ida

B. Wells. Students of history who've taken the house tour, however, will know that tucked away beyond the garden gates of fine mansions stand the living quarters of enslaved people who tended the gardens and cleaned the elegant homes. Those Black gardeners in Holly Springs and Natchez likely did the same kind of work John Cameron did when he was enslaved in Jackson, Mississippi, as "the yard boy" in Howell Magee's garden. "I he'ped keep de yard pretty an' clean, de grass cut, an' de flowers tended to an' cut," Cameron told a WPA interviewer in the mid-1930s. "I taken dat work 'cause I lak's pretty flowers. I lake to buil' frames for 'em to run on an' to train 'em to win'roun'. I could monkey wid 'em all de time."*

What started as a unified plan to tell the stories of the enslaved in Holly Springs, however, has dissipated. For more than a decade, the Slave Dwelling Project partnered with Preserve Marshall County and the Holly Springs Garden Club to present a four-day "Behind the Big House" tour of three mansions and their adjacent slave dwellings to the public. Initially, the partnership blossomed as the groups incorporated the interpretation of slave dwellings into the annual house tours. The first year, 2011, was a success. Since then, however, the relationship has withered on the vine. The Garden Club of Holly Spring prefers the *Gone with the Wind* hoopskirt, mint julep version of history like the folks in Natchez. The club allows access to the architecturally significant homes each April, but it does a poor job of interpreting the human bondage that existed within the garden walls.

---

* Cameron also called Magee a good slave owner, describing in detail how he was good to the people he enslaved.

Despite the diminishing relationship between the two groups, the slave dwelling tour has scored some Mississippi wins. The Mississippi Humanities Council supports the Slave Dwelling Project and the University of Mississippi's Department of History recruits student guides and monitors. Schoolchildren learn about the enslaved ancestors at three properties whose owners have consistently allowed access to the slave dwellings.

A similar "Behind the Big House" tour has been staged across the Mississippi River at the Historic Arkansas Museum in Little Rock; Historic Washington State Park in Hope, Arkansas; and Lakeport Plantation in Lake Village, Arkansas. I did a similar program called "Beyond the Big House" in Charleston with the Historic Charleston Foundation.

A true test of the Slave Dwelling Project's effectiveness comes when I am invited back to a site. An invitation to return is a sign that I am not the only person who believes preserving and interpreting former slave dwellings is the right thing to do. Jenifer Egleston, my coworker at the National Trust for Historic Preservation, and her husband, Chelius Carter, an architect, helped me launch the "Behind the Big House" tour in Holly Springs. They own the Hugh Craft House. In the first year, the tour didn't include students. During the tour's second year in 2012, schoolchildren heard the story, too. Through the years, students stepped inside the space where the enslaved lived at the Hugh Craft House, Burton Place, and Magnolia. Being at the scene of the crime of slavery at these properties evokes a special power of place that moves the emotions.

Dressed in my blue Civil War reenactor's uniform, I was ready for the high school students on April 11, 2012, when they arrived at the Hugh Craft House, built in the middle of the nineteenth century. Because of my experience as a Fort Sumter park ranger, I feared the students would misbehave. Their teachers, however, prepared them, and the orientation they received in the big house by guide Alex Mercedes and Chelius Carter also readied them for the power of the place. The property has a unique wooden slave dwelling with three rooms, a loft, and a basement that oddly served as a smokehouse. The dwelling's white exterior is in stark contrast to the unpainted brown interior. A line of questions about slavery streamed from one student, stirring her emotions to the point that she cried. Her classmates graciously gave her time to recover. This was a true testament of the power of place.

The following day, I was ready for another wave of students at Burton Place, a historic house owned by Jim Pearson, a retired lawyer. Burton Place's redbrick slave dwelling is divided into three compartments, each with a chimney and exterior doors. As the third graders filed in, they too were filled with pertinent questions that I answered in a manner appropriate for a young audience. But then for the second time in two days, the power of place led to tears. The power didn't grip a student. A volunteer chaperone felt it.

In 2013, Memphis firefighter Frank Busby and his wife, Genevieve, a paramedic, owned Magnolia. The previous year, when I initially toured the house, I saw its potential. The Busbys worked frantically to prepare the house for the tour. Extensive renovations by a series of previous owners had attached the once-separated kitchen and slave dwelling to the main house. As a result the average person would not readily identify the space as a place that once housed enslaved people. This attachment meant the space would come with a bed, electricity, and an indoor full bathroom. Joining the structures also made interpreting them much more interesting, giving me the opportunity to explain to the visitors how some spaces that once housed enslaved people are sometimes hidden in plain view. The main house was the filming location for the 1999 movie *Cookie's Fortune*.

Later in the day, I returned to the Hugh Craft House, where I spent the night. During the tour of the slave quarters, a visitor tried to make the point that labor was not free for the slave owner. "The slave owner was economically liable for the feeding, clothing, housing, and healthcare of his slaves, even the nonproductive ones like the young and elderly," the man said. I replied that he can justify slavery economically, but can he justify it morally? Another visitor supported my view and did not allow the economic justification for slavery to carry the day.

Holly Springs' "Behind the Big House" tours are continuing to convince some people and entities that the tour and the Slave Dwelling Project mean no harm. Telling the stories of the enslaved is the right thing to do. I challenge well-established historic house tours across the country with slavery as an element of their histories and an extant slave dwelling to step out of the comfort zone. By doing so, we can present a complete story of this nation's history. Natchez, are you listening?

* * *

The story of what the Igbo people (also known as Ebo or Ibo) from what is now Nigeria and other West African countries did along coastal Georgia to resist slavery is embedded in Gullah Geechee folklore. The actual event in 1803 at a site known as Igbo Landing on St. Simons Island, Georgia, is remembered as the "Myth of the Flying Africans," an enchanting tale of the Africans' courage to face death over enslavement. When St. Simons resident Wallace Quarterman, who was born into slavery in 1844 near Savannah, was asked in 1935 if he knew the story of Igbo Landing, he replied, "Ain't you heard about them? Well, at that time Mr. Blue he was the overseer and . . . Mr. Blue he go down one morning with a long whip for to whip them good. . . . Anyway, he whipped them good and they got together and stuck that hoe in the field and then . . . rose up in the sky and turned themselves into buzzards and flew right back to Africa. . . . Everybody knows about them."

Quarterman shared this metaphor of the Africans' ability to transform the hardships of slavery into the magical ability of flight. It has inspired writers and filmmakers, including Toni Morrison, who adapted the myth of the flying Africans for her novel *Song of Solomon*.

The event unfolded in the spring of 1803, when Igbo people arrived in Savannah, where they were sold into slavery and placed on a smaller boat for the transfer to St. Simons Island. During the journey down the coast, about seventy-five Africans rebelled, forcing the two white slave agents to jump from the boat to their deaths. Once on shore, the Africans sang. They marched with their chief into Dunbar Creek to die en masse.

Sixteen years before Quarterman's birth, Julia Rush was born on St. Simons. It is unknown whether they were acquainted, but it's likely she also heard the Igbo Landing story. Unlike the Africans who took their lives to escape slavery, Rush faced the humiliation of bondage. As a child Rush played with the daughter of her owner from the morning until night. When Rush grew older, she worked in the white family's kitchen. She and the other enslaved people, Rush said, were treated well. They didn't want for food, clothing, or time off to tend to their own interests. But that changed suddenly for Rush when her owner's wife died. He divided his slaves among his children. Rush became the property of her former white play-mate, who had married and was living in Carrollton, Georgia. Her former playmate beat Rush for the slightest offense. She thought her husband had been intimate with Rush. Rush's owner even ordered her husband to beat Rush with a cowhide whip. The white woman cut Rush's long straight hair. It is stories like these that are fading from the Black consciousness of St. Simons, where develop-ment has overtaken the island.

The island's Cassina Garden Club is preserving the island's Black history as the proud stewards of two slave cabins at the Hamil-ton Plantation. The garden club invited me to the island in March 2015 to help raise $400,000 to restore the cabins to be as historically accurate as possible. A garden club with the desire to restore extant slave dwellings surprised me. I envisioned garden clubs with retired and well-kept white women interested only in plants. Well, maybe not. The women in Natchez don't care about plants.

The restoration of the tabby slave cabins, the only slave dwell-ings remaining at Hamilton Plantation, reversed more than a cen-tury of weather and wear. To my surprise, the plantation grew more Sea Island cotton than rice. One of the cabins still had its original chimney in the middle of the structure, a sign it was built for two families. The second cabin is now the club's meeting space. It is adorned with exhibits that interpret the cabins and slavery.

To raise the money, the club organized several activities, including a Cabin Fever Weekend, which included island tours and a stop at Igbo Landing. Would I have followed the chief into the river? I don't think I would have done that. I would have wanted to live and take my chances with bondage. Similar acts of mass suicide occurred on slave ships when Africans jumped overboard. The post–Civil War freedom song "Oh Freedom" that later became a civil rights anthem includes the line "Before I'd be a slave I'd be buried in my grave." The Africans who took their lives gave early meaning to those lyrics.

FIFTEEN

ℱAMILY ℛEUNIONS

AFTER EMANCIPATION, BLACK PEOPLE IN FREE STATES PLACED ads in newspapers to find their formerly enslaved relatives. The notices served as testaments to their enduring hope and determination to regain what slavery stole from them. Four months after the end of the Civil War, Saml (Samuel) Dove in Utica, New York, once a leading abolitionist city, placed an ad in the *Colored Tennessean* newspaper in Nashville to seek information about his family.

SAML. DOVE wishes to know of the whereabouts of his mother, Areno, his sisters Maria, Neziah, and Peggy, and his brother Edmond who were owned by Geo. Dove, of Rockingham county, Shenandoah Valley, Va. Sold in Richmond, after which Saml. and Edmond were taken to Nashville,

Tenn., by Joe Mick; Areno was left at the

Eagle Tavern, Richmond

Respectfully yours,

SAML. DOVE.

Utica, New York, Aug. 5, 1865-3m

It appears (Samuel) Dove may have also been enslaved by Geo (George) Dove in Virginia, but he may have escaped to New York state. It's unknown whether Dove found his mother and siblings. It's also unknown how many of the thousands of ads placed after Emancipation led to reunions. The Last Seen database, however, contains nearly one hundred ads announcing searches that ended happily. One of them appeared in the *Reading Times and Dispatch* in Reading, Pennsylvania, on July 26, 1871.

POTTSTOWN has an Enoch Arden* in the

shape of a colored man named James Dogan,

who was a slave prior to the rebellion, and,

escaping into the Union lines, afterwards be-

came [became] a soldier and fought all through the

war. He became separated from his family,

and not hearing from them for several years,

subsequently married again. Recently he

learned of the whereabouts of his first wife

---

* "Enoch Arden" is a poem by Alfred, Lord Tennyson. In it, a happily married fisherman suffers financial problems and becomes a merchant seaman. He is shipwrecked, and after ten years on a desert island, he returns home to discover that his beloved wife, believing him dead, has remarried and has a new child.

and family, and is about to return to them,
his second wife giving her hearty consent.

Dogan's reunion with his family is likely the first in a series of small and intimate Black family gatherings at the dawn of freedom. Since then Black family reunions have become popular summertime celebrations. We gather most often at hotels or other venues that cater to large groups. We've also met with family in parks, church basements, and backyards. The Atlantic slave trade, domestic slavery in North America, and the Manifest Destiny doctrine that more than doubled the size of the United States has scattered African DNA across this continent and beyond. The twentieth century's Great Migration also sent us fleeing the segregated South for northern states in pursuit of happiness and better-paying jobs. Rejoining these dispersed kinship pieces is a challenging puzzle. Black families have used plantation records to find loved ones, but when they don't exist and census records offer limited information, the chances of finding a family's past is slim.

Genealogy and DNA matches, archaeology, and archival primary sources are helping families fill those gaps. For one family, a slave auction bill of sale led them to a seventeen-year-old girl who arrived in Charleston on a vessel from Cameroon.

According to Martin family oral history and documents, when she arrived in America, the girl was named Trasie. The bill of sale shows that Marie Louise Imbert, a new resident of Charleston, sold Trasie to Burnette Martin, the wife of Louis Martin, for $300 on July 1, 1799. Trasie was subsequently sold on December 17, 1799, to John Martin, a planter from Jenkinsville in Fairfield County,

South Carolina. Around 1802, Trasie gave birth to Katie, and Katie had at least six, possibly seven children, who are said to have been fathered by the enslaver Martin. Katie's children with Martin were Vara, Benjamin, Ellen, Moses, Jerry, and John. She also had a son, Nathan, whose father is unknown. Katie Martin Lattie died on August 26, 1892, at age ninety. Today, more than seven thousand of her descendants live in thirty-eight states, Washington, DC, and overseas. They include educators, engineers, medical professionals, businesspeople, judges, politicians, and an astronaut, Charles F. Bolden Jr., who flew on four space shuttle missions. In 1966, the United Martin Family, with chapters in seven states, held its first family reunion at Hampton, Virginia. Since then the Martins have met nearly annually to celebrate their heritage and kinship and to proudly recognize their family's accomplishments.

I've attended my own family reunions, and through the Slave Dwelling Project I've participated in family celebrations at McCollum Farm in Davis County, North Carolina, and James Madison's Montpelier. During my first visit to Bacon's Castle in 2012, I met Barbara Anderson and her sister, Judy Anderson. They are related to Camellia Pierce, who was enslaved at Bacon's Castle. The sisters were reluctant to participate in the Bacon's Castle sleepover. They only came on the advice of their pastor. After hearing the story of their ancestor, however, they organized a reunion at Bacon's Castle the following year. Some of the owners of former plantation sites also encourage family reunions on their property. Larry Faulkenberry, owner of Goodwill Plantation near Columbia, South Carolina, invites residents from the nearby Eastover community to hold family reunions at Goodwill. Middleton Place,

Magnolia's neighbor on the Ashley River northwest of Charleston, has reunions that include the white Middletons and the descendants of the people who were enslaved there. Some in the descendant community have the Middleton surname.

Not all African Americans, however, have accepted known family ties to plantations. It's disappointing that some Black people don't want to have family reunions at plantation sites. Community organizer Louis Smith of Summerville, South Carolina, is one of them. He believes plantations should be forced to go away. He once told me plantations should be burned to the ground. Not all former plantation sites have opened their gates to Black family reunions. The fear of demands for reparations has built a wall between them and the descendants. I am hoping that number will decline. Descendants of enslaved people can possibly find their roots if more former plantation sites interact with them.

By the third year of the Slave Dwelling Project, managers of historic sites were inviting me to their properties. I had gained a good reputation helping to highlight responsible stewards of slave dwellings and those who've accurately interpreted the enslaved people who lived in those dwellings. My position as a program officer with the National Trust for Historic Preservation also gave me an entrée with site managers. The Slave Dwelling Project's wave of media attention also helped to spread my message across the country. Somerset Place Historic Site in Creswell, North Carolina, is an example of a former plantation site that has opened its gates to its descendant community and invites Black families to hold reunions on the property. When Karen Hayes, Somerset's site manager, presented me with the idea of doing a sleepover there during a family reunion, I immediately accepted her offer. I agreed on the condition, however, that I assist in planning the event. I was not involved with setting the activities of other family reunions. Nevertheless, I did not want the Slave Dwelling Project to detract from the family's plans at Somerset. Wilhelmenia "Mina" Wilson of El Cerrito, California, in the San Francisco Bay area, was my liaison to the Dickerson-Wood family, whose origins in America began at Somerset. They subsequently agreed to merge the Slave Dwelling Project with their reunion. To enhance it further, I added living historians to the public part of the event. The living historians were presenting as the family arrived. Jerome Bias, a Mebane, North Carolina, furniture maker, was demonstrating cooking in the kitchen's hearth. Sparks flew as blacksmith Gilbert Walker of Savannah, Georgia, pounded hot metal. North Carolina actress and storyteller Carolyn Evans joined Dontavius Williams, a York County, South Carolina, storyteller, to give voice to the ancestors.

At Somerset the threads that tie the Dickerson-Wood family's African past to their American present began on June 10, 1786, with Kofi and Sally. They were aboard the *Camden*, a two-masted brig owned by Josiah Collins and his family. The ship held them and seventy-eight other captured West African men, women, and children. The vessel arrived at Edenton in eastern North Carolina, where the Africans began the arduous and dangerous work to transform swampland into cropland.* The Collins family watched as the Africans dug by hand a six-mile canal through dense timberland to

---

* According to the family's history, Kofi died in 1843. Sally was born in 1775, and she died in 1850.

connect the Scuppernong River with Lake Phelps, later used to irrigate rice fields at Somerset. Josiah Collins, newly arrived from Somersetshire, England, with his son, Josiah Collins II, and two local businessmen partnered to use the free labor to turn one hundred thousand acres into a rice-growing plantation. The elder Collins bought his partners' shares before he died in 1819. Josiah Collins III, one of his seven grandchildren, inherited five thousand acres, including Somerset and its one hundred enslaved workers. The skilled Africans made Somerset one of the South's most profitable plantations, which in turn positioned Collins as the third-largest slaveholder in North Carolina with 328 enslaved workers. Prior to 1865, about eight hundred people had been enslaved at Somerset.

Africans died during the canal's construction. Only eleven of the original eighty Africans brought to North Carolina survived to 1819, and only five of them lived to produce multigenerational families at Somerset, according to the family's history. Among them are Guinea Jack and his wife, Fanny, and Kofi and his life mate, Old Aunt Sally, a Guinea Negro. She was eleven years old when she and Kofi arrived at Somerset. At age fourteen Sally gave birth to a daughter they named Hannah, who was the first of five children, followed by daughters Betty, Murriah, and Neisa, and son Kofi Jr.[*]

---

[*] According to the Dickerson-Wood family, the birth and death dates for Sally's children are Hannah, July 9, 1789–June 21, 1828; Betty, November 20, 1797–May 6, 1850; Murriah, June 1, 1800, to sometime prior to 1843; Neisa, June 10, 1803, to sometime between 1840 and 1843; and Kofi Jr., 1807 to sometime between 1839 and 1843. Betty and Murriah produced multigenerational families, with the Dickerson-Wood family being descendants of Murriah's son George Dickerson (1826 to before 1900), who was the father of Lucy Dickerson Wood.

For most African Americans, their ancestors' departure port and country of origin remain unknown, leaving their African roots open for speculation. Michael Gomez, author of *Exchanging Our Country Marks*, shows that Africans brought to Somerset were Igbo from today's southeast Nigeria, Cameroon, and Gabon. The Igbo/Biafrans have a reputation of resisting slavery by suicide, like their countrymen who took their lives in 1803 at Igbo Landing on St. Simons Island, Georgia. In John S. Bassett's 1899 book, *Slavery in the State of North Carolina*, he presents an account from a former Somerset overseer who watched Africans drown themselves. "At night they would begin to sing their native songs, and become so wrought up that, they would grasp their bundles of personal effects, swing them on their shoulders, and setting their faces towards Africa, would march down into the water singing as they marched till recalled to their senses only by the drowning of some of the party."

The Dickerson-Wood family had not gathered together for a family reunion in nearly three decades, but after months of planning the reunion was set for August 3, 2019, at Somerset. Lucy Dickerson and Arthur R. Wood were both born in North Carolina a few years prior to the end of the Civil War. They had ten children, five boys and five girls. Mina Wilson's maternal grandfather, Arthur Lorenzo Wood, was the second-born child. Wilson's mother, Lucy Wilhelmina Wood, and her first cousins, who are the grandchildren of Lucy Dickerson and Arthur R. Wood, had organized previous reunion events. Most of them had passed away. That presented the moment for Wilson and the other Dickerson-Wood great-grandchildren to follow their elders' example to inculcate the younger relatives with the importance of family connections. The reunion's theme "Honoring the Legacy of Our Ancestors—Restoring Family Connections" encircled the reunion logo printed on different colored T-shirts to represent the four family lines. Organizers expected forty-five people, many of whom had never met.[*]

The family's first reunion in 1987 came a year after the release of Dorothy Spruill Redford's book *Somerset Homecoming: Recovering a Lost Heritage*. In addition to connecting the family to Kofi and Sally, her research also uncovered other branches of the family's lineage. The book got author Alex Haley's attention. He wrote a blurb for its cover. "Dorothy's study is the best, most beautifully researched, and most thoroughly presented Black family history that I know of," Haley wrote. Redford only knew Haley through his groundbreaking family saga *Roots*, a bestselling novel and the basis of the 1970s television miniseries of the same name that follows his African ancestor Kunta Kinte's journey from the Gambia to America. Redford had invited Haley to the reunion, but there was no guarantee he would attend. But Haley did come to the event, surprising Redford, who shocked Haley with a back-crushing embrace. North Carolina governor James Martin stepped from a helicopter to greet the family. He asked them, "Did you hear it? Did you hear the sound in your head calling you home?"

For the 2019 reunion, family members in California, Georgia, Maryland, New York, North Carolina, Texas, and Virginia

---

[*] Lucy Dickerson, 1863–April 26, 1927; Arthur R. Wood, March 13, 1861–March 28, 1925; Arthur Lorenzo Wood, 1886–1962; Lucy Wilhelmenia Wood, February 2, 1918–August 14, 2016. Lucy Wilhelmenia Wood is the daughter of Arthur Lorenzo Wood.

rendezvoused at a Raleigh, North Carolina, hotel a day before the event at Somerset. Mina Wilson flew in from San Francisco with her teenage children, Ma'lia Gibson and Malcolm Gibson. Mina Wilson and her brother Charles Wilson and their sisters Margaret Hasan and Deborah Najee-ullah also attended the reunion. They are the great-great-grandchildren of George Dickerson, Murriah's third child and Sally's daughter.

When they all arrived at the hotel, concerns rose that the weather might ruin the following day's events. Flash flood warning alerts pinged cell phones as thunderstorms rolled through central North Carolina. The next morning, they began a 150-mile caravan under cloudy skies and intermittent rain to Creswell in northeastern North Carolina.

If the showers continued, the family had no backup plan for the outdoor reunion at a site some of them considered inappropriate for a Black family celebration. Why were they meeting at Somerset, a former plantation where four generations of their family had been enslaved? One of the family's matriarchs, ninety-six-year-old Essie McCullough of New York City, and sixteen-year-old Malcolm Gibson questioned the decision to hold the event at Somerset. Mina Wilson, Kofi and Sally's seventh-generation great-granddaughter, attempted to explain Somerset's relevance to her son. But Malcolm only shook his head, unable to comprehend her message. That message became clear, however, when the family arrived at Somerset. A black sign at Somerset's entrance displayed "Welcome Descendants" in large gold letters. Karen Hayes and the Somerset staff greeted the family warmly. Michelle Lanier, executive director of the North Carolina Division of State Historic Sites, which manages Somerset, presented McCullough with a colorful bouquet. Then Lanier told McCullough and the rest of the family about her enslaved ancestors. Part of Lanier's childhood was spent in a Gullah community on Hilton Head Island, South Carolina. She told the family a story she's shared many times before. Lanier's philosophy of connecting people to the sites she manages might explain why she greeted the family and why she has vigorously supported the Slave Dwelling Project's efforts in North Carolina. As Lanier shared her story with McCollough and her relatives, she also told them they stood in a place of power. Then McCollough spoke with pride as she recognized the importance of the family's ties to the former plantation.

Charles Lorenzo Wilson and his wife, Leslie Bell-Wilson, however, immediately knew why Somerset was important to his family. The Wilsons were married in 2003 at Somerset, where his mother, Lucy Wood Wilson's, paternal ancestral lineage began in the United States. Charles and Leslie Wilson experienced the same resistance from some of their relatives and friends prior to their African-themed wedding at Somerset Place. He is also a seventh-generation descendant of Kofi and Sally. Returning for the 2019 reunion was his seventh visit to Somerset, his "maternal ancestral home." The family reunion was just another opportunity for Wilson to introduce his younger relatives to some of their American roots. By noon the weather miraculously cleared to present an ideal day for the celebration, a gift some attributed to the ancestors.

As the greetings ended, family members began to peel away to mingle with the public and observe the living historians who offered vignettes into the lives of the enslaved, who built a culture of survival.

They told the stories of enslaved field workers who prepared a quick meal cooked under the hot sun on the blade of a hoe, giving rise to the term "hoecake." They talked about abolitionists whose hidden symbols guided freedom-seekers to safety and who showed runaways how to conceal their scent from pursuing bloodhounds. Then Dontavius Williams performed "The Chronicles of Adam." Williams began with Adam's master telling him he was getting to be a big boy. The plantation owner asked Adam to show a visitor how fast he could run and how high he could jump. Adam was so proud when he received applause. Then the visitor told the plantation owner, "I'll give you $300 for him." At that moment Adam felt the light drain through his feet into the dirt. "The last thing I heard was my mother crying," Adam said. "Please don't take my boy!" Adam's mother pleaded. "That was the last time I saw or heard my mother," Adam said. "But I still have this stocking doll she made for me to keep me safe." The living historians invoked deep thought in Margaret Hasan and a greater appreciation of her ancestors. For her the presentations were a "come-to-self moment" that helped her appreciate the level of pride and mother wit they possessed. Dontavius's portrayal of Adam also made her aware that her ancestors couldn't shape their futures and that she should strive for self-determination to honor their memory.

Mina Wilson felt an embrace from behind. Her son, Malcolm, squeezed her and whispered, "Mom, I get it. This is really cool!" That message Wilson shared with her son began to resonate with him during a hike around Somerset with newfound cousins. Three-year-old Mubeen Ali Najee-ullah, son of Tariq and Muslimah Najee-ullah of Catonsville, Maryland, made a different kind of connection. The fiercely independent child talked as he walked the fence line along the property's perimeter. He paused for a toddler's soliloquy. The adults watched and listened from a distance. Muslimah Najee-ullah was not concerned because it was her son's habit to be alone. Then she concluded Mubeen Ali was holding conversations with his ancestors.

The bustling activities of the day slowed. The heat waned as the setting sun kissed the horizon along the 16,600-acre Lake Phelps rimmed with old cypress, where enslaved workers injured clearing the swamp were left overnight and found dead the next morning. At night the frog-cicada chorus swelled and flying insects buzzed louder. But then a peacefulness descended under a star-studded sky. After dinner, most of the family members returned to the Raleigh hotel. Margaret Hasan and Deborah Najee-ullah, Mubeen's grandmother, Charles and Leslie Wilson and Charles Wilson's sisters, Mina Wilson and family friend Hazel Reid, remained to sit for a fireside chat before the sleepover. They were among a dozen people who moved into position for the conversations. The racially mixed group included the staffs at Somerset and Historic Stagville, another former North Carolina plantation site Lanier manages, the Slave Dwelling Project living historians, and a law enforcement officer, who acknowledged his ancestors were overseers at Somerset.

Charles Wilson observed that the family approached the fire with reverence, knowing the ancestors rejoiced at their willingness to pause and walk in their footsteps, listen to their souls, speak their words, and see their truths. The people around the circle engaged in a heartfelt discussion about the day's experience with the living historians. Then the conversation returned to another Black family's rift with the living historians. That family is also descended from enslaved people at Somerset. They held a separate family reunion that coincided with the Dickerson-Wood reunion. Some members of the other family took issue with the living historians dressed in period attire. They called their portrayals of enslaved people disrespectful buffoonery.

Charles Wilson concluded the different view is a matter of perspective. "Are you the descendants of Africans who were enslaved or are you merely the descendants of slaves?" he asked. Mina Wilson said her family didn't come from slavery, but they came through slavery.

Leslie Bell-Wilson paid homage to all of the ancestors who survived being chained and inhumanely transported across the Atlantic from their African homelands to America, where they and their descendants were stripped of human identity "only" because of the color of their skin.

Mina Wilson listened as the family discussed their lived experience and reflected on the history and legacy of their ancestors. They talked about the socioeconomic realities of their lives that emanate from the wealth stolen from their ancestors. She observed as the white people in the circle "assumed a posture of deep listening. They created space to understand more deeply the reality that we, as the descendants of the enslaved people, shared. They created space within themselves to fully hear our voices. Their positioning of themselves in such a way made us feel heard, honored, relevant, and important; a gift given to us in the space where we sat and in the conversation in which we were engaged."

Deborah Najee-ullah also noted the white people were silent, a behavior she has seen often in discussions that include slavery and other racial issues. Were they too intimidated to speak? "It is, however, a curious phenomenon to me and a little disconcerting," she said. "The exchange becomes one-sided, imbalanced, incomplete, and cloaked. Yet the fireside chat deeply inspired and moved me with a heightened sense of connectedness to Somerset Place."

At midnight the group sang "Happy Birthday" to Deborah before settling in for the night. The living historians joined me in one of two replicas of the original slave dwellings. The family slept in the plantation's hospital. Charles and Leslie Wilson prepared their bedding in the operating room. Mina and her sisters, Deborah and Margaret, slept in the sickroom with a family friend, Hazel Reid of New York City. As they labored to inflate air mattresses, they chastised themselves for complaining about lowering their middle-aged bodies to the floor. The ancestors had it even harder, harder than they could ever imagine.

Falling asleep was easy. Staying asleep was a challenge. Throughout the night Mina, her sisters, and Hazel rose to scurry across an open field to a distant outhouse. On the third trip, the sisters complained the facility was not nearby, but then they spontaneously burst into a collective laugh when they realized the inconvenience was just for one night and not a lifetime. "Sally and Kofi, we ain't," Mina said. That realization solidified another poignant moment of appreciation for what the ancestors endured when they had to pull up their skirt tails to tromp across wet grass in the dark to answer nature's call.

After sunrise, they stood in a circle to pray to the ancestors. Between each invocation, they poured a libation. Charles Wilson gave the final prayer, an appreciation for the ancestors who endured with a sense of purpose. With tears streaming down his cheeks, he expressed gratitude for them. The ancestors could suffer two deaths. The first came when they died. The second could occur if their descendants forget them.

SIXTEEN

IMPRESSIONS OF THE ENSLAVED

THIS TALE FROM A SLAVE CABIN IS A BLEND OF MEMORIES FROM PEOPLE WHO WERE ENSLAVED ON SOUTH CAROLINA PLANTATIONS. IN THE MID-1930S, THEY SHARED STORIES ABOUT THEIR ENSLAVEMENT WITH WRITERS FROM THE WORKS PROGRESS ADMINISTRATION'S FEDERAL WRITERS' PROJECT.

People back in slavery times had a way to forecast the weather and even death. They said when the old rain crow stayed in the air and hollered like "goo-oop, goo-oop" it's going to rain soon. Then they say when you heard a cow cry mournful somebody was going to die. The people used to have a bird for cold weather, too. Folks said, "Don' you hear dat cold bird? Look out, it gwine be cold tomorrow." The cold bird, he's a brown bird. When I saw that brown bird I ran for the woods to do what my pappy told me to do to help him get a fire in the fireplace cause if I didn't I'd be in trouble. I fetched chips and kindling wood and piled a good size bundle outside our cabin.

My pappy name was Ned, and my mammy name Jane. I had brothers, Tom and Gill and sisters, Lizzie and Nary. Pappy would tell me: "Elmer, cut de chip out de whiteoak: you better git up to keep frum gitting a whipping." I did what my old pappy say do so I gave him the wood to start the fire in the wooden chimney dabbed with mud. The whole cabin was made of long logs dabbed with mud. It had no windows. Just one door. The chimney was always catching afire and the wind coming through filled the little cabin with smoke and cinders. Our cabin was the only one made of logs with a dirt floor. Other people had cabins made with boards and plank floors, windows and brick chimneys. But my mammy was an African-born woman. She didn't want no plank wood under her feet. She wanted to feel the dirt.

One day the master put my mammy on the banjo table with a red handkerchief around her head. She was sold to a man in Alabama. When they herded all the niggers together she got away and spent months making her way back to South Carolina. Those Africans sure were strong. Mammy said she stayed in the woods at night. Negroes along the way gave her bread. She would beat anyone that tried to stop her from coming back.

When she did get back she was lanky, ragged and poor, but master was glad to see her. He told her he was not going to sell her away again. But she was afraid he would send her back to Alabama so she skedaddled into the woods. Pappy took food to her. A month later the master asked pappy where she was. Pappy just looked sheepish and grinned. The master told pappy to bring her back. Mammy had been gone for three months until she came back to the cabin to shuffle her tired feet on the dirt floor then lay her head on a soft pillow stuffed with chicken feathers. But she never felt well anymore. Then I heard the mournful cry of the cow. In about three more months my mammy was dead.

* * *

These memories describe a basic slave dwelling with a dirt floor, no window, one door, and a fragile chimney that posed a constant fire hazard. I've seen dirt floors in slave cabins, like the rustic dirt-floor cabins at Historic Sotterley Plantation at Hollywood, Maryland, where I shared an upper-level space with an active wasp nest. I am afraid of dirt floors. I don't want to lay my head in dirt. But I've seen well-built slave dwellings that were so beautiful I'd gladly live in them, if I had been enslaved, like the two-story brick dwelling at Bellamy Mansion in urban Wilmington, North Carolina. The restored 1844 main house at Laurelwood Plantation near Columbia, South Carolina, is such a stunning place to see that it prompted Isaiah Scott, a Lower Richland High School student, during my visit to the plantation, to remark that it is a "beautiful eyesore." Isaiah saw the physical beauty of the big house alongside the ugly history it represents. His poetic choice of words touched me, prompting me to think about structures I've seen that are on the extremes. For the time enslaved people had to spend in their cabins, there is beauty, even in the ones with dirt floors and smoky, rickety chimneys.

The positioning of slave dwellings on the landscape sometimes seems just as irregular as a leaning chimney. Cabins along slave streets are often aligned in neat rows, like the cabins at Magnolia and McLeod Plantations, both in Charleston. Symmetrical alignment of cabins indicates the white overseers or plantation owners may have imposed their Western logic to establish clearly defined and uniform spaces for enslaved people. However, when enslaved workers were given the opportunity to build their quarters, they were sometimes more inclined to place structures in random arrangements in secluded spaces, much more consistent with their natural worldview. Early slave dwellings were also likely much smaller than many of the dwellings I've seen. As famed landscape architect Frederick Law Olmsted traveled through South Carolina in the 1850s, he was shocked to see minimal one-room dwellings. "The negro-cabins, here, were the smallest I had seen—I thought not more than twelve feet square, inside. . . . They were built of logs, with no windows—no opening at all, except the doorway, with a chimney of sticks and mud." Olmsted saw even "meaner conditions" in eastern Texas, where dwellings were "rough [enclosures] of logs, ten feet square, without windows, covered by slabs of hewn wood four feet long. Great chinks are stopped with whatever has come to hand—a wad of cotton here, and corn shuck there."

Whether cabins were neatly aligned in rows or haphazardly placed on the landscape, in those dwellings and their clean-swept yards, enslaved people crafted independent communities in which some of them sold produce, chickens, and hand-crafted boats to build material wealth. That independence was far more evident on plantations with large enslaved populations, like Stagville Plantation in Durham, North Carolina, a community of more than one thousand enslaved workers. John Michael Vlach, author of *Back of the Big House: The Architecture of Plantation Slavery*, notes that Leslie Howard Owens is one of the few scholars to make the connection between slave dwellings and a vigorous autonomous slave culture.

According to Owens, "The Quarters, sometimes partially, some-times entirely, and often mysteriously, encompassed and breathed its own special vitality into these experiences, frequently assuring that bondage did not snuff out the many-sided existence slaves cre-ated for themselves." Those independent enslaved people, like Aunt Phillis, who was formerly enslaved on the Pope Plantation near Beaufort, South Carolina, realized their owners' success was a result of their labor and achievement. Aunt Phillis was among an estimated eight thousand to ten thousand enslaved people who were freed after the Union navy took control of Beaufort months after the attack on Fort Sumter. She was confined to bed when she talked about her enslavement in the spring of 1863 with New York journalist Charles Nordhoff. He presented her with a provocative question that caused her to sit up in bed. Nordhoff asked Aunt Phillis where her former enslaver got the $20,000 to build his house. Aunt Phillis pushed her sleeve up, pointed to her arm, and replied, "You see dat . . .? Dat's whar he got he money—out o' dat black skin he got he money."

In the mid-nineteenth century, Starling Yours owned McCol-lum Farm, a tobacco farm in Madison, North Carolina. During its two-hundred-year history, McCollum Farm had seventeen enslaved people who lived in three log houses. One of the houses has sur-vived. It's a windowless, one-door cabin with a sleeping loft and a stone chimney. By the mid-twentieth century, the floor was likely removed when the structure became a chicken coop. I was con-fronted with this rough snake-infested cabin in May 2014. I hated it. The cabin was in such bad shape that it was on a slippery slope toward demolition by neglect. I didn't go looking for this cabin; it found me, in an odd way.

Jonathan Williams, an educator in Mayodan, North Carolina, was waiting in an orthodontist's office when his random reach for something to read placed the October 2013 issue of the *Smithsonian Magazine* in his hands. As he flipped through the pages, his eyes landed on Tony Horwitz's article on the Slave Dwelling Project. He read with growing interest about my mission to sleep in every extant slave dwelling in the United States. Williams, a social studies teacher and principal intern at McMichael High School in Mayodan, found me on Twitter. We initially communicated via social media, and then phone calls led to a plan for a sleepover at McCollum Farm.

Jonathan took me seriously when I suggested I wanted to maximize my time in Mayodan. He prepared a whirlwind schedule that began at his school, where I joined four other speakers for a fast-paced history fair. Historians, authors, preservationists, a museum director, and Mayodan's mayor sat at stations, while small groups of students rotated past each station every seven minutes. It was like speed dating. Once I got into a groove, I saw that format as a very effective way to talk to three hundred students about the Slave Dwelling Project. The school's history club and football team cleaned the cabin. But volunteer hands couldn't sweep or brush away that scary dirt floor or repair walls with gaping cracks. I know the ancestors slept on dirt floors, but that gene didn't reach me. I've concluded that my fear of dirt floors may indeed have something to do with genetics. The ancestors' DNA could very well be mingled in with the soil; that thought troubles me. I don't try to commune with the ancestors. That is not my mission. My purpose is to honor them.

Dick Cartwright, McCollum's owner, cooked turtle stew in a huge black pot over an open fire. One of the local school board members also prepared a traditional dinner of cornmeal mush, pinto beans, greens, and fatback. Cartwright is a descendant of the original owners of the property. His daughter and her husband were also there with descendants of those who were enslaved on the property. Cartwright took us on a tour of the unoccupied side of the big house. One side of it had renters. The big house, built in 1812, the slave cabin, a meat house, a corn crib, and a few other outbuildings were sturdy but needed restoration.

Jonathan organized a public event at McCollum with some of the speakers who presented at the high school. About five minutes into my presentation, a strange storm whipped the winds. We retreated to the cabin. Instead of coming inside the cabin, most of the audience left before the event ended. Eight of them remained. Did the others leave because of the weather, or did the cabin scare them as much as it frightened me?

Then the time came for the sleepover. Kimberly Proctor, executive director of the Rockingham County Historical Society and Archives, and her grandson, Jones Gresham, joined me and Jonathan. We covered the dirt floor with a tarp and then arranged our sleeping bags on it. The tarp made it easier to sleep on the dirt floor, and the unrelenting desire to sleep eased my earlier apprehensions.

BELLAMY MANSION

Tillie's mother was enslaved on Dr. John Dillard Bellamy's Grovely Plantation in Brunswick County near Wilmington, North

Carolina. "It was the begges' place anywhere hereabouts," she told a Works Progress Administration (WPA) interviewer in the mid-1930s. "I was raised on it too. Of co'se it was in the country: but it was so big we was a town all to ourselves." Bellamy had property in Wilmington, and like his country home, his city house was also grand with proportioned Corinthian columns and exquisitely carved capitals. Bellamy and his family didn't get a chance to live in the house but for a few years before they fled briefly from the advancing federal troops. During the Civil War, Union soldiers may have been held at a makeshift prisoner-of-war camp under the Fourth Street Bridge in Wilmington, according to John H. Jackson's boyhood recollections. White women carried baskets of food to the prisoners. "De all had plenty of food," Jackson told an interviewer in the 1930s. "A warehouse full of everything down there by the river nigh Red Cross Street." Years later the US Army arrived just across the river. Federal troops prepared to bombard the city, but Wilmington raised the white flag, Jackson said. After the white people fled, the Northern army "told the colored people that any house in Wilmin'ton they liked, that was empty, they could go take it, an' the first one they took was the fine Bellamy Mansion on Market an' Fifth Street. . . . A lot of common colored folks was in it because I seen 'em sittin' on the piazza an' all up an' down those big front steps. I seen 'em. . . . But Dr. Bellamy came home soon with his family an' those colored people got out. They wan't there long."

I entered the 2015 Slave Dwelling Project season with my second visit in four years at the Bellamy Mansion. The ornate big house is impressive, but the unique two-story brick slave dwelling behind it fascinated me. The Bellamy Mansion Negro House is divided into four compartments with a five-seater indoor privy. This dwelling was clearly designed by Bellamy to flaunt his wealth but, in doing so, he unintentionally provided uncommon comforts for enslaved people. Bellamy had enslaved craftsmen build it around 1859 for nine people who toiled for him in the city before his mansion was completed in 1862. The female workers in the quarters included nurses, housekeepers, and a cook and housekeeper named Sarah, along with two men who worked as a butler/coachman and a handyman. Bellamy's big house and slave dwelling had a spatial relationship found throughout the South. Enslavers often had their homes positioned so they could see into the enslaved community. Bellamy had that in mind, too. From his big house, Bellamy could monitor movement around the slave dwelling and other structures in a complex that included a carriage house, brick stable, and laundry room.

An invitation to visit Bellamy followed the National Trust for Historic Preservation's conference in 2010 in Austin, Texas. Plans for lectures in January 2014 at Bellamy Mansion and the University of North Carolina Wilmington (UNCW) morphed into a sleepover at Bellamy and a partnership with Dr. Tammy Gordon, an associate professor of history, and some of her UNCW students. The students were creating a traveling exhibit on preserving and interpreting extant slave dwellings. Six graduate students and a Bellamy staff member signed up to join me and Terry James in the dwelling. While the lectures were increasing in popularity, I never passed up an opportunity to sleep in extant slave dwellings, even if it meant doing so in the winter. The ancestors did not have a choice. Gareth Evans, Bellamy's executive director, provided space heaters and extension cords to bring some warmth to the space. The dwelling was in a much better condition than when I first saw it in 2011 with Terry. The redbrick dwelling had been painted a salmon color. A new staircase rose to the second floor. Bellamy's commitment to interpret this space was evident by the money spent to restore the structure.

Wrapped in blankets, we sat on the floor huddled in a circle on the apartment's first level. The students asked focused questions well past midnight. We delved into how slavery has affected this nation. As they talked about their lives, the students realized they were in a place that once separated families and attempted to stop the growth of enslaved people and their communities. That epiphany inspired gratitude for their contemporary circumstances.

At the Bellamy Mansion, Terry was on his twentieth night in a slave dwelling with me, and as usual, he came prepared to sleep in shackles. The young inquiring minds quizzed Terry, a descendant of slaves, about what motivates him. They also wanted more details on why I started the Slave Dwelling Project and what motivates me. This was certainly a great exercise in how these sacred spaces can serve as classrooms; the students engaged in the deepest thoughts about race and slavery before they fell asleep.

The lives of the people who had lived in the dwelling were on Elizabeth Mae Bullock's mind. She tossed and turned on the hard floor and woke up periodically, anticipating the morning, when she could go home and take a warm shower. But then she contemplated the previous inhabitants and how, at the end of a night, they could not leave. As she stood to stretch stiff limbs, she reflected on those rising from uncomfortable nights' rests to perform daylong manual tasks.

The dwelling's historic meaning filled Joshua Christian Cole, the only male in the group, with despair and isolation. He slept alone and stared at the ceiling. Then he realized he and his fellow students had established a self-imposed gender segregation that closely matched the gender mix of the enslaved people who had lived in the dwelling. It is believed that two men lived in the carriage house adjacent to the slave quarters, and as many as nine women could occupy the slave quarters. Even though the enslaved workers at Bellamy lived in one of the largest cities in North Carolina, slavery had isolated them within an urban setting. He felt isolated at boarding school. But then an enslaved person who felt isolated could only dream of freedom. He always knew he'd return to his beloved family, and he possessed a sense of self and calmness even in the most traumatic situations, foreign feelings for an enslaved person. During the night it occurred to Joshua that he had gone to bed in a building that was designed more as a storage unit for human property than a home. The building was expressly designed to keep subjugated people nearby to work in service to the big house. This blatant attempt to systematically destroy individual agency and identity, he concluded, is what made slavery so cruel. He admits, however, it would be an absolute joke for him to claim he had any idea what an enslaved person went through after just one night in a slave dwelling. He rose the next day with a better understanding of what he truly valued and how fortunate he was to have been born in this time and place.

In the stillness ideas fumbled around Leslie Ann Randie-Morton's mind. She watched the shadows from the magnolia near the window dance across the plastered walls. A night in the dwelling lit a desire to know more about her ancestors in Mississippi. When she moved to North Carolina, she was asked where she was from. She'd loudly and proudly said Mississippi, never thinking that where she was born could brand her as an ignorant racist. Friends and colleagues later admitted their first impression of her was just that—she *had* to be a bigoted, closed-minded racist if she was a white Mississippian. Her graduate program cohorts later sheepishly admitted their misplaced preconception of her. Then they asked if her family had owned slaves, a question she could not answer. She had only heard the good stories about her family. Her father, a newly minted attorney in the early 1960s, was targeted by white businessmen because he represented African Americans. Then she heard that her grandfather enlisted in the National Guard to protect James Meredith as he enrolled at the University of Mississippi. Was her father a civil rights champion or simply in need of clients as the new lawyer in town? Did her grandfather proudly stand up for equality at Ole Miss, or did he resent being mobilized to protect a Black man? She never asked those questions that are now important for a budding historian. She wants to know more. Not to atone. Not to harbor guilt. Just to understand.

25 Longitude Lane

Eighty-two-year-old Thomas Campbell was told that according "to de writin' in de Book," presumably the Bible, he was born on March 15, 1855, in a section of South Carolina that in 1800 was called the Fairfield District. Sixty-eight years later it became Fairfield County. Campbell does not know how he and his mother, Chanie, became

John Kennedy's property or how they ended up in Charleston. But there he was as a child, 140 miles from Fairfield on the Battery in Charleston with a view of the distant Fort Sumter at the entrance to the city's harbor. He stood there "seein' a big ocean of water, wid ships and their white sails all 'bout, de waves leapin' and gleemin' 'bout de flanks of de ships in de bright sunshine, thousands of white birds flyin' 'round and sometimes lighting on de water." John Campbell's mother held his hand, and with her other she gripped "de handle of a baby carriage and in dat carriage was one of de Logan chillun. Whether us b'long to de Logans [a white family] or whether us was just hired out to them I's unable to 'member dat. De slaves called him Marster Tom." Eventually, Campbell and his mother went back to Fairfield County under Kennedy's control.

In August 2013, I stood with Terry James on the Battery (or the Bat'tre as a Gullah speaker would pronounce it), where seabirds soar and the sun dances on rippling waves. We wore our blue Union reenactor uniforms. Tour guides and tourists were astonished to see two Black men in Union blue at the Battery, an outdoor shrine to the old Confederacy at the tip of the Charleston peninsula. Until recent years, nothing on the Battery spoke of Black history. Vintage cannons and artillery pieces from the War of 1812 and the Civil War point toward Fort Sumter three miles away at the entrance to the harbor. Stunning pastel-colored mansions, once the homes of slave owners, rim the boulevard along the Battery's seawall. In this antebellum setting, we certainly looked like two pelicans on the wrong perch. People asked why we were there. We told them we came to sleep in a nearby urban slave dwelling along one of the city's most picturesque alleys.

The 540-foot-long Longitude Lane is near the tip of Charleston's peninsula, just a few blocks north of the Battery. Lined with ivy-covered facades and fence columns shaded under moss-draped trees, the alley is just a foot wider than a tractor-trailer rig. In the eighteenth century, railroad tracks ran along the alley to join street-side warehouses with the wharfs on the Cooper River. But now the alley's weatherworn cobblestone footpath with slate runners over the tracks makes this lane a visual treat for tourists wanting Charleston's charm. The beauty of this lane and probably that of the entire city, however, can only faintly mask slavery's indelible stain. College of Charleston history professor emeritus Bernard Powers Jr. reminds us that in Charleston the past is always present.

Maria Jenkins shared some of that pain of the past in the 1930s with a WPA interviewer. As a child enslaved at a Wadmalaw Island plantation near Charleston, she was taught how "to wash de baby clean and put on he dipa [diaper], and if I ain't do um good he [her owner] konk my head," said Jenkins, who was nearing ninety years old when she was interviewed at 17 Longitude Lane. Her relationship with the property and its owner is unknown. It is likely 17 Longitude Lane may have been a dependency or former slave dwelling for one of the nearby larger homes that surround the alley. Terry and I left the Battery for 25 Longitude Lane, where we had arranged a sleepover. Susan Heape, the home's owner, said her father always called 25 Longitude Lane a "slave quarters." Her father, Branford Heape, was the city's first licensed tour guide in 1952.

Built in 1780, the seven-hundred-square-foot one-bedroom house at 25 Longitude Lane sits at the west end of the alley near

Church Street and a few blocks south of the famed Dock Street Theater, which boasts the distinction of being America's first theater. With handblown original glass windows, heart-of-pine wood floors, and a double fireplace, the house also has a private walled garden and a basement, a rarity in low-lying Charleston. Heape asked the question that's perhaps on the minds of most people when they learn she owns and lives in a dwelling that possibly was once the home of enslaved people, although she has no documentation to prove it. She considers herself a steward of the property, who bears the duty and honor to protect a property someone else might want to neglect or destroy. Before she bought the house in April 2006, Heape knew it needed repair, but she saw potential in its stout brick walls in spite of dreary dark shutters, overgrown vines, and messy mulberry trees. Heape said the house needed her and she needed it. Previous owners had tried to modernize it, but by doing so, they masked its authentic slave dwelling origins. She restored the dwelling's original features. She removed modern plastic light fixtures and stripped away glossy paint that hid interior brick walls. Then she laid down heart-of-pine floors identical to the few remaining original planks. She did much of the work herself, except for the electrical and plumbing systems. Outside she installed a traditional African American folk art garden of heirloom plants with natural elements such as seashells and antique farming implements.

When Terry and I returned to Longitude Lane from the Battery, Susan's friend Mary Ellen Millhouse had arrived. Mary Ellen attended my lecture the previous day at the College of Charleston. She had asked interesting questions about how many enslaved people stayed in Charleston after they were freed. Mary owns a house in Beaufort, South Carolina, that once housed slaves. Since the start of the Slave Dwelling Project, I had been trying to identify extant slave dwellings in Beaufort. It was as if Beaufort was in denial of its slaveholding past. The result of the conversation with Mary was that a stay at the property will occur, but we have yet to determine the right date to maximize its effectiveness. The conversation continued over Susan's tasty stew, but it soon shifted away from extant slave dwellings to a football game on the TV. When that happened, Susan decided to leave for her second home on Edisto Island, south of Charleston. She also was convinced she might lose sleep because the snoring from me or Terry or both of us would keep her awake. I took the couch. Terry spread his sleeping bag on the kitchen floor. He donned the shackles and then tossed throughout the night in a futile attempt to find a comfortable posture for sleep.

OLD CITY PARK

It's likely that many people who do not live in Dallas, Texas, had not heard of Dealey Plaza until November 22, 1963, when an assassin's bullet killed President John F. Kennedy. The presidential motorcade was winding through the plaza when the fatal shot was fired from high up in the Texas School Book Depository. The plaza now draws rubbernecking tourists who scan the site where the nation's thirty-fifth president was mortally wounded. Adjacent to the three-acre Dealey Plaza, however, is a much smaller and far lesser-known Martyrs Park. It is perhaps just as obscure as Dealey Plaza had been before Kennedy's death.

In Dallas on July 8, 1860, the temperature soared to 110 degrees. Around 1:30 p.m. a fire started in a rubbish pile in the young frontier village. Within hours the wind had pushed the blaze through Dallas, consuming nearly all of the wooden homes and businesses. Spontaneous fires had occurred before in that part of Texas. They were normally blamed on the new technology of phosphorus-tipped matches that could ignite in extreme summer heat. White people, however, had their own suspicions about what caused the fire. Just as fast as the blaze swept through Dallas, so did rumors among its nearly seven hundred white residents that the fire was the result of a slave and abolitionist uprising. The year before the fire, abolitionist John Brown swung from the gallows following a failed uprising in West Virginia. In Dallas, some one hundred enslaved people were rounded up, interrogated, and tortured. Then the blame for the fire fell on three enslaved men: Patrick Jennings, an accused agitator owned by a Dallas attorney; Sam Smith, an enslaved preacher with alleged ties to visiting abolitionist preachers; and Cato, who operated a mill owned by the Overton family, a job that some whites said gave him an uncomfortable level of responsibility. At 4:00 p.m. on July 24, sixteen days after the fire, the doomed men were escorted from the brick jail and led through the blackened ruins of Dallas to three nooses at the Trinity River. Reportedly, Patrick, with a wad of tobacco in his mouth, nonchalantly reviewed the village. His death took the longest of the three to achieve. As life drained from his body, the tobacco remained in his mouth.

John Kennedy was assassinated in Dealey Plaza, one hundred yards from the site where the enslaved men were executed. Established in 1963, the park has no marker to acknowledge where

Jennings, Smith, and Cato were hanged in 1860.* To spark the memory of the forgotten Martyrs Park, a reader of the *Dallas Morning News* called the area the "invisible park . . . that no one can see." The men did not receive a trial, and no evidence was offered to prove they had set the fire. One member of a citizens committee who investigated the blaze, Judge James Bentley, doubted the men had burned the village, but then he justified the hysteria-driven lynchings when he said, "Somebody had to hang."

While Martyrs Park and the events that happened there have become a nearly forgotten footnote in Dallas's history, the Millers, an African American family, have timed their annual family reunion each July to mark the anniversary of the 1860 fire. According to a newspaper account, at least one person linked to the alleged revolt was enslaved at William Brown Miller's plantation in the city's Oak Cliff community. The Miller family ancestors were enslaved at the Millermore Plantation. According to the 1860 census, Miller enslaved thirteen African Americans, including three couples: Arch and Charlotte, John and Lucy, and Clayton and Betsy. Dallas genealogist and historian Donald Payton said John and Lucy Miller were his great-great-grandparents who remained in Dallas after the Civil War.

At the Millermore Plantation the one-room Miller Cabin, built in 1847, was the first home for the white family before the main house was erected. The white Miller family lived in the cabin and then moved to the main house after its completion in 1862. When

---

* In 1991, the site of the lynchings was named Martyrs Park. The City of Dallas has plans to install a memorial in Martyrs Park to the victims of racial violence.

they moved out, Arch and Charlotte moved in. They lived in the cabin with their family until after the Civil War. The cabin and the main house that were once on the Millermore Plantation were disassembled and moved to Old City Park (OCP).* The cabin had been a frontier dwelling, a pioneer family's house, a neighborhood school, the home of enslaved people, and a home of freed people; now it is a preserved historic structure at an outdoor museum exhibit at OCP, which features twenty historic buildings.

Payton had planned to spend the night with me in the one-room dwelling that resembles a giant Lincoln log cabin, but he declined when the temperature dropped to near freezing. At the start of the Slave Dwelling Project in 2010, I committed to only seek extant slave dwellings in the places where they were originally built. Context is important to maintain historical integrity. Had I held true to that rule, however, I would not have slept at three presidential and several national, state, and local historic sites, as well as OCP.

When the Slave Dwelling Project was in its infancy, C. Preston Cooley and his wife, Bonnie, were my coworkers at Magnolia Plantation and Gardens in Charleston. The Cooleys left Magnolia in 2012 to move to Dallas, where Preston is executive director of Old City Park. Early in 2018, Preston invited me to the site as part of a plan to tell more of the site's Black history. Preston also extended that invitation to the living history team. I had traveled out of state with the living historians before, but never with more than two of us

---

* The site was previously called Dallas Heritage Village.

flying together.* We also planned a conversation around the camp-fire with thirty-five people before the sleepover. After the fireside conversation, only three people joined me for the night in the cold Miller Cabin. Luckily, the cabin had a functional fireplace. I got up three times during the night to put wood in the hearth. I thought about enslaved people who may have slept in the big house on pal-lets, where their purpose was not to keep the fire going at night for their warmth but for that of those who enslaved them.

Bonnie Cooley joined me and Elizabeth Qualia, OCP's cura-tor of collections and interpretation, and Melissa Prycer, OCP's president and executive director, for the sleepover. Elizabeth chose to join us for the unique experience. As she lay on the wooden floor snug in her sleeping bag, music played softly in her ears. She could not warm her nose, but she tried to calm her mind and think about the enslaved people who called the log cabin home. She struggled to imagine the daily life contained within the cabin's walls. Espe-cially the lives of Arch and Charlotte. Her mind began to chant: Arch and Charlotte . . . Arch and Charlotte . . . Arch and Charlotte. The refrain changed to: You won't be forgotten . . . You won't be forgotten . . . You won't be forgotten.

Over fifteen years, Melissa has done a little bit of everything at the outdoor museum, except spend a night in one of the historic buildings. My visit presented her with an opportunity she had to take. She didn't sleep well. She slept on a cot, but the below-forty-degree

---

* The living historians were Jerome Bias, the lead cook; Dontavius, assistant cook and storyteller; Gilbert Walker, blacksmith; and Rodney Prioleau, brick maker. They had an option to spend the night with me in the slave cabin, but they chose hotel rooms.

temperature spoiled it for her, and the fireplace didn't help. Throughout the night she thought of the people who had also slept in the cabin: whites and Blacks, young and old. Nevertheless, in the morning she rose reinvigorated. She began to think of the Miller Cabin differently and the array of stories it can tell.

Before I arrived in Dallas, I asked Preston to maximize my time at the OCP. He scheduled a lecture for me with a diverse audience of nearly one hundred people. Because of time constraints, Dr. Deborah Fripp, president of the Teach the Shoah Foundation in Carrollton, Texas, did not have an opportunity ask me a question following my lecture. Instead, she shared her thoughts in a blog she posted on the *Times of Israel* website. Here's an excerpt from her blog:

> Like the standard narrative of the Holocaust, the standard narrative of slavery is written from the perspective of the perpetrators, with the victims a faceless flow of bodies with no wills or voices of their own. Black slaves are primarily portrayed as strong field hands, mostly capable only of unskilled work, desired for their brawn, not their brains.
>
> The full story is very different. Enslaved blacks were capable, skilled laborers who could be trusted with the running of a plantation. The standard image of enslaved people in America reminds me of the difficulty Jews have with the standard image of Jews in the Holocaust. Jews in the Holocaust are typically portrayed as helpless, passive victims. We know this story to be false. Jews in the Holocaust were smart, strong, active movers in their own lives.

Enslaved people in America are often portrayed as broken victims, passively doing what they were told to do. We do hear stories of skilled slaves but they are described as the exception, not the rule. We know this to be false too. Enslaved people were smart, strong, active movers of their own lives, just as the Jews in the Holocaust were.

We are, actually, taught stories of resistance to slavery in school. Harriet Tubman and the underground railroad is a favorite topic in many elementary schools. The bravery of people like Tubman is another essential point in this narrative. People who had escaped slavery returned to help others. Many of the black soldiers fighting for the Union in the Civil War were escapees from slavery, returning to danger to help their fellows. Again, this reminded me of the stories of people returning to, or remaining in, the ghettos and camps in the Holocaust in order to help others when they could have escaped.

When we talk about resistance in the Holocaust, however, we mean more than simply physical resistance. We also talk of spiritual resistance. Spiritual resistance is the seemingly simple act of continuing to celebrate your own faith when it is forbidden. Enslaved people continued to practice their beliefs as well.

In my extended family tree, I have both victims (of the Holocaust) and perpetrators (of slavery). I also have relatives who liberated the death camps and who taught in some of the first integrated classrooms in the American South. If you go further out, you will find German soldiers as well. This full nuance of both victim and perpetrator is the story of families in America. Nor is my family unique in this way.

Those of us who are related to perpetrators have nothing to fear from telling the victims' stories. Those of us who are related to victims have nothing to fear from fleshing out the perpetrators' stories. Neither diminishes us. Rather, understanding the nuances in everyone's stories helps us avoid cardboard caricatures of complex people.

The stories of the powerful are the easy stories to tell. These are the stories of people who left behind antebellum turkey platters that we still use today. The stories of the oppressed are less accessible. We must go digging for them, like the Oneg Shabbat Archive which preserved a deeply nuanced story of Jewish life in the Warsaw Ghetto. We must dig deep enough to find the stories of courage, hope, strength, and skill that are missing from our current narrative of slavery in America. Even if that story is merely fingerprints on a brick.

I do not remember the year when I began to look for fingerprints in the bricks of stately houses that were once the homes of enslavers. But I was focused on them by the time I visited Monticello and Montpelier, and my search for them at every site has become a passion. On occasion my hosts have pointed to those bricks with the evidence that an enslaved person had touched them. Those impressions in the bricks are a testament that the architectural structures we admire were built by enslaved people, which adds to the richness of sleeping with the ancestors in their former homes.

The impressions in bricks are not the only markings of the ancestors that guide us to their stories. If they were buried in wooden coffins, the tops of them eventually collapsed, leaving indentations in the soil. Those depressions are telltale signs of the existence of our enslaved ancestors. They didn't get headstones etched with messages from the past. Their loved ones could not afford it, and if they could, it's likely they could not read it. I am thankful to archaeologists who are finding the tangible items that prove our ancestors' existence, such as discarded copper slave tags that are only in the Charleston soil. Those items show that the enslaved had skills and responsibility. They were blacksmiths, cooks, millers, midwives, musicians, and hostlers. It was the carpenters, too, who fashioned the wooden beams that support the antebellum structures. They used an adze, a short-handled tool that resembles a hatchet, to hand-hew a tree trunk into a support beam. Unlike a hatchet's blade, the adze's sharp curved blade is turned perpendicular to the short handle. I've used one before, and it requires skill to carefully chip away the wood to shape a log. Our ancestors used these tools with precision, and the markings left on antebellum logs is another testament to their existence and craftsmanship.

Many of the historic sites I've visited, like Old City Park, are beginning to appreciate the stories of the enslaved, accounts that have unfortunately been hidden for too long. As these stories emerge, they might encourage more Black families like Donald Payton's family in Texas to become curious about their ancestors. Unfortunately, cold weather prevented me from spending a night with Donald Payton in the Miller Cabin. I missed out on an opportunity to hear his homespun stories of his family and how we as Black people should access our past. He captured it succinctly, however, in 2018 when he told a Dallas newspaper reporter, "You have to know your grannies and your great-grannies. You can't just go through life believing that you made yourself."

CONCLUSION

I N THE SUMMER OF 2022, I FOLLOWED WITH GREAT INTEREST THE ongoing comments on social media from people upset that an 1830s slave dwelling on the Belmont Plantation in Greenville, Mississippi, was being rented through Airbnb. I was on the side of those strongly opposed to this cabin or any antebellum property being advertised online as a short-term rental. Twelve years into the Slave Dwelling Project, I can speak with authority that this was an opportunity for Airbnb to do the right thing to honor our enslaved ancestors. Instead, they and the owners of this property commercialized the memory of the African ancestors and their enslaved descendants. This problem is not new. Other antebellum properties have been rented before in other locations. But it took a young TikTok audience to shine a spotlight on Airbnb's offensive rental.

American history has become so distorted that some people still prefer a *Gone with the Wind* version of the brutality inflicted on enslaved people. We have become so desensitized that some still believe that using these places as vacation rentals is a good idea. The controversy was not limited to social media. Mainstream news outlets around the world ran the story, and by the early fall of 2022, I found myself on the fringes of this Airbnb slave cabin controversy.

The company emailed me to seek my advice on what they should do. I felt honored to be asked for my recommendation. It was somewhat of an unexpected positive recognition that produced in me a feeling of accomplishment that my work had enough of an impact that Airbnb, an international company, had reached out to me. During my first and only conversation with two company representatives in the early fall of 2022, I suggested that the company not list slave dwellings on their site. Airbnb took my advice. I am sure others made a similar suggestion.

When I launched the Slave Cabin Project in May 2010, I had no reason to believe that a big company like Airbnb would notice me. But since then I have traveled to twenty-five states and the District of Columbia and spent more than two hundred nights in slave dwellings. In this quest I have brought much-needed attention to the lives of the enslaved ancestors. This journey has taught me that I'm not the best at arithmetic or coloring within the lines. My initial intent was to pursue slave cabins for one year just in South Carolina. I broke that rule in the first year. Enduring the discomfort of a slave cabin for one-night increments pales in comparison to what enslaved people endured for a lifetime. Their lives are often dismissed by the uninformed, ignorant, arrogant, or simply racist people who would prefer that people like me would just get over slavery and move on. They also want to dismiss some of the reasons why their white privilege is rooted in a system based on purging Native Americans and enslaving Africans and their descendants.

I understand what happens when someone is misinformed because they haven't been properly taught how racial segregation was shaped by slavery. Until high school, I looked forward to going to the county fair when it came to my hometown of Kingstree, South Carolina. I did not understand why most of the Black residents in the 1970s went on Thursdays. That day was set aside for the Black fairgoers. It was an unwritten yet understood Jim Crow rule in South Carolina that the fair was a segregated event. That revelation would come later in my life.

My upbringing in a segregated community, along with the images of whites on television where they were always the victors, implanted in my young mind that white people were the enemy. I didn't know that rage was contained in me until I had to conform to life in the US Air Force. When I left a predominantly Black Kingstree, I often found myself as the only Black airman in military activities. I had to grow up fast. I encountered many white people and liked most of them. It was a six-year journey that prepared me well for the Slave Dwelling Project.

There is a reason why some people are ignorant about slavery. They lack knowledge about this most fundamental and horrific aspect of American history because public schools and institutions of higher education have either overlooked this history or given it short shrift. I saw it firsthand when my only child, Jocelyn McGill, toured Clemson University in Clemson, South Carolina, to decide if she wanted to become a Tiger. During the tour I had to force myself to keep my mouth shut because the guide was not telling her and the other Black students in the group what I thought they should hear about Clemson's troubled past. The university was built on John C. Calhoun's Fort Hill Plantation by convict labor in 1889. That's an important fact that potential students should know. Having the Calhoun mansion on its grounds is worthy of note, too. Calhoun was an American statesman from South Carolina and vice president of the United States for John Quincy Adams and Andrew Jackson. He adamantly defended slavery and sought to protect the interest of the white South. Also on the campus is a building named for Benjamin Ryan Tillman Jr., who was South Carolina's governor from 1890 to 1894 and a US senator from 1895 until his death. He was a white supremacist and led a paramilitary group of Red Shirts during South Carolina's violent 1876 election during Reconstruction. During the tour, I struggled to remain silent as the guide expounded on the history and attributes of Clemson but left out these telling and important facts about its history. I can only hope that Clemson and other institutions of higher learning are now beginning to reckon with their history and tell potential students the truth about slavery.

A Time for Truth Telling

In my twelve years of following in the footprints of slavery, I have encountered many people who voluntarily disclose they are the descendants of slave owners. They seem to be attracted to the uniqueness of the Slave Dwelling Project, which gives them a neutral ground to have conversations around campfires with people who don't look like them. I have refereed many of these talks and have sometimes felt like a priest taking confessions. Did I help them absolve themselves of their guilt or the guilt of their enslaving ancestors? It was a surprise at first to hear these revelations from everyday white people. But now I wonder about those people who have slave-owning ancestors, who would much rather conceal that information for whatever reason. When actor Ben Affleck's slave-owning ancestors came to light during the production of an episode of *Finding Your Roots*, hosted by the noted historian and scholar Dr. Henry Louis Gates Jr., Affleck persuaded the program not to include those ancestors. When this was discovered, PBS postponed the episode, which the network never aired. That is one prominent example, but there are countless individuals who want to deny or hide their ancestors' past. I want everyone to be forthcoming to the public. Descendants of enslavers may possess the information that can help the descendants of enslaved people trace their ancestry.

Prior to the Slave Dwelling Project, I was a nine-to-five program officer based in Charleston, South Carolina, with the National Trust for Historic Preservation. My 2013 release from the Trust three years after launching the Slave Dwelling Project was not of my choosing, but it gave me the push I needed to take my work to another level. The pandemic didn't stop me from conducting sleepovers, and my persistence prompted a woman to comment on my Facebook page. She said I was bold. But what did I do to warrant that description? Maybe she felt I had no fear of speaking before an audience or calling out racism when I saw it. Maybe she labeled me bold because I have no fear of the unknown, and I overcame my fear of spending nights alone in slave cabins. Whatever the reason, being bold is necessary for me to continue my search for slave dwellings.

My first of many Facebook restrictions came when I posted a historic photograph of a lynching. Facebook labeled it as promoting hate, but I wanted to use it to illustrate the violence that was inflicted on our ancestors. Some view my honoring of the enslaved ancestors as an assault on American history. Nikole Hannah-Jones was viciously verbally attacked when she introduced the *1619 Project,* an ongoing initiative by the *New York Times Magazine* that began in August 2019 on the four hundredth anniversary of the beginning of American slavery. It aims to reframe the country's history by placing the consequences of slavery and the contributions of Black Americans at the very center of our national narrative. Countering the white male narrative always brings scrutiny, a lesson I learned during my years as a National Park Service ranger at Fort Sumter when I was confronted by Confederate sympathizers.

The Evolution of the Slave Dwelling Project

If you hold on to something too tightly, or you do not allow it to evolve and flourish, you can deprive it of its ability to survive. The Slave Dwelling Project is no exception. It has evolved beyond my imagination and expectations. During the project's evolution, conferences have played an important role in bringing together students, scholars, educators, artists, and the public. The seven Slave Dwelling Project conferences were convened to change the narrative of American history, address the legacies of slavery, and promote education about slavery and the contributions of African Americans. From our first conference in 2013 in Savannah, Georgia, to our 2022 conference in Charleston, South Carolina, our keynote speakers have included Colson Whitehead, author of eight novels, including the 2016 novel *The Underground Railroad*, and Edda L. Fields-Black, author of *Deep Roots: Rice Farmers in West Africa and the African Diaspora*. These conferences have forged many partnerships with colleges and universities, including the University of Virginia, Middle Tennessee State University, Clemson University, and the College of Charleston. The 1772 Foundation, which works to ensure the safe passage of our historic assets to future generations, has so far been the primary donor for these forums.

Through all of this success of conducting seven conferences, there is regret. None of them have been held in a northern state. Of the twenty-five states where I've spent nights in slave dwellings, eight of them have been northern states. The Slave Dwelling Project board of directors has agreed that we will not hold a conference in 2023, but in 2024 we will schedule a conference in a northern state.

WHOSE STORY IS IT?

I have had a consistent problem with white costumed interpreters at historic sites who portray enslavers and their families. These characters remind me of the real-life enslavers who abused our ancestors. Some historic sites have used costumed white interpreters to demonstrate the work that historically would have been the task of an enslaved person. They've portrayed crafters, cooks, blacksmiths, brick makers, carpenters, barrel makers, and wheelwrights. Using white interpreters to demonstrate the tasks of enslaved people softens the story. A white person can't authentically communicate the good, bad, or ugly parts of the African American story. Twenty years ago these sites did not hire many—if any—Black interpreters, and Black people also weren't standing in line to volunteer for these roles.

Historic sites would use information from outdated and misleading history books to present their incomplete vignettes to an unsuspecting audience composed mostly of white folks seeking sugarcoated versions of history. These sites catered to people eager to consume an interpretation of antebellum history that kept them in a comfortable place. The Slave Dwelling Project now offers an alternative.

The project has evolved to provide a more authentic presentation of slavery through "Inalienable Rights: Living History Through the Eyes of the Enslaved." Since 2016, talented Black living historians have traveled with me as far north as Maryland and as far west as Texas. They demonstrate cooking, blacksmithing, and brick making, and storytellers present compelling insights into the lives of enslaved people.

Most people I've interacted with since 2010 have embraced what we do. The consistent message to honor the enslaved ancestors has received widespread support. The audience has been growing, which is a testament to the project's success and its ability to evolve. The support has been aimed at the project and at me personally.

While I have received widespread support, I have also been criticized for my direct approach. Some white southerners hate me because I call out their treasonous enslaving ancestors. I gave a presentation at a Charleston church and got a "thank you" letter that criticized me for being negative. The gentleman said he would have preferred that I talked about the accomplishments of enslaved people. He wanted me to tell a story that did not make him feel uncomfortable. Along with the letter, the envelope included a check for one hundred dollars made out to the Slave Dwelling Project. We cashed it. These southern sympathizers would much rather fly their Confederate flag and keep Confederate monuments in public view than acknowledge that slavery is the foundation of their white privilege. Some of these southerners also received the same incomplete history lesson I got, which portrays enslaved people as happy and enslavers as benevolent. Their white ancestors have passed down to them through oral traditions and textbooks the false narrative that they treated their enslaved property like family.

Some white northerners hate me because I call out the founding fathers for allowing slavery to exist and persist in Northern states. At a presentation at Hampton Plantation in McClellanville, South Carolina, a gentleman disrupted my talk when I said Thomas Jefferson enslaved six hundred people and had children with an enslaved woman. Northerners are quick to acknowledge the Underground Railroad, but they are ignorant of or don't talk about their ancestors' participation in chattel slavery. Their limited knowledge of colonial history does not include purging Native Americans and enslaving people. Some northerners want the information about slavery that existed in their states to remain hidden or incomplete. For example, at Stenton, the country home of James Logan, the colonial mayor of Philadelphia and later chief justice of the Pennsylvania Supreme Court, the staff consistently recognize Dinah, an enslaved woman, for saving the house from being burned by the British. While I applauded Stenton, I reminded the staff that the stories of all who were enslaved at Stenton should be included in the narrative. The staff took it more as an insult when I tried to be instructive. In November 2019, all was forgiven, and I spent a night at Stenton with one of the most diverse audiences ever assembled.

When I call out the impact of slavery in the North and the role Northerners played in slavery, white northerners dispute what I have to say. But I have learned that the economics of slavery was not limited to the South. Northern banks, insurance companies, cotton factories, and shipping businesses were all complicit in supporting slavery in the South. Some northerners would prefer to ignore the idea their ancestors either enslaved people or provided economic comfort for those who did. This kind of exploitation was not limited to people of African descent. Indigenous people also were victimized in the North and the South.

Some Black people, believe it or not, hate me even when I am telling the stories of "our" ancestors. They are misinformed when they think we've "overcome" racism in this country that has held us back as a people before and after Emancipation. They don't want to be reminded of slavery, or they don't want white people to be reminded of it, for fear it will make them feel uncomfortable. They would rather that we as Black people conform to the majority's way of thinking and accept their interpretation of our history. I was told once by a Black executive at Boeing's aircraft manufacturing plant in North Charleston that my message was too radical for Boeing employees.

Then there's another group of Black people who hate me for different reasons. They think I am not Black enough and that my method of teaching isn't hard enough on white people. I've been criticized for having too many white people on the Slave Dwelling Project's seven-member board of directors. The project has been a not-for-profit organization since May 5, 2014. The board currently is composed of five Black people and two white people. The board's racial mix has remained the same since its inception.

Even after twelve years, I am still getting opposition from surprising places: public schools. In Tillar, Arkansas, on Friday, December 2, 2022, I looked into the eyes of about seventy-five diverse middle schoolers who joined me at the Hollywood Plantation. Those young eyes lit with enthusiasm as we exchanged our thoughts about slavery in Arkansas and this nation. Some even said they would spend a night with me in a slave cabin at the plantation, if given the opportunity.

That group was half the size of what I had anticipated. The size of the group was diminished when the usual social media advertising for the event went awry with negative comments from opponents of critical race theory. It got so bad that two days prior to the event, someone in the school's chain of command decided they did not want the children to learn about slavery at the nearby plantation. That led to only half of the students attending the program.

My visit was supported by Preserve Arkansas in Little Rock. Comments were posted on the group's Facebook page. Lance wrote: "Poor white ppl were slaves also." Mercedes said: "All countries had slaves. Sold by their own people. If they want to hate they need to go and find those peoples." Carol chimed in: "Many of the plantation owners in the South treated their slaves well and after they were emancipated they refused to leave and stayed on as share croppers. On the other hand, the people of the north used whips and chains. Chaining the women sewing in their factories to the sewing machines they were using!" Then Carol wrote: "I wouldn't want any of my family treated the way the North treated their slaves and didn't have to free them until years later! It's over, it's done with, no one who is alive lived during that time! You certainly didn't so don't judge people today by what their ancestors did about two hundred years ago! We have a very mobile population and those who live in the south may have northern ancestors and vise [sic] versa, also many others have no ancestors who lived in the Us [sic] at that time! Get over all your hurt feeling [sic] about something that didn't happen to you?"*

These comments took me back to the place of anger I was in twelve years ago when I started the project. These comments also took me back to an earlier moment that sparked my anger, as a lad

---

* The use of the question mark at the end of this sentence is part of the original text.

learning South Carolina history from a 1964 history book written by a white woman whose version of history was not kind to the people who gave me my DNA.

Critical race theory (CRT) is an academic concept that is more than forty years old. The core idea is that race is a social construct and that racism is not merely the product of individual bias or prejudice but is embedded in legal systems and policies. CRT has never been taught in grade schools, but many red states are legislating to stop it even though there is no "it" to stop. They call their effort anti-critical race theory. Florida and Texas lead this effort. School boards are being infiltrated with anti-CRT supporters whose intent is to ban the teaching of any history that will make white children feel uncomfortable or make them hate themselves or America.

In 2010, Tom Johnson, who was the director of Magnolia Plantation and Gardens, supported my idea of spending a night in the newly restored slave dwelling at Magnolia. I have not delved deeply into his reason for saying yes. Maybe he knew more about the power of place than I did. Maybe he saw the slave cabins as the future classrooms that I continue to use today.

Following the footprints of slavery has not always been easy, but it has always been a joy. I had no road map to follow while doing something that had never been done before. Being told that you and your idea are not welcome doesn't feel good. Engaging in campfire conversations about slavery and the legacy it left on this nation with people who don't look like or think like you is not an easy task. Bringing others into the fold to share and manage the idea requires the ability to trust others and hope they have your best interests at heart. Some good ideas die because those who have them wait for the right time to launch. The right time may never come, so sometimes you have to fix a plane in flight and learn as you go along.

With no precedent to follow, I'm free to cut my own path. I get paid for sleeping around. (LOL!!!) I have made my passion my job and my job my passion. I get to sleep in places some people fear. Using social media to reach a broader audience also is invigorating.

The Future

My current campaign is to encourage historic sites to pay reparations to the descendants of those who were enslaved there. It will keep a lot of genealogists busy with proving who they are. In many cases, that research has already been done. Those paid reparations should not be forced. It should be done voluntarily. Every historic site that once enslaved people and now charges an entrance fee should contribute a portion of every admission ticket to a reparation fund. A portion of every fee paid to have a wedding on a plantation also should be contributed to a reparation fund. But who controls this fund? Every bank, insurance company, newspaper, college, and so on that benefited from the institution of slavery should contribute a portion of every sale to a reparation fund. The New York City clothier Brooks Brothers comes immediately to mind because it sold material and clothing to enslavers who outfitted the people they enslaved. There will be pushback to this bold proposal, like there was to removing Confederate monuments from public places, but it's getting done.

Conclusion

And just when I thought I had it all figured out with the Slave Dwelling Project, I was reminded that the war is not over. Congressman Kevin McCarthy, a Republican from California, is the current Speaker of the United States House of Representatives. He proclaimed in his acceptance speech for the Speaker's gavel that the Republicans will pass laws to address the "woke agenda in our schools." (It is so funny how white people misappropriate cool Black terms like "woke" and then use them against us.) That attack on this so-called woke agenda is now aimed directly at the Slave Dwelling Project and other efforts to teach an inclusive and truthful history. McCarthy's agenda is a new and improved version of the United Daughters of the Confederacy's program. I refuse to go back to that place where the youth of America are taught that enslavers were benevolent and enslaved people were happy. McCarthy's agenda is a continuation of white supremacy and absolving white folks of their continued contributions to systemic racism.

I've probably got more sleepovers behind me than I have ahead of me, but as long as I have a voice, I will continue to advocate for and love on the enslaved ancestors and tell their stories truthfully and respectfully. If you've read this book, I imagine you are with me. Use your powers, your skills, and your influence for good and avoid evil. We have more campfire conversations, living history programs, lectures, conferences, and sleepovers to do. That includes the White House. Because our ancestors built it! Peace!

ACKNOWLEDGMENTS

One of my biggest flaws is knowing how to say thank you without sounding ungrateful. I will attempt to express my heartfelt gratitude to the many people who've supported me and assisted in making this book and the Slave Dwelling Project a reality.

My gratitude begins with the late author Tony Horwitz, who saw me, a young Black park ranger at Fort Sumter, as interesting enough to include in his book *Confederates in the Attic*. Because of Tony's book, Glen Kirshbaum featured me in his 2001 History Channel documentary *The Unfinished Civil War*. This documentary gave me the courage to sleep in my first slave cabin alone at Boone Hall Plantation in Mount Pleasant, South Carolina. That experience led to the Slave Dwelling Project.

Tom Johnson, the former executive director of Magnolia Plantation and Gardens, and the Drayton family, the property's owners, allowed me to spend a night in one of the site's newly restored slave cabins to launch my project in 2010. The Drayton family's continued support has given me and the Slave Dwelling Project the time to grow and has allowed me to take the show on the road.

Acknowledgments

Elizabeth Johnson, deputy state historic preservation officer at the South Carolina Department of Archives and History, understood what I wanted to do, and she provided me with a list of extant slave dwellings in South Carolina.

Living historians have traveled with me to demonstrate the agency of the enslaved ancestors through cooking, blacksmithing, brick making, and storytelling. Thank you, Jerome Bias, Cheyney McKnight, Sara Daise, Christine Mitchell, Tammy Denease, Carolyn Evans, Tammy Gibson, James Brown, Jamal Hall, Rodney Prioleau, and Gilbert Walker for your phenomenal work to represent enslaved people.

Not-for-profit organizations cannot function without a board of directors. Thanks to present and former board members Nicole Moore, Tanya Timmons, Amber Mitchell, Rachael Finch, Frederick DeShon Murphy, Jonathan Williams, Patt Gunn, Angela Dickey, Leslie Stainton, Donald West, Terry James, Katherine Haskel, Melanie Edwards, Prinny Anderson, and Elon Cook.

Site stewards do a great job allowing the public to interact with their historic properties. Some have gone above and beyond to give me and the Slave Dwelling Project access to their sites. Thank you, Chelius Carter and Jenifer Egleston, for creating the "Behind the Big House" tour in Holly Springs, Mississippi. Begun in 2011, the tour has been offered every year since then, except during the pandemic. Thank you, Kristen Laise and Shannon Moeck, for allowing me and the living historians to interact with your audiences for six consecutive years. Thanks to the Louisville crew—Teresa Lee, Shirley Harmon, Patti Linn, and Kathy Nichols—for our ongoing coalition. The Historic Charleston Foundation and the Charleston Museum gave me sole access to their properties when we knew very little about the COVID-19 virus. Through technology and social media, we conquered that crisis together.

Tanya Bowers, former director for diversity at the National Trust for Historic Preservation, dragged me kicking and screaming onto a national stage at the Trust's convention in Texas. She then helped me write a blog. Thank you, John Hildreth, for being the best boss at the Trust and for giving me the room to create the Slave Dwelling Project.

The Slave Dwelling Project would not have lasted if it had not been for our donors. Mary Anthony at the 1772 Foundation has been the largest donor to the project. In my world, unsolicited and unrestricted donations are the best. Thank you, Elizabeth Morton and the Elhapa Foundation, for believing in the Slave Dwelling Project. Theresa J. Wallace has been looking out for us at the South Carolina Humanities. A South Carolina Humanities grant enabled the Slave Dwelling Project to start "Inalienable Rights: Living History Through the Eyes of the Enslaved."

Thank you, Julie Hussey, Cathy Werner, and Greg Garvin, for serving on our development committee and conducting all our fundraising campaigns. Thanks to everyone who bought a Slave Dwelling Project T-shirt or hoodie. And thank you, Sharon Clemmons, for sending the mountain of thank-you notes to everyone who contributed through the regular mail.

Matthew Reeves and Terry Brock, thank you for the great work at Montpelier. Because of you, I love archaeology.

Sheri Jackson and Diane Miller, thank you for nurturing our National Park Service Network to Freedom partnership.

Peter Wood, Carroll Van West, and Bobby Donaldson, thank you for being pro bono keynote speakers at three of our conferences.

Thank you, Chris Lese, for being a great history teacher. For the past nine years, I've met you and your students in many places throughout the United States during slave dwelling sleepovers. Thanks also to the Marquette University High School students for joining me at several locations.

Michael Twitty, thank you for teaching me the magic of food and how it can inspire us to seek the company of people who don't look or think like us.

Jodi Skipper, thank you for getting me that first lecture with an honorarium at the University of South Carolina. I realized then that the project had staying power. Thanks also for the lecture opportunity at the University of Mississippi. You've played an important role in helping to sustain the "Behind the Big House" tour in Holly Springs, Mississippi, and creating the "Behind the Big House" tour in Arkansas with Rachel Patton and Jodi Barnes.

Rhonda Thomas, you made our sixth conference happen in partnership with Clemson University. Carroll Van West, you organized our fifth conference at Middle Tennessee State University with the Jubilee Singers and novelist Colson

Acknowledgments

Whitehead. Thank you, Marcus Martin and Kirk von Daacke for hosting our fourth conference at the University of Virginia. The remarkable Arianne King Comer curated the artwork for three of our conferences. Corie Hipp, along with the board of directors, protected my blind spots. Nothing happens without Corie's input.

To Charleston mayor John Tecklenburg, the city's proclamation naming November 12, 2019, as Slave Dwelling Project Day, is one of my fondest memories.

I'm not a writer, but I've got a story to tell. Enter Herb Frazier. Thank you, Herb, for inspiring me to do this book. Those weekly Tuesday-night conversations and writing sessions paid off. We did Uncle Nearest proud.

Joseph McGill Jr.

Thank you, Joseph McGill Jr., for allowing me to help you share your incredible story with the readers of this book. It has been a long journey. We held our first book meeting on November 17, 2017. A few years later, those occasional conversations evolved into weekly Tuesday-night sessions over food with Uncle Nearest. Hundreds of hours later, this book has emerged as a testament to your devotion to our African ancestors.

And Steve Hoffius, your review of the early chapters set us on the right path.

When I asked my grandmother, Mable McNeil Frazier, how to spell a word, she threw the dictionary at me and said, "Look it up!" My father, Benjamin Frazier, who opened my eyes to a world beyond Charleston, bought me a typewriter when I was twelve. He encouraged me to tell stories. My mother, Albertha Nelson Frazier, who joined the ancestors during this writing project, left me with her commonsense wisdom.

I'd also like to thank my wife, Adrienne Troy Frazier; my daughters, Angela Thomas, Amanda Frazier White, and Adrienne Nicole Frazier; my stepsons, Asim Hamilton and Seth Hamilton; and the rest of my family and friends who've supported me. This work is not over yet. There are more books to write!

Herb Frazier

Sources

Introduction

Publications

Federal Writers' Project: Slave Narrative Project, South Carolina. This account is a compilation of stories writers in South Carolina recorded from Henry Brown, Charleston; Richard "Dick Look-up" Jones, Union County; Jerry Hill, Spartanburg; Charley Barber, Winnsboro; Uncle Sabe Rutledge, Georgetown County, and Sam Polite of Beaufort County.

Harrison, Renee K. *Enslaved Women and the Art of Resistance in Antebellum America.* New York: Palgrave McMillan, 2009.

Mooney, Barbara Burlison. "Looking for History's Huts." *Winterthur Portfolio* 39, no. 1 (Spring 2004): 49–70. https://www.journals.uchicago.edu/doi/10.1086/431009.

Rhea, Gordon. "Fellow Southerners!" *North and South* 13, no. 5 (January 2012): 12–17.

Frazier, Herb, Bernard Edward Powers, and Marjory Wentworth. *We Are Charleston: Tragedy and Triumph at Mother Emanuel.* Nashville: W. Publishing Group, 2016.

"An American Secret: The Untold Story of Native American Enslavement." *Hidden Brain,* November 20, 2017. https://www.npr.org/2017/11/20/565410514/an-american-secret-the-untold-story-of-native-american-enslavement.

Sources

Chapter One: Dusting Off an Old Idea

Interviews

Elaine Nichol, Suzannah Smith Miles, Michael Allen

Publications and Film

Nichols, Elaine. *Sullivan's Island Pest Houses: Beginning an Archaeological Investigation*, unpublished master's thesis, 1989.

Roberts, Sam. "Tony Horwitz Dies at 60; Prize-Winning Journalist and Best-Selling Author." *New York Times*, May 28, 2019. https://www.nytimes.com/2019/05/28/obitu aries/tony-horwitz-dead.html.

Nye, Doug. "Documentary about Playing Soldier Digs Up the Roots of the Civil War." *Chicago Tribune*, February 18, 2001. https://www.chicagotribune.com/news/ct-xpm -2001-02-18-0102180455-story.html.

Pierce, John. "The Reasons for Secession: A Documentary Study." American Battlefield Trust, accessed February 13, 2023. https://www.battlefields.org/learn/articles/reasons -secession.

Kirschbaum, Glenn, dir. *The Unfinished Civil War*. Greystone Television / The History Channel, 2001.

Chapter Two: Embarking on a Yearlong Project

Interviews

Deborah Grace, Elizabeth Johnson, Caroline Howell, Kelly Logan Graham, Jacob "Jake" Martin, Robert S. Jones Jr.

Publications

Ad for an enslaved woman who ran away, *City Gazette*, Charleston, South Carolina, Friday, June 21, 1816.

Antebellum Register of St. Andrew's Parish Church, 1830–1859.

Sources

Porwoll, Paul. *"In My Trials, Lord, Walk with Me": What an Antebellum Parish Register Reveals about Race and Reconciliation.* Charleston, SC: Saint Andrew's Parish Church, 2018.

Moore, John Hammond. *Carnival of Blood: Dueling, Lynching, and Murder in South Carolina, 1880–1920.* Columbia: University of South Carolina Press, 2006.

Bartelme, Tony. "Restoring History." *Post and Courier,* February 28, 2009. https://www.postandcourier.com/news/restoring-history/article_913a8f84-a555-524f-90b1-8656dc59018d.html.

"The Great Expedition." *Chicago Tribune,* November 14, 1861.

Olsen, Christopher J. "July 21, 1861: First Major Battle of the Civil War." The History Reader, July 21, 2011. https://www.thehistoryreader.com/military-history/july-21-1861-first-major-battle-civil-war/.

Ung, Jenny. "False Quote on Freed Slaves Wrongly Attributed to Harriet Tubman." AP News, October 4, 2018. https://apnews.com/article/archive-fact-checking-2312300417.

Yorkville Enquirer, Yorkville, South Carolina, December 5, 1861.

Welles, Gideon. *The Union Navy's Attack on Bluffton, Report of the Secretary of the Navy,* 1863.

Chapter Three: Honoring the Ancestors

Interviews

Ernest Parks, Eugene Frazier, Larry Faulkenberry, Tom Milligan

Publications. Video

"McLeod Plantation Timeline." Charleston County Parks, accessed February 13, 2023. https://www.ccprc.com/1779/Historical-Timeline.

Halifax, Shawn. "Calling Them by Name: The Story of McLeod Slaves' Transition to Freedom." *Post and Courier,* February 10, 2017. https://sponsored.postandcourier.com/web/charleston-county-park-recreation/calling-them-by-name-the-story-of-freed-slaves-transition-to-freedom/.

Frazier, Eugene Sr. *A History of James Island Slave Descendants & Plantation Owners: The Bloodline.* Charleston, SC: History Press, 2010.

McGill, Samuel D. *Narrative of Reminiscences of Williamsburg County.* Columbia, SC: Bryan, 1897.

Sources

Heyward, Duncan Clinch. *Seed from Madagascar*. Chapel Hill: University of North Carolina Press, 2018 (1937).

Edgar, Walter. *South Carolina: A History*. Columbia: University of South Carolina Press, 1998.

"Bluff Road and Kingville Road." Historic Columbia, accessed February 24, 2023. https://www.historiccolumbia.org/tour-locations/1001-kingville-road.

"The Wateree Indians." Carolina—The Native Americans, Carolana, accessed February 24, 2023. https://www.carolana.com/Carolina/Native_Americans/native_americans_wateree.htm.

Koger, Larry. *Black Slaveowners: Free Black Slave Masters in South Carolina, 1790–1860*. Columbia: University of South Carolina Press, 1985.

"Cowasee Basin." *2013 LCV Cities Tour*, Book TV, C-SPAN. https://www.c-span.org/video/?312306-1/cowasee-basin.

Slave Narratives: A Folk History of Slavery in the United States from Interviews with Former Slaves, South Carolina Narratives, Federal Writers' Project of the Works Progress Administration, 1941.

Sicard, Sarah. "Harriet Tubman Led a Badass Raid in 1863." *Task & Purpose*, March 7, 2016. https://taskandpurpose.com/history/harriet-tubman-led-a-badass-raid-in-1863/.

Grigg, Jeff W. *The Combahee River Raid: Harriet Tubman & Lowcountry Liberation*. Charleston, SC: History Press, 2014.

"Historical Sketch of Eastover." Town of Eastover, South Carolina, accessed February 12, 2023. https://www.eastoversc.com/about-us/pages/historical-sketch-eastover.

The State (Columbia, South Carolina), July 20, 2013.

"SCDNR Receives Three Tracts to Add to Heritage Preserve WMA System." *Carolina Sportsman*, accessed February 12, 2023. https://www.carolinasportsman.com/hunting/scdnr-receives-three-tracts-to-add-to-heritage-preserve-wma-system/.

142. *List of Field Slaves—1854–1856, Heyward and Ferguson Family Papers, 1806–1923*. Heyward and Ferguson Family Papers, 1806–1923, Lowcountry Digital Library, College of Charleston Libraries. https://lcdl.library.cofc.edu/lcdl/catalog/lcdl:39031.

Chapter Four: A Homecoming

Interviews

Lee Brockington, Eric Frazier, Michael Bedenbaugh, Terry James, Jodi Skipper

Sources

Publications, Map, Website

"Remembering Florence Kaster and Her Fight Against Prejudice." *Stories of Faith from Catholic Extension* (podcast), January 18, 2018. https://catholicextension.libsyn.com /remembering-florence-kaster-and-her-fight-against-prejudice.

Boddie, William Willis. *History of Williamsburg: Something About the People of Williamsburg County, South Carolina, from the First Settlement by Europeans About 1705 Until 1923.* Columbia, SC: State Co., 1923.

A map showing the location of Pynes along the Seaboard Coastline Railroad in Colleton County, South Carolina. Heyward Family Association, accessed February 24, 2023. https://www.heywardfamilyassociation.org/wordpress/wp-content/uploads/2016/06 /acereduced.jpg.

"Rev. Samuel Girard Earle." Find a Grave, accessed February 13, 2023. https://www.finda grave.com/memorial/56226551/samuel-girard-earle.

"Elias John Earle (1823–abt. 1897)." WikiTree, accessed February 13, 2023. https://www. wikitree.com/wiki/Earle-1377.

Slave Narratives: A Folk History of Slavery in the United States from Interviews with Former Slaves, South Carolina Narratives, Federal Writers' Project of the Works Progress Administration, 1941.

"This Place Matters: A Short Documentary About Historic Preservation Centering Around Slave Cabins Identified in Anderson, SC." Produced by Alex Stephens and Linda Lavold. Dead Horse Productions, 2013. Video, 17:42, October 7, 2013. https://www. youtube.com/watch?v=uzMP9tGQfi0.

Chapter Five: A Chapel for the Enslaved

Interviews

John Rutledge Parker, Terry James

Publications

Slave Narratives: A Folk History of Slavery in the United States from Interviews with Former Slaves, South Carolina Narratives, Federal Writers' Project of the Works Progress Administration, 1941.

SOURCES

Boyle, Christopher C. *Mansfield Plantation: A Legacy on the Black River*. Charleston, SC: History Press, 2014.

McDermott, John. "Mansfield Plantation Back with Family." *Post and Courier* (Charleston).

Vlach, John Michael. *Back of the Big House: The Architecture of Plantation Slavery*. Fred W. Morrison Series in Southern Studies. Chapel Hill: University of North Carolina Press, 1993.

CHAPTER SIX: ANOTHER STATE

INTERVIEWS

Carole King, Dorothy Walker, Teresa Paglione, Tania Cordes, Chris McWhirter, Caius McWhirter

PUBLICATIONS

Slave Narratives: A Folk History of Slavery in the United States from Interviews with Former Slaves: Volume I, Alabama Narratives. Work Projects Administration, 2011.

Erbach, Elizabeth. "Dexter Avenue Baptist Church, Montgomery, Alabama." January 5, 2009. blackpast.org.

Kambhamptay, Anna Purna. "Annie Leibovitz on the Democratization of Photography, Her Influences and Her Google Pixel Campaign." *Time*, October 22, 2019. https://time.com/5706141/annie-leibovitz-google-pixel-4/.

CHAPTER SEVEN: EXPANDING MY HORIZON

INTERVIEWS

Wali Cathcart, Nicole Moore, Lisa Bratton, Strauss Moore Shiple, Terry James, Dontavius Williams, Danny Drain, Kevin Lynch

Sources

Publications

Lehmhouse, Zachary A., and Joseph C. Mester. *A Historical Background and Context*. Unpublished.

"Learn About Historic Brattonsville's African-American History." Explore York County Blog, York County Visitors Center, February 1, 2021. https://www.visityorkcounty. com/blog/post/learn-about-historic-brattonsvilles-african-american-history/.

Burkins, Glenn. "Historic Brattonsville Honors the Enslaved and Their Descendants." Q City Metro, September 7, 2017. https://qcitymetro.com/2017/09/07/historic -brattonsville-honors-living-descendants-enslaved-families/.

Banks, Lindsey. "New Exhibit at Historic Brattonsville." *Charlotte Ledger*, July 31, 2021.

Vernon, Amelia Wallace. *African Americans at Mars Bluff, South Carolina*. Baton Rouge: Louisiana State University Press, 1993.

Chapter Eight: What History Tells Us

Interviews

Bryan McAuley, Naomi Carrier, Bud Northington, Ted Ellis, Geneva "Candi" Richardson Flora, Hank Ward, LaSandra Sanders, Toni Carrier

Publications

Slave Narratives: A Folk History of Slavery in the United States from Interviews with Former Slaves, South Carolina Narratives, Federal Writers' Project of the Works Progress Administration, 1941.

"Early Statehood: Slavery." Texas State Library and Archives Commission, last modified December 5, 2017. https://www.tsl.texas.gov/treasures/earlystate/slavery-01.html.

Slave Narratives: A Folk History of Slavery in the United States from Interviews with Former Slaves: Texas Narratives, by Work Projects Administration.

Haywood, Felix. "Federal Writers' Project: Slave Narrative Project, Vol. 16, Texas, Part 2, Easter-King." 1936. Iowa Department of Cultural Affairs, courtesy of the Library of Congress. https://iowaculture.gov/history/education/educator-resources/primary -source-sets/african-americans-and-civil-war/narrative.

Sources

Baumgartner, Alice L. *South to Freedom: Runaway Slaves to Mexico and the Road to the Civil War*. New York: Basic Books, 2020.

Barker, Eugene C., and James W. Pohl; revised by Mary L. Scheer. "Texas Revolution." Texas State Historical Association. Last modified June 17, 2021. https://www.tshaonline .org/handbook/entries/texas-revolution.

Cutrer, Thomas W. "Heard, William Jones Elliott (1801–1874)." Texas State Historical Association. Last modified October 24, 2019. https://www.tshaonline.org/handbook /entries/heard-william-jones-elliott.

Rodemann, Katharyn. "Happy Trails: The History of Egypt." *Texas Monthly*, October 2003. https://www.texasmonthly.com/articles/happy-trails-37/.

Staples, Brent. "A Fate Worse Than Slavery, Unearthed in Sugar Land." *New York Times*, October 27, 2018. https://www.nytimes.com/2018/10/27/opinion/sugar-land-texas -graves-slavery.html.

Young, Barbara L. "Egypt, TX (Wharton County)." Handbook of Texas, Texas State Historical Association, accessed February 13, 2023. https://www.tshaonline.org/handbook /entries/egypt-tx-wharton-county.

"Naomi Carrier at Egypt Plantation, Texas." Tracey Silverman, video, 2:00, March 30, 2011. https://www.youtube.com/watch?v=fs3xCZVP0gM.

"Caroline Seward." Find a Grave, accessed February 13, 2023. https://www.findagrave. com/memorial/95523957/caroline-seward.

Jones, Nancy Baker. "Annie Mae Hunt." *Texas Women's History Moments* (audio). Women in Texas History, Ruthe Winegarten Memorial Foundation for Texas Women's History, accessed February 12, 2023. https://www.womenintexashistory.org/audio/annie -mae-hunt/.

Chapter Nine: Higher Learning

Interviews

Simon Lewis, Bernard Powers, Lynn Rainville, Crystal Sterling Jones Rossson, Terry James, Kirt von Daacke, Grant Mishoe, Mary Jo Fairchild.

Publications

Nesbit, Scott. "The Education of William Gibbons." 2004. https://www.latinamerican studies.org/slavery/Gibbons_William.pdf.

Sources

Wilder, Craig Steven. *Ebony and Ivy: Race, Slavery, and the Troubled History of America's Universities*. New York: Bloomsbury, 2013.

Ruane, Michael E. "A Brief History of the Enduring Phony Science That Perpetuates White Supremacy." *Washington Post*, April 30, 2019. https://www.washingtonpost.com/local/a-brief-history-of-the-enduring-phony-science-that-perpetuates-white-supremacy/2019/04/29/20e6aef0-5aeb-11e9-a00e-050dc7b82693_story.html.

Dillingham, Richard. "The Story of Joseph Anderson." Mars Hill Anderson Rosenwald School, accessed February 12, 2023. https://andersonrosenwaldschool.com/the-story-of-joseph-anderson/.

Dillingham, Richard, Dan Slagle, and Sarah Weston Hart. *The Historic Mars Hill Anderson Rosenwald School: Our Story, This Place*. Asheville, NC: Pisgah, 2022.

A Basic Biography, Benjamin Rush.

Rainville, Lynn. *Invisible Founders: How Two Centuries of African American Families Transformed a Plantation into a College*. New York: Berghahn Books, 2019.

Farrell, Jessica. "History, Memory, and Slavery at the College of Charleston, 1785–1810." *Chrestomathy: Annual Review of Undergraduate Research, School of Humanities and Social Sciences, School of Languages, Cultures, and World Affairs, College of Charleston* 7 (2008): 52–71. https://chrestomathy.cofc.edu/documents/vol7/farrell.pdf.

Greene, Harlan. "Addlestone Library & Rivers Green." Discovering Our Past: College of Charleston Histories, accessed February 12, 2023. https://discovering.cofc.edu/items/show/4.

"A Brief History of the College." College of Charleston, accessed February 12, 2023. https://www.cofc.edu/about/historyandtraditions/briefhistory.php.

Laudenslager, Chase. "1800's Slave Badge Found on College of Charleston Campus." WCBD-TV (Charleston, South Carolina), June 15, 2021. https://www.counton2.com/news/local-news/1800s-slave-badge-found-on-college-of-charleston-campus/.

"Universities, Slavery, Public Memory and the Built Landscape." School of Architecture, University of Virginia, November 1, 2017, https://www.arch.virginia.edu/ccl/ccl-news/universities-slavery-public-memory-and-the-built-landscape.

Slavery and Justice: Report of the Brown University Steering Committee on Slavery and Justice, Brown University.

"President's Commission on Slavery and the University." University of Virginia, 2013. https://slavery.virginia.edu/.

McGuffey Cottage, University of Virginia: Historic Structure Report. John G. Waite Associates, Architects, 2018. https://officearchitect.virginia.edu/sites/officearchitect/files/2020-12/McGuffeyCottageHSR.pdf.

Sources

Chapter Ten: Presidential Slaveholders

Publications

Brady, Patricia. "Daniel Parke Custis (1711–1757)." Encyclopedia Virginia, accessed February 13, 2023. https://encyclopediavirginia.org/entries/custis-daniel-parke-1711-1757/.

"Biography of George Washington." George Washington's Mount Vernon, accessed February 13, 2023. https://www.mountvernon.org/george-washington/biography/.

Kearse, Bettye. *The Other Madisons: The Lost History of a President's Black Family.* New York: Houghton Mifflin Harcourt, 2020.

O'Neill, Aaron. "Number of Slaves Owned by U.S. Presidents 1789–1877." Statista, June 21, 2022. https://www.statista.com/statistics/1121963/slaves-owned-by-us-presidents/.

"The Life of Paul Jennings." James Madison's Montpelier, accessed February 13, 2023. https://www.montpelier.org/learn/paul-jennings.

"Dolley Madison Rescues George Washington." George Washington's Mount Vernon, accessed February 13, 2023. https://www.mountvernon.org/george-washington/artwork/dolley-madison-comes-to-the-rescue/.

Burke, Kathleen. "Witness to History: The First Memoir by a White House Slave Recreates the Events of August 23, 1814." *Smithsonian Magazine*, March 2010. https://www.smithsonianmag.com/history/witness-to-history-7507369/.

Hicks, Hilarie M. "The Naming Project: Milly." Montpelier's Digital Doorway, May 21, 2021. https://digitaldoorway.montpelier.org/2021/05/21/the-naming-project-milly/.

"Montpelier's Log Cabin Workshop Short." James Madison's Montpelier, video, 4:08, October 8, 2014. https://www.youtube.com/watch?v=yKuN7AWWa-Y.

Hicks, Hilarie M. "Putting People in the Picture." Montpelier's Digital Doorway, April 9, 2020. https://digitaldoorway.montpelier.org/2020/04/09/putting-people-in-the-picture/.

"Sawney A. Early, Sr." Geni.com, last updated January 12, 2022. https://www.geni.com/people/Sawney-A-Early-Sr/6000000019026756350.

Roberts, Nigel. "Descendants of James Madison's Slaves Fight for Equal Power of Foundation Overseeing His Former Plantation." BET, April 25, 2022. https://www.bet.com/article/2h67cm/descendants-james-madison-slaves-battle-equal-power-over-plantation.

Stanton, Lucia C. "Appendix H: Sally Hemings and Her Children, Report of the Research Committee on Thomas Jefferson and Sally Hemings." Thomas Jefferson Foundation, last updated June 6, 2018. https://www.monticello.org/thomas-jefferson/jefferson

SOURCES

-slavery/thomas-jefferson-and-sally-hemings-a-brief-account/research-report-on
-jefferson-and-hemings/appendix-h-sally-hemings-and-her-children/.

"The Life of Sally Hemings." Monticello, accessed February 13, 2023. https://www
.monticello.org/sallyhemings/.

CHAPTER ELEVEN: LIVING HISTORY IN OUR FEDERAL, STATE, AND COUNTY PARKS

INTERVIEWS

Peri Frances, Terry James, Julia Rose, Lynda Davis, Stephanie Sperling

PUBLICATIONS

Schafer, Daniel L. *Anna Madgigine Jai Kingsley: African Princess, Florida Slave, Planta-tion Slaveowner.* Gainesville: University Press of Florida, 2018.

Visiting Kingsley Plantation, National Park Service.

Landers, Jane. *Black Society in Spanish Florida.* Champaign: University of Illinois Press, 1999.

"Fairbank Plantation." Daniel Island Historical Society, accessed February 13, 2023. https://dihistoricalsociety.com/fairbank-plantation/.

"Gullah Jack." Timucuan Ecological & Historic Preserve, National Park Service, last updated May 26, 2022. https://www.nps.gov/timu/learn/historyculture/gullah-jack.htm.

McFarland, Kenneth. "Stagville." NCPedia, January 1, 2006. https://www.ncpedia.org/stagville.

Slave Narratives: A Folk History of Slavery in the United States from Interviews with Former Slaves, North Carolina Narratives, Federal Writers' Project of the Works Progress Administration, 1941.

Born in Slavery: Slave Narratives from the Federal Writers' Project, 1936 to 1938, Appendix II: Race of Interviewers, Library of Congress.

Onion, Rebecca. "Is the Greatest Collection of Slave Narratives Tainted by Racism?" *Slate,* July 6, 2016. https://www.slate.com/articles/news_and_politics/history/2016/07

/can_wpa_slave_narratives_be_trusted_or_are_they_tainted_by_depression_era.
html.

North Carolina Historic Sites.

"Historic Stagville Presents 'Freedom 150' May 30." North Carolina Department of Natural and Cultural Resources, May 20, 2015. https://www.ncdcr.gov/press-release
/historic-stagville-presents-%E2%80%9Cfreedom-150%E2%80%9D-may-30.

Inge, Leoneda. "Freedom 150: Commemorating the Lives of Former Slaves After the
Civil War." North Carolina Public Radio, May 29, 2015. https://www.wunc.org
/arts-culture/2015-05-29/freedom-150-commemorating-the-lives-of-former
-slaves-after-the-civil-war.

Hill, James. "Horton Grove Slave Quarters and the New Old South." *Talking Buildings*
(blog), September 5, 2016. https://talkingbuildings.com/horton-grove-slave-quarters
-and-the-new-old-south/.

"Abner Jordan Shares His Life as a Slave." The History Engine, accessed February 24,
2023. https://historyengine.richmond.edu/episodes/view/4847.

Stagville Plantation, Plantations of North Carolina, a list of enslaved people at Stagville.

Thomas, William G., and the Center for Digital Research in the Humanities. *Mima Queen
v. John Hepburn. Minute Book Entry.*

Fede, Andrew T. "Not the Most Insignificant Justice: Reconsidering Justice Gabriel
Duvall's Slavery Law Opinions Favoring Liberty." *Journal of Supreme Court History*
42, no. 1 (March 2017): 7–27. https//doi.org/10.1111/jsch.12132.

"Descendants of Mareen Duvall of Middle Plantation." Geni.com, accessed February
13, 2023. https://www.geni.com/projects/Descendants-of-Mareen-Duvall-of-Middle
-Plantation/145.

"Marietta House Museum." Maryland-National Capital Park and Planning Commission,
accessed February 13, 2023. https://www.pgparks.com/3072/Marietta-House
-Museum.

Thomas, William G., and the Center for Digital Research in the Humanities. *Thomas
Butler, Sarah Butler, Matilda Butler, Airy Butler, Reason Butler, Sally Butler, Liddy
Butler, & Eliza Butler v. Gabriel Duvall.*

"The Butler Family's Freedom Petition." Rose Notes, Marietta Historic House Museum,
January 27, 2022. https://www.rosenotes.net/blog/the-butler-familys-freedom
-petition.

Sources

Chapter Twelve: Above the Mason-Dixon Line

Publications

Newman, Richard S. *Freedom's Prophet: Bishop Richard Allen, the AME Church, and the Black Founding Fathers*. New York: New York University Press, 2009.

"Allen Enslaved." Historical Society of Pennsylvania, accessed February 13, 2023. https://hsp.org/history-online/exhibits/richard-allen-apostle-of-freedom/allen-enslaved.

McGill, Joseph. "Slavery in the North: Cliveden Historic Site, Philadelphia, PA." *Lowcountry Africana* (blog), July 12, 2011. https://lowcountryafricana.com/slavery-in-the-north-cliveden-historic-site-philadelphia-pa/.

McGill, Joseph. "They Lived Where They Worked." *The Slave Dwelling Project* (blog), November 16, 2015. https://slavedwellingproject.org/they-lived-where-they-worked/.

"In Loving Memory of David Allen Pettee (August 18,1957–September 13, 2020)." Unitarian Universalist Ministers Association, accessed February 13, 2023. https://uuma.org/remembering-the-living-tradition/in-loving-memory-of-david-allen-pettee-august-181957-september-13-2020/.

Swarns, Rachel L. "Insurance Policies on Slaves: New York Life's Complicated Past." *New York Times*, December 18, 2016. https://www.nytimes.com/2016/12/18/us/insurance-policies-on-slaves-new-york-lifes-complicated-past.html.

Wilder, *Ebony and Ivy*.

"The Decline of Northern Slavery and the Rise of the Cotton Kingdom." US History I (AY Collection), OER Services, accessed February 13, 2023. https://courses.lumenlearning.com/suny-ushistory1ay/chapter/the-decline-of-northern-slavery-and-the-rise-of-the-cotton-kingdom/.

Slavery in Northern U.S., Perceived to Have Ended Early, Persisted Well into 19th Century. University of Arkansas.

Klein, Christopher. "Deeper Roots of Northern Slavery Unearthed." History Stories, History.com, updated February 5, 2019. https://www.history.com/news/deeper-roots-of-northern-slavery-unearthed.

Thompson, Kathleen Logothetis. "When Did Slavery Really End in the North?" *Civil Discourse: A Civil War Era Blog*, January 9, 2017. https://civildiscourse-historyblog.com/blog/2017/1/3/when-did-slavery-really-end-in-the-north.

History of Slavery in New York. Historical Society of the New York Courts.

"Bush-Holley House." Greenwich Historical Society, accessed February 13, 2023. https://greenwichhistory.org/the-bush-holley-house/.

McGill, Joseph. "Descendants of Slaveholders, Descendants of Slaves Share Overnight Stay at Bush-Holley House, Greenwich, CT." *Lowcountry Africana* (blog), April 10, 2012. https://lowcountryafricana.com/descendants-of-slaveholders-descendants-of-slaves-share-overnight-stay-at-bush-holley-house-greenwich-ct/.

Dionne Ford. National Endowment for the Arts.

Hammon, Jupiter. "An Evening Thought: Salvation by Christ, with Penitential Cries." Poets.org, accessed February 13, 2023. https://poets.org/poem/evening-thought-salvation-christ-penitential-cries.

Rosin, Viha. "Jupiter Hammon's 'An Evening Thought: Salvation by Christ with Penitential Cries': An Analysis." *IOSR Journal of Humanities and Social Science* 23, no. 11 (November 2018): 24–26. https://www.iosrjournals.org/iosr-jhss/papers/Vol.%2023%20Issue11/Version-2/D2311022426.pdf.

Brown, Shannah. *Jupiter Hammon's An Evening Thought: Finding Identity Through Religion*. Shannah Brown, Art, Design, Literature, 2014.

Morris, Deborah S. "Joseph Lloyd Manor, Home of Renowned Slave Poet, Named Literary Landmark." *Newsday*, October 11, 2020. https://www.newsday.com/long-island/suffolk/slave-writer-landmark-jupiter-hammon-q43772.

"Student Finds New Work by First Published African-American Poet." *Tell Me More*, National Public Radio, March 12, 2013. https://www.npr.org/2013/03/12/174100708/first-african-american-poet-still-showing-new-work.

Schuessler, Jennifer. "Confronting Slavery at Long Island's Oldest Estates." *New York Times*, August 12, 2015. https://www.nytimes.com/2015/08/14/arts/confronting-slavery-at-long-islands-oldest-estates.html.

Chapter Thirteen: Resistance

Publications

Vlach, *Back of the Big House*.

Young, Peighton L. "African and African American History at Bacon's Castle." *Preservation Virginia* (blog), June 27, 2019. https://preservationvirginia.org/african-and-african-american-history-at-bacons-castle/.

"Sir William Berkeley." Britannica.com, last modified January 1, 2023. https://www
.britannica.com/biography/William-Berkeley.

"Inventing Black and White." Facing History and Ourselves, last modified August 11,
2017. https://www.facinghistory.org/resource-library/inventing-black-white.

McCulley, Susan. "Bacon's Rebellion." Historic Jamestowne, National Park Service, June
1987, last updated February 26, 2015. https://www.nps.gov/jame/learn/historyculture
/bacons-rebellion.htm.

"Preservation in Action: Bacon's Castle." Preservation Virginia, video, 1:56, November 19,
2018. https://www.youtube.com/watch?v=EsBkw-QY6nI.

Williams, Allison T. "Surry Residents, Historians Sleep at Bacon's Castle's Slave Quarters." *Daily Press*, October 8, 2012. https://www.dailypress.com/news/dp-xpm
-20121008-2012-10-08-dp-nws-slave-dwelling-project-20121008-story.html.

Lehman, Christopher P. "Slaveholder Investment in Territorial Minnesota." *Minnesota
History* (Fall 2017): 264–274. https://collections.mnhs.org/MNHistoryMagazine
/articles/65/v65i07p264-274.pdf.

Rosen, Robert N. "An American Moses, Harriet Tubman, in the Lowcountry." *Post and
Courier*, May 8, 2016. https://www.postandcourier.com/opinion/an-american-moses
-harriet-tubman-in-the-lowcountry/article_4cdde266-59e6-593a-b614-890b67
4724c2.html.

Lowe, Frederick H. *Virginia Highway Marker Will Honor Dred Scott*. The NorthStar
News & Analysis.

"Nat Turner's Insurrection." Historical Marker Database, last modified March 20, 2022.
https://www.hmdb.org/m.asp?m=22796.

Chapter Fourteen: Garden Clubs

Publications

*Slave Narratives: A Folk History of Slavery in the United States from Interviews with Former
Slaves, Mississippi Narratives*. Federal Writers' Project of the Works Progress Administration, 1941.

Davis, Jack E. "A Struggle for Public History: Black and White Claims to Natchez's Past."
Public Historian 22, no. 1 (2000): 45–63.

Sources

Cardon, Dustin. "'Still Learning': Natchez Reckons with Its Racist Past and Celebrates Local Black History." *Mississippi Free Press*, February 11, 2022. https://www.mississippi freepress.org/20766/still-learning-natchez-reckons-with-its-racist-past-and -celebrates-local-black-history.

Grant, Richard. *The Deepest South of All: True Stories from Natchez, Mississippi.* New York: Simon & Schuster, 2021.

Powell, Timothy B. "Ebos Landing." New Georgia Encyclopedia, last modified July 17, 2020. https://www.georgiaencyclopedia.org/articles/history-archaeology/ebos -landing/.

Slave Narratives: A Folk History of Slavery in the United States from Interviews with Former Slaves, Georgia Narratives. Federal Writers' Project of the Works Progress Administration, 1941.

Chapter Fifteen: Family Reunions

Interviews

Mina Wilson, Charles Lorenzo Wilson, Montez Martin

Publications

Last Seen: Finding Family After Slavery. Saml. Dove searching for his mother Areno, sisters Maria, Neziah, and Peggy, and his brother Edmond. *The Colored Tennessean* (Nashville, TN), August 12, 1865.

Kates, Cheryl Baker. *Martin Family History: From Africa to America—Reflections on a Rich History: The Martins of Jenkinsville, South Carolina.*

Bassett, John Spencer. *Slavery in the State of North Carolina.* Baltimore: John Hopkins Press, 1899. https://archive.org/details/slaveryinstateof00bass.

Gerard, Philip. "The 1980s: A Reunion for the Ages." *Our State*, August 29, 2022. https:// www.ourstate.com/the-1980s-a-reunion-for-the-ages/.

Ewen, Ilina. "Bearing Witness: Michelle Lanier's Unique Perspective on History." *Walter Magazine*, November 2021. https://waltermagazine.com/community/people/michelle -lanier/.

Sources

Chapter Sixteen: Impressions of the Enslaved

Interviews

Jonathan Williams, Dick Cartwright, Susan Heape, Donald Payton, C. Preston Cooley

Publications

Vlach, *Back of the Big House.*

Raver, Anne. "In Georgia's Swept Yards, a Dying Tradition." *New York Times*, August 8, 1993. https://www.nytimes.com/1993/08/08/us/in-georgia-s-swept-yards-a-dying-tradition.html.

Owens, Leslie H. *This Species of Property: Slave Life and Culture in the Old South.* Oxford: Oxford University Press, 1977.

Litwack, Leon F. *Been in the Storm So Long: The Aftermath of Slavery.* New York: Vintage Books, 1979.

Nordhoff, Charles. *The Freedmen of South-Carolina: Some Account of Their Appearance, Character, Condition, and Peculiar Customs.* African American Pamphlet Collection. New York: Charles T. Evans, 1863. https://www.loc.gov/item/12005602/.

Slave Narratives: A Folk History of Slavery in the United States from Interviews with Former Slaves, North Carolina Narratives. Federal Writers' Project of the Works Progress Administration, 1941. In the narrative, Tillie is only identified as "Tillie, daughter of a slave."

The Bellamy Mansion: Dr. John D. Bellamy and His Mansion, by Dr. John D. Bellamy. Cape Fear Historical Institute Papers, 1941.

"The Bellamys." Bellamy Mansion Museum, accessed February 13, 2023. https://www.bellamymansion.org/the-people.html.

McGill, Joseph. "Slave Dwellings as Classrooms." *Slave Dwelling Project* (blog), February 8, 2015. https://slavedwellingproject.org/slave-dwellings-as-classrooms/.

Slave Narratives: A Folk History of Slavery in the United States from Interviews with Former Slaves, South Carolina Narratives. Federal Writers' Project of the Works Progress Administration, 1941.

Tommy Dew's Walking Tour—Charleston SC. "Longitude Lane is an alley located on the lower part of the peninsula in downtown Charleston and actually runs east and west."

Sources

Facebook, September 17, 2018. https://www.facebook.com/405075929544801
/photos/a.439755889410138/1991597497559295/.

Wilonsky, Robert. "If Dallas Hates Erasing History So Much, Why Doesn't Anyone Know About Park Honoring Three Slaves Who Were Hanged?" *Dallas Morning News*, October 6, 2017. https://www.dallasnews.com/opinion/commentary/2017/10/06/if -dallas-hates-erasing-history-so-much-why-doesn-t-anyone-know-about-park-honor ing-three-slaves-who-were-hanged/.

Pocta, Benj. "160 Years Ago This Month, a Fire Engulfed Dallas." Central Track, July 21, 2020. https://www.centraltrack.com/160-years-ago-this-month-a-fire-engulfed-dallas/.

INDEX